IN THE SHADOW
OF ANTICHRIST

IN THE SHADOW OF ANTICHRIST

The Old Believers of Alberta

by

David Scheffel

broadview press

For those peasants, buffoons and
simpletons at first seeming, are like those
dolls within a doll, secrets within secrets
concealing.

Yevgeny Yevtushenko

Cataloguing in Publication Data

Scheffel, David, 1955-   .
  In the shadow of antichrist: the Old Believers of Alberta

ISBN   0-921149-71-9 (bound)   ISBN 0-921149-73-5 (pbk.)

1. Raskolniks — Alberta. I. Title.

BX601.S34   1991   281.9'7123   C90-095245-8

broadview press   in the US, broadview press
P.O. Box 1243   269 Portage Rd.
Peterborough, Ontario   Lewiston, NY
K9J 7H5   Canada   14092   USA

printed in Canada

This book was published with the assistance of the Province of Ontario,
through the Ontario Arts Council.

Contents

List of Illustrations

List of Tables and Figures

Foreword

The Old Believers present us with a set of issues and themes central to human culture. These have been embodied in their historical and contemporary life in a most unusual way.

The author of this book has two goals: to provide a detailed "thick description" of the cultural life of a contemporary Old Believer community, its actions and their meaning; and to show, as the best field work in the still quite young discipline of anthropology has done, that careful attention to the details of culture and experience in a living community has consummate value because it deepens our appreciation of culture and human experience, whether or not it is deemed relevant and applicable to the dominant culture, contemporary life, or the scholar's own society.

The Old Believers challenge our notions of freedom and liberty. They seek, on the one hand, a social landscape which will leave them in peace to pursue a thoroughly disciplined life, a life, as the Apostle Paul puts it, "as a slave of Christ." In this pursuit the modern democratic state is as much a threat, if not more, as was the totalitarian control of a Czar 300 years ago. The freedom the Old Believers seek is simply the opportunity to live a meaningful life through, and I mean *through*, the ritual forms of a tradition that has structured life and thought in a coherent way. For the faithful every thought, word, and deed participates in mythic meaning, in what Old Believers call the truth. The purpose of life is not to conform to the fallen world which no longer understands its purpose and reason for being. Rather, it is to be a living model, an *icon*, of what the Creator intended for this world. To this extent the Old Believers are a vivid example of Orthodox Christian culture which calls its faithful, not out of this world to some transcendent paradise or isolated kingdom of nostalgia, but to live in the created order as sacred tradition would have it. This is a liturgical life, an Orthodoxy and an Orthopraxia, right praise, practice and reflection. It is a life in the "image and likeness of God," as the Old Believers put it, a real life, a Christ-like life, not anti-life, Anti-Christ. It is nothing short of reality. At the same time it is a life in some sense timeless. And as the reader of this book will readily grasp, this does not mean a life frozen in time, a life based on obsolete historical models: Old Believer culture, like virtually all cultures, is a playground of meaning, of encounter and adaptation. It is timeless because it does not take its cue from cultural fashions or the innovations offered by modernity either for changing the forms of the culture or the understanding of them. Rather, the vagaries of history are understood in the context of the mythic meaning and character of sacred tradition.

Old Believer culture has texts and traditions, knows them, and has its own hermeneutic. The faithful treasure and use on a daily basis the teachings of Scripture and of the Church Fathers—St. Cyril of Jerusalem and many others. Sacred tradition is a living presence: the memory of their civilizing hero, archpriest Avvakum, is as present among the Old Believers in Northern Alberta as he was in the battle with Patriarch Nikon three centuries ago. They live a pattern of life prescribed in ancient texts, in the *ustav* which orders daily prayer, feasting and fasting, and in the *kormchaia kniga*, canon law which structures the path of life. *Psalter* and a rich folk tradition animate the meaning of their daily encounters in the world and are pathways to communion with God. And all this without apology.

In the Shadow of Antichrist : The Old Believers of Alberta opens the door to a rich oral tradition. We glimpse a living relationship to ancient texts, and life formed and informed by ritual patterns. From birth to death, in work, eating, fasting, sleeping and sexual life, leisure and worship, ritual shapes and provides the context of meaning. All becomes real in ritual. The rich historical context necessary for our understanding of Old Believer custom and world view is marshalled and runs like a golden thread through this book so that we can understand this people for whom the past is a living presence. And I think we see, as well, just how significant Eastern Christianity, long the forgotten sister of

Western Christianity, is for a full understanding of Christian culture. It nudges us another step away from the assumption that Christian culture is adequately understood through its Latin—whether Roman Catholic or Protestant—expressions.

The study of human culture in Western Canada is in its infancy. While various historians, sociologists, and anthropologists have written on immigration, tolerance and prejudice, acculturation, etc. in the context of this recently settled part of North America, we have not had a full ethnographic description of any immigrant culture in this part of the world. This book is the first to provide us with a thick description of a culture in Western Canada. It makes a theoretical contribution to our understanding of Christian culture and traditional culture in the modern world, a contribution which highlights the shadow of so much of our scholarship to date. It lets us reach out and touch—as the best scholarship can—the living body, the iconic form, of a people whose life has taken on such clear meaning perhaps because it has been lived on the shadow side.

David J. Goa
Curator of Folk Life
Provincial Museum of Alberta

Acknowledgements

This book is partly based on my doctoral dissertation in anthropology, which was defended at McMaster University in May 1988. I wish to reiterate my gratitude to Dr. Christopher Hallpike for his dedication in supervising the project, to McMaster University for funding it, and to Dr. Stephen Dunn for helpful comments on how to turn the dissertation into a book.

While in the field, I was fortunate to be surrounded by many people who were interested in the research and my welfare. I must single out Della and David Goa, Lee Grimmer and Barnabas Walther, and my immensely accommodating hosts, Lina and Daniel Plamondon. Among the Old Believers who overcame their traditional distrust of strangers and made my work possible, I wish to express my indebtedness to Anastasia Reitova and her family, and to Vasily Kuznetsov. They taught me a lot not only about Old Orthodoxy but also about the gentle side of religious fundamentalism.

My deepest gratitude is reserved for my wife, Anita Scheffel, who took an active interest in the writing of this book, improved it by eliminating some of the clumsiness of my English, and gave me the time to finish it. The book is dedicated to her.

Introduction

21 June 1981. I arrived here today. Josephville is a pleasant little village of some three hundred people, with a gas station, a Roman Catholic church, and a small hotel, which I moved into for fifteen dollars a night. If you follow the main street, you come to a gravel road that ends in the settlement of the Old Believers. Already in Josephville, I ran into the Russians: youngsters (mostly boys) in colourful outfits, driving around in pick-up trucks, with no apparent purpose in mind. Some were hiding in a corner store, smoking cigarettes secretly.

The road to the settlement leads through forests and fields, here and there a farm, then none at all, and suddenly a bridge across a narrow river. On the bridge were perhaps ten children, all in pretty and colourful embroidered shirts. Boys with cropped hair, girls with long tresses, most of them blond and incredibly "Russian" looking.

Past the bridge, you can turn left or right. I took the left road and followed the edge of what used to be a forest whose trees had been cut down to make room for fields. That must have happened at least a year ago, because the wood seemed rather dry. But cultivated fields are nowhere to be seen. To the left of the road stand houses with much space between them. They are not unusual in their appearance, but the surrounding outbuildings and vegetable patches have an air of Eastern Europe. I followed the road and counted approximately ten homes before reaching its end, then turned around and explored the area to the right of the bridge. This seemed to be the actual heart of the settlement; between fifteen and twenty houses, closer together but again surrounded by vegetable gardens, with the same semi-cleared fields across the road. It was here that I met adults walking along the road, but only a few, probably because most would stay at home on a Sunday. The adults too look typically Russian, the men with long beards, short hair and colourful shirts, the women matronly and stern. They appear slightly stoical but nod in response to my greetings. The road came to an end, so I turned around and returned to Josephville. I feel excitement and relief— they have not left after all! But I am also afraid, having no idea how to penetrate this isolated and closely knit community! It will be terribly difficult.

This diary entry sums up my first impressions of the people described in this book. I had first heard of their settlement in 1979, but it took me two years to identify the exact location of this recently founded community. Despite my exhaustive enquiries of government agencies, newspapers, and universities, it seemed that the arrival of a group of Old Believers in Canada had gone entirely unnoticed. By the fall of 1980, I had been admitted to a doctoral program in anthropology, with the Old Believers as my planned dissertation topic. Needless to say, I had to locate the people in order to proceed with my studies.

When I was almost ready to give up the search and choose another topic, a letter from a museum curator in Alberta confirmed the existence and described the location of the elusive community. I was ecstatic. At a time that anthropologists were coming to terms with the rapid disappearance of exotic and isolated tribes to study, I was about to discover and describe an almost completely unexplored society!

At this time, my knowledge of the Old Believers was rather limited. I had read some historical works dealing with the schism of seventeenth- century Russian Orthodoxy, the tragic *raskol* which split the church and people into two factions: one of tradition-oriented Old Believers, the other of western-oriented builders of modern Russia. I had also read the classic works of

Tolstoy, Gorky, Leskov, and several other writers, which impressed upon me the influence of the Old Believers on Russia's history, culture, and politics. Gradually, I realized that the people I was about to meet face to face were not an isolated and unknown "tribe", but rather the offshoot from a mighty tree with very long roots. The more I learned, the less secure I grew about my ability to comprehend the culture and society of the Old Believers during the one year of field work that anthropologists use for the collection of ethnographic data.

This apprehension intensified when in the summer of 1981 I finally reached the people I was about to study, in order to make preliminary arrangements for my year-long sojourn.

As my diary entry demonstrates, I had mixed feelings about the research plan. Understandably, I was exhilarated at having finally found the enigmatic Old Believers of Alberta. Simultaneously, the visit helped me understand the difficulty of gaining entry into a community whose explicit goal was isolation. As it turned out, the Old Believers opened their doors, answered my questions, invited me to meals, and tolerated my presence in their church. But the hospitality stopped short of allowing me to take up residence in the Russian village. For the next six weeks, I was obliged to commute every day from the nearest Canadian town. When asked about the possibility of my returning and spending a full year in their midst, my informants shrugged as if to express benevolent indifference.

In addition to filling me with uncertainty concerning the planned field work, the exploratory visit impressed upon me the necessity of not viewing the Russian community and its residents as a self-contained entity explicable by means of the traditional ethnographic method. While the Old Believers were fairly isolated from the surrounding society, they were anything but self-contained in a historical sense. Unlike their North American neighbours, the Old Believers do not watch television, listen to the radio, or read newspapers as a way of expanding their perception of the world. Instead of letting in the outside *synchronically*, they do it *diachronically*. They learn about their place in the world predominantly through history, and the past serves as the preferred method for reducing the burden of voluntary isolation. Instead of chatting and drinking with their neighbours, the Old

Believers communicate with saints and ancestors. Instead of fearing the old and glorifying the new, they fear the future and glorify the past.

The importance of history was reflected in almost every answer to my questions. Asked about the significance of his costume, a man would point out hand-painted icons as ancient models of proper appearance. Quizzed about the structure of dietary prohibitions, a woman would refer to "old books" as their source. Interrogated about specific features of religious ritual, an elder automatically opens an ancient liturgical tome and searches for the appropriate answer. This tendency of the Old Believers to see the present *only* as an appendage to the past threatened the feasibility of my planned ethnographic study. I realized that in order to grasp the essence of the local culture, I would have to unearth its entangled roots. And that would require a depth of historical analysis for which anthropologists are not trained, and which cannot be accomplished in the course of normal field work.

As if methodological problems were not enough, someone had started the rumour that I was a spy. Unwittingly, I had prepared the ground for the allegation by using the term *raskolniki* (schismatics) in my first encounter with the Old Believers. This unintended insult—a legacy of nineteenth-century scholarship—associated me with the tsarist inquisition and its Soviet progeny. Eventually, my poor command of Russian persuaded most residents that I was not likely a Soviet spy. But there remained the possibility of my working for the Canadian government, a prospect equally unappealing to my reluctant hosts.

By the end of the short summer visit, I had identified a core of seemingly reliable informants who appeared willing to help with my research regardless of the rumours about my alleged spying. However, I was becoming increasingly apprehensive about the ethical aspects of the planned field work. Granted, every anthropologist is likely to encounter some degree of suspicion and perhaps resistance in the field. We are prepared for this in our training, which underlines the need for following not only scientific but also moral standards. With the Old Believers, however, established procedures, such as informing the community about the purpose of the research and seeking collective permission to embark on it, seemed inappropriate. I learned very quickly that no one in the settlement spoke for any one else; if I wanted approval for the research I was about to initiate, I had to ask for it individually rather than collectively. Did this mean that if more than fifty per cent of the residents consented, I had satisfied ethical considerations and could go ahead with the project? I didn't know.

My worries about the ethics of the planned research were manifold. For one, I was afraid that my alleged spying might be a divisive factor in the relationship between those who consented to my presence and those who didn't. Related to this was the concern that if my informants believed in the fictitious connection between me and the government, they would be likely to withhold some information and perhaps fabricate data that could seriously distort the outcome of my work. Pondering this possibility, I realized that although I was not a spy, the field work could make me into one against my will. What if I discovered illegal immigrants among the people I wanted to study? And how would I deal with other types of criminal or deviant behaviour? Should it be made public, thus exposing my informants to potential harm? Or should I compromise academic honesty by failing to disclose the material?

These questions and doubts contrasted greatly with the euphoria I had felt upon arriving. The exhilaration of having discovered a community and a people unknown to anthropologists and other social scientists, waiting to become *mine*, had been displaced by fears of professional and personal inadequacy. I had to face the fact that the welcome extended to me was less cordial than I would have liked, and that methodological and ethical pitfalls threatened the planned field work.

Such thoughts were responsible for my sombre mood upon ending the visit. To clear my mind, I invited a friend to a canoe trip through a nearby stretch of northern wilderness. Several days into the adventure, the canoe capsized in unexpectedly heavy rapids, and we spent the next three days evading bears and praying for another chance at life. Finally, help arrived in the form of a police helicopter, and soon I was back with the Old Believers, ready to say good-bye to the few friends I had made.

The reception I received took me completely by surprise. The news of my adventure had spread through the community, and wherever I went, people shook my hand, offered food and drink and enticed me to recount all details of the trip. My story elicited their own, and soon I was bombarded with recollections of rafting on treacherous Manchurian rivers, tiger-hunting accidents in the taiga, and related experiences from the Old Believers' colourful past. It seemed that my short stay away had brought about a degree of intimacy which the previous weeks of intensive explanations of my role could not achieve. I realized then how abstract I must have appeared in my role as a university scholar. No one from among the Old Believers had ever been to a university, and the idea of collecting vast quantities of facts for the purpose of advancing knowledge seemed hard to fathom. I had to be a government spy. The river adventure tore off the abstract mask of an unintelligible and therefore dangerous outsider and transformed me into another adventure-seeking but vulnerable human being. In the best anthropological tradition, my presence became a source of entertainment. As I was to find out later, my informants enjoyed taking risks, and my foolish trip reminded them of episodes in their own lives.

Once we had found a common language, the spy hypothesis faded. Even the most reticent residents conceded that few governments would pay their agents to go on risky wilderness trips, and I was encouraged to come back the following summer. Although my request to live in the community itself remained ungranted, there were enough indications of goodwill to encourage the planning of the real field work.

I returned in the early summer of 1982 and spent several long weeks persuading my hosts to allow me to live in their midst. Finally, after numerous futile attempts at finding a family that would rent me a room or an unused shed, I was told that local Old Believers would never consent to an outsider's moving into their village. If I seriously wished to learn about their culture, they would consider allowing me to convert and to really become "one of them". Another way of gaining acceptance did not exist, according to my informants. Before I knew it, the conversion option was raised at a church meeting, and some of my acquaintances started looking for a suitable bride for me. At last it dawned on me that my determination to follow the traditional principles of anthropological field work would drive me either to violate the trust of my hosts by faking interest in the conversion option, or to cease being an anthropologist and become an Old Believer instead.

I resolved the dilemma by giving up the desire to live in the Russian community. I rented a room in the closest Canadian outpost, Josephville[1] and made preparations for an uneventful year in which I would study the Old Believers as a daily commuter from the outside. At the time of this "capitulation" I felt that I was compromising my status as a budding anthropologist, for I had lost the chance at "going native" and at gaining more than a superficial impression of the lives lived by "my people". There can be no doubt that my residence some fifteen kilometres down the road from the actual object of my study deprived me of some valuable insights into the home life of the Old Believers. On my almost daily visits, I caught glimpses of the private domain, but these do not add up to the usually rich texture of intimate knowledge displayed by ethnographers living in the midst of the described societies. I remained a visitor, albeit a very frequent one, whose presence modified the observed environment. I tried to minimize the effect of my presence by always speaking Russian, dressing in local garb, letting my beard grow long and full, and adhering as conscientiously as possible to the numerous rules that regulate the Old Believers' daily life. But these expressions of sympathy and tolerance were understood as nothing more than that. Far from propelling my assimilation, these gestures of goodwill merely camouflaged the considerable gap between "my people" and me.

Ironically, this gap seemed to widen every time my hosts tried to make me feel at home. As everywhere else, the sharing of food is considered a token of respect and friendship by the Old Believers, who made a point of inviting me to elaborate meals served after the demanding Sunday prayer sessions. On these occasions, an outside observer would have believed me a perfect example of an anthropologist gone native. With my long beard, embroidered shirt, enough Russian to get by, I would be sitting at a long table, surrounded by a large family, fitting in as anybody else. Only an Old Believer would have noticed the one detail that marked my foreign status: I was using a separate set of dishes, a set literally called *pagan*, which my hosts never touched for fear of defilement. This *pagan* plate and cup ensured that I remained a pariah even when everything else pointed to the contrary.

It was only when I had begun to appreciate the extraordinary significance attached to the concept of paganism by my hosts that I stopped blaming myself for failing to conduct the field work from within the community. I finally realized that as long as strangers continue to be classified as polluting pagans, their attempts at gaining insider status without conversion must be doomed. This insight helped me come to terms with my "banishment" and to set realistic research goals.

Every anthropologist who has carried out full-scale field work is likely to remember it as a very interesting but also extremely demanding period of professional and personal development. Not a day goes by without a discovery, and hardly a week goes by during which one doesn't experience alternating feelings of exhilaration and dejection. The anthropologist is separated from his or her normal milieu, surrounded by people with unfamiliar values and beliefs, forced to speak a poorly understood language and expected to make a significant discovery, which will justify the energy and funds that sustain the year in the field. Even under the best of circumstances, field work demands all of one's resources.

Although my year with the Old Believers exposed me to the usual experiences of anthropological research in the field, the requirement to commute daily between the periphery and the centre of the studied society introduced some unexpected features which are not always encountered in more traditional settings. Unlike other anthropologists who enter the field, go native and remain on the inside for as long as possible, I felt condemned to lead a double life for this period, continually commuting between "Canada" and "Little Russia", unable to find peace in either. My base in Josephville served as a much-needed refuge from the emotional and physical strains of research, and it provided another vantage point for observing the Old Believers, namely from the perspective of their immediate neighbours. But because of my intimate and somewhat mysterious association with the residents of the Russian enclave, the people of Josephville were not altogether certain whether I should be regarded as friend or foe. Hence whether I was at work or at home, I was viewed with a degree of suspicion, which always reminded me of my marginality.

Although that marginality weighed heavily on me, it also served as a source of strength that enabled me to gain unusual insights into the culture of the people I studied. Given the Old Believers' tendency to dogmatism and ethnocentrism, integration into the community presupposes the acceptance of a whole range of values and beliefs as unshakable truths that cannot be questioned. Had I gone native more completely than I did, the pressure to see and to portray my hosts as they wanted to be seen would have escalated, thereby threatening the elusive goal of objectivity expected by the academic community. By remaining a "fence sitter", I retained the freedom to ask questions many Old Believers considered silly, useless, and even dangerous.

I hope that this book will achieve at least two goals. Firstly, the material offered here provides an introduction to a fascinating people who have been curiously neglected by anthropologists and other social scientists. The ethnographic description which spans chapters 3 - 7 is thick with Russian and Church Slavonic terms, and with at times painfully detailed summaries of local beliefs and customs. These data are presented with a minimum of interpretive distortion, in the hope that they will provide an empirical base for future comparative research. I make a small step in this direction in chapters 2 and 8, which combine my own material with ethnographic and historical data from other locations and periods, and help place "my people" in a much larger context. This insistence on the comparative method may at times disturb the reader, who is expected to digest a considerable volume of seemingly obscure material spanning many centuries and regions. But I am confident that the extra demand will lead to a deeper grasp of the complex identity of the people portrayed here.

Although the primary purpose of this book is to lift the cloak of obscurity to which the Old Believers seem to have been condemned by history and modern scholarship, I also hope to provide inspiration and perhaps justification for the study of other seemingly insignificant societies and communities. My research could not have been carried out had it not been for the anthropological tradition of refusing to evaluate societies on the basis of their military, economic, political, or technological influence on the investigator's society. What this tradition holds dear is the conviction that all cultures are equally valuable as objects of scholarly scrutiny and as sources of enlightenment. Such a view cannot be reconciled with the manifold calls heard these days demanding "relevant" and "applied" research, which is usually conducted from an alarmingly ethnocentric perspective.

The present study demonstrates, I hope, the unexpected links between an isolated and obscure community and societies far removed in time and space. The imaginative reader will have no difficulty using this case study as more than a description of a little-known people. Whether he or she displays an interest in the culture of Byzantium, Muscovy, eighteenth-century Russia, contemporary Soviet Union, or in the more general topics of religious fundamentalism and the politics of purism, the Old Believers will never be far away, inviting parallels to be drawn and comparisons to be made, forever resembling "those dolls within a doll, secrets within secrets concealing."

A few of these parallels and comparisons are attempted in chapter 8, where I identify a number of theoretical issues in anthropology, history, and religious studies to which this study may be relevant. Of particular importance is the transmission of culture in general and religious orthodoxy in particular by means of ritual. For many decades, anthropologists have criticized the western bias against viewing ritual as the backbone of religion (Douglas 1973; Radcliffe-Brown 1952:155-165) or even of culture as a whole (Connerton 1989). The Old Believers, who in Russian are referred to as Old "Ritualists", testify to the importance of ritual in several key areas of their culture: the distinction between orthodoxy and heterodoxy, the communication and transmission of dogma, and even the relationship between the past and the present cannot be articulated without ritual.

The focus on the practical aspects of religion invites comparison with a spate of recent studies devoted to "folk religion" in various European settings (see Badone 1990). The number and quality of these studies indicate that, at last, anthropologists are ready to give Christianity more than a passing glance. But they also demonstrate the need for shedding the popular misconception that Christianity, particularly in Europe, is synonymous with Roman Catholicism and Protestantism. As I try to show in this book, especially in chapter 8, Eastern Orthodoxy must receive serious attention in anthropological models of Christianity. This I consider the main theoretical contribution of the present work.

Prelude in Muscovy

Unquestionably the most difficult thing about introducing the Old Believers is an explanation of their origins. This is not because their past is devoid of fascinating and illuminating episodes or because it remains undocumented; although there are few English-language introductions to the subject, Russian scholars have compensated for the dearth of western interest with dozens and dozens of reputable treatises. What, in fact, makes the emergence of the Old Believers so hard to explain is not a lack of reliable material, but rather the absence of shared reference points between the commentator and the reader.

Anybody writing about Russian history for a western audience must overcome the widely held notion that it began with Peter the Great, samovars, and vodka. Once it is accepted that Russia, albeit known as Muscovy, existed prior to the eighteenth century, other barriers must be surmounted in order to fill a vacuum left by professional historians. Muscovite, that is, pre-eighteenth century, history as it is taught by western academics is long on military campaigns, economic developments, and dynastic squabbles, but short on religion and popular culture. Consequently, even readers with some background in Russian history are far more likely to have heard of Dmitrii Donskoi, Ivan the Terrible, and Boris Godunov than of Patriarch Nikon, Archpriest Avvakum, or, indeed, the *raskol* itself.

The historical synopsis provided in this chapter may seem tedious, because most of the material will not have been encountered before. Who has heard of the difference between *dvoe-* and *troeperstie*, double and triple *alleluia*, or *krest* and *krizh*? Yet it is these seemingly obscure historical details which, to this day, have preoccupied the Old Believers and have shaped their relationship with the surrounding society. But the scope of this introduction extends beyond the Old Believers. It enables the reader to look at Russian history from an unaccustomed angle, and, perhaps, to gain a better understanding of the roots of Russian and Soviet culture.

The Appropriation of Orthodoxy

Described in the ninth century as a "barbarous, nomadic, leaderless...nation of no account" (in Geanakoplos 1984:350), the entity known later as Russia emerged in the sixteenth century as a powerful nation, and came to play an important role in European affairs. Russia's rise from obscurity was marked by three events of lasting significance: the acceptance of Greek Orthodoxy as the country's state religion; the lifting of the Tatar yoke, which set the stage for territorial expansion; and the appropriation of the position occupied by the Byzantine Empire following the latter's demise.

The baptism of Prince Vladimir of Kiev into Greek Orthodoxy predestined Russia to become entangled in the web of disputes between the Christian East and West, Since the division of the Roman Empire into a Greek and a Latin hemisphere, political and theological disputes had favoured separate development of the two sibling empires, with their centres in Constantinople and Rome respectively. Byzantium, erected on a foundation of Hellenism and Oriental Christendom, established hegemony in southeastern Europe and Asia Minor. The Latin empire carved out its sphere of influence in Italy and western Europe. The Roman inheritance was claimed by both entities.

The rivalry between the Greeks and the Latins reached the boiling point in the ninth century. The loss of Byzantine territory in Italy, the coronation of Charlemagne as Roman Emperor, and the attempt by the Pope of Rome to attain control over the entire Christian church challenged the Greek view of political realities in Europe. The estrangement erupted into an open conflict after the decision of the Latin church to modify the common Christian creed by the addition of the word *filioque*, an innovation fiercely opposed by Greek theologians.[2] The *filioque* dispute, inflamed by further divergences in the interpretation and conduct of liturgical practices, drove a wedge between eastern and western Christians, which has yet to be removed. A formal schism separated Greek Orthodoxy and Roman Catholicism into autonomous churches, headed by the Patriarch of Constantinople and the Pope of Rome respectively, and prepared the ground for the cultural and political polarization of Europe.

The Greek-Latin animosity was exported to Russia by Greek missionaries. Having become a vassal of the Byzantine Empire, Prince Vladimir of Kiev and his successors accepted the Orthodox version of Christianity and the Greek view of the West. Roman Catholics, referred to collectively as *"Latins"* or *"Franks"*, were accused of having suppressed authentic traditions of the early church and of following heterodox practices, which threatened their Christian status. As in Byzantium, the *filioque*, the composition of the Eucharist, and the manner of performing baptism constituted the theological core of Russian reservations. But in addition, there emerged a vast periphery of secondary accusations, which converted seemingly harmless habits associated with the West—such a shaving, kneeling, dancing, or the eating of sausages—into further evidence of the Latins' spiritual decline. In due time, virtually any cultural difference came to be regarded as an expression of heresy, which militated against friendly relations between the Orthodox and the Roman Catholics, or, later on, the Protestants.[3]

The anti-western sentiments supplied an important building block for Russia's political culture following the lifting of the Tatar yoke in the fifteenth century. The ensuing process of "nation-building", which culminated in the unification of several principalities within the entity known as Muscovy, was propelled by a sense of religious mission, which facilitated the appropriation of territories controlled by heterodox rulers. While Muscovy's Christian status legitimized and compelled raids on Moslem lands, its Orthodox status justified westward expansion at the cost of Ukraine, Poland, Lithuania, and Sweden.[4]

The Muscovite version of the Byzantine sense of manifest destiny became formalized in the well-known belief in Moscow being the "Third Rome", which in turn fertilized the notion of "holy Russia". Although the formulation of this twin doctrine seems to have been prompted by the fall of the "Second Rome", that is, Constantinople, in 1453, rumblings of Russian nationalism predate the demise of the Byzantine Empire.[5] With Muscovy's rise to power, it was inevitable that the tutelage exercised by the Greek mother church over its Russian dependency would eventually be challenged.

The signal for Moscow's rebellion came from Italy in 1439. The imminent threat of a Turkish conquest of the remnants of Byzantium had prompted the eastern emperor to seek military assistance from the West in exchange for settling the schism between Greek Orthodoxy and Roman Catholicism to Rome's advantage. The short-lived Union of Florence brought about neither the survival of the ailing eastern empire nor a lasting peace between Constantinople and Rome. But it supplied a powerful rationale for the Russification of the Muscovite branch of the Orthodox church and for Russia's role as the self-appointed protector of the Christian faith. The Greek bishop who had endorsed the union on behalf of Russia was arrested upon his return to Muscovy and replaced with an anti-unionist Russian prelate. The Patriarch of Constantinople was not asked for his blessing (Arkheograficheskaya kommissiya 1897).

The suspicion cast upon the Greeks by their temporary reconciliation with the papists seemed confirmed by the final demise of Byzantium in 1453, which was widely interpreted as God's punishment for the Florentine Union (Koncevicius 1927). The niche vacated by the Second Rome could now be openly claimed by Moscow.

The modification of the relationship between Muscovy and the Greek mother church was not aimed at its termination. The Ecumenical Patriarch, who continued to reside in Constantinople even after the Turkish conquest, and the other three eastern patriarchs of Jerusalem, Antioch, and Alexandria, were still recognized and paid respect. But instead of genuine power, the post-Byzantine Greek church retained merely an advisory role, displayed primarily in the field of what might today be called "theological consulting". In exchange for this service, Russia supported the impoverished mother church and its numerous dignitaries financially. By the end of the sixteenth century, the Russification of the national church and faith seemed to have

Russia's first Christian princes depicted as saints.

been brought to a successful end. Muscovy finally had its own pantheon of *Russian* saints and a set of doctrines defining *Russian* Orthodoxy (Koch 1962). The evolution towards cultural independence was crowned by the elevation of the Moscow-based metropolitan see to an autonomous patriarchate in 1589.

The appropriation of Orthodoxy during the Muscovite period promoted an ever-closer overlap between the state and the church. The outward manifestation of the links binding the two realms can be seen in the role played by the head of the state. At first a mere prince, the ruler of Muscovy gradually elevated himself to a Grand Prince and, after the fall of Byzantium, to tsar, a title which derives from the Latin Caesar. The farther the ruler rose, the more likely he became to justify his exalted position in religious terms. The observation of a shocked English visitor that the tsar was respected "not as [a] prince, but as a God" (in Fuhrmann 1982:154) is echoed by virtually every western traveller. Folk sayings such as "the tsar neither burns nor drowns", or "the heart of the tsar lies in God's hand" (in Staden 1964:60), reinforced the popular belief in the semi-divinity of the ruler. In keeping with this status, the tsar was granted privileges allowed no other layman, such as access to sacred space and the performance of various church rituals (Aleppo 1873).

The extraordinary fusion achieved in Muscovy between the goals of the state and those of the church permeated the entire society with a degree of religiosity that astonished foreign commentators. As one of them put it after a long visit in the 1650s, "Undoubtedly all these Russians are saints, surpassing in devotion the hermits of the deserts" (Aleppo 1873:253)! But the acceptance of an ideology which equated religious and civil service also blurred the line between heresy and political crime or even simple dissent (Hoesch 1975:123). It cannot be overemphasized that because of the symbiosis between the spiritual and the political domain, exemplified by the tsar in his combined role of church- and statesman, any type of protest against any type of authority was likely to be interpreted as an attack on the very core of Muscovite culture (Raeff 1984:2-3).

Muscovite Xenophobia

Muscovy was an isolated country whose inhabitants knew little about the world surrounding them. Very few people were allowed, as a rule, to travel abroad, and the handful of visitors who came to Muscovy every year were so closely supervised that they could hardly serve as a source of information about their respective countries of origin. The little knowledge Muscovites possessed about other peoples derived either from religious propaganda or from rumours based on chance encounters with foreign residents.

Limited knowledge of other cultures predisposed even the highest segments of Muscovite society to a level of chauvinism that was rare in other European countries. The appropriation of Orthodoxy as something of a Russian national trait—aptly reflected in the term *holy* Russia—was partly the result but also a source of Muscovite ethnocentrism. It favoured a sense of manifest destiny that usually accompanies a nation's belief in being God's "chosen people". Since proper Christianity was assumed to be restricted to the Orthodox, the differences between animists, Moslems, Jews, Roman Catholics, or Protestants mattered relatively little. All these "unbelievers" were lumped into a single class of *pogany* (pagans) (Goetz 1905:139; Popov 1875:70-75; Smirnov 1914:134,144-146), and treated accordingly. This status justified, for example, the slaughter of Jewish and Roman Catholic residents of conquered Polish cities (Aleppo 1873:84) or the sale of western prisoners of war into Turkish slavery (Staden 1964:53).[6]

Comparable to a bacillus within a healthy body, foreigners of all colours posed the threat of infecting Muscovy with the numerous vices attributed to infidels. Besides their theological objections to heterodox religious practices, Russian critics attacked astronomy and astrology as a form of sorcery (Olearius 1656:184-185), accused foreign scientists of magic (*ibid*.:186), and felt greatly perturbed by the influx of secular art forms spreading from the West. Visitors from abroad attributed the Muscovite xenophobia to barbarism stemming from scientific and artistic ignorance (Olearius 1656:184), thereby overlooking the genuine threat western innovations posed to Muscovy's survival. After all, the country's rise coincided with the Renaissance, with its tremendous potential for emancipating the individual from the grip of the church. In view of the Orthodox symbiosis between church and state, the process of secularization which was, albeit in a piecemeal fashion, being exported from western Europe to Russia threatened to undermine Muscovy's very foundation.

Because the country's expansion, achieved largely through military means, depended to a considerable degree on technology transfer from the West, Muscovy could not curb the impact of acculturation by simply sealing its borders. Not unlike contemporary Islamic fundamentalist societies, Muscovy needed western know-how and experts in order to attain and maintain political and cultural independence from the surrounding world. To fulfill this need, the tsar recruited foreign soldiers, officers, craftsmen, and scientists who received various privileges in exchange for their help in modernizing the Russian army, economy, and system of administration (Staden 1964). Hence the problem faced by state officials was not how to keep foreigners out of the country, but rather how to confine their influence to the fields slated for modernization.

Foreigners were isolated from the native population and closely watched in all their activities. The strategy of containment began at the border, where visitors from abroad were met by an official and conducted to Moscow in order to allow the tsar to be the first to learn about the purpose of the visit (Aleppo 1873:92; Herberstein 1926:206). Foreign envoys were assigned supervised quarters and guides who prevented unofficial contact with the local population (Aleppo 1873; Staden 1964:112). These tight controls extended even to private correspondence: mail from abroad was routinely scrutinized by the foreign office (Fuhrmann 1982:103).

Western soldiers and experts who lived in Moscow more or less permanently were confined to a ghetto walled off from the rest of the city. Because they were barred from Orthodox churches (Olearius 1656:303), foreign residents were free to practise their own religion, but only to the extent that this privilege did not influence Russian subjects (Staden 1964:109). However, those who desired to win the confidence of the tsar felt compelled to convert to Orthodoxy. After the conversion, a foreigner was not likely to receive permission to leave Muscovy ever again. For, as one sixteenth-century western resident put it, "The road into the country is wide, but the road out is very narrow" (Staden 1964:109).

Of all foreign visitors and residents, the Greeks alone received the privilege of participating in Russian religious services (Olearius 1656:45,295). But they too were closely watched by their hosts, and even members of the clergy were discouraged from unsupervised contact with their Russian counterparts (Aleppo 1873:65,92,130). Thus, in spite of the willingness to recognize some distinctions within the vast class of foreigners, the tendency to polarize the universe into "us" and "them" prevailed on all but the most formal occasions. In times of crisis, the ever-present xenophobia manifested itself in various forms of scapegoating, which expressed the widespread demand that Muscovite society be healed by purging it of all alien elements. In one instance, a terrible outbreak of pestilence in the early 1570s was attributed to the presence in Moscow of an elephant given to the tsar by the Persian shah. The popular outcry against this alien creature was so strong that the exotic animal had to be killed (Staden 1964:43). On another occasion, the Patriarch of Moscow ordered his people to collect and burn imported musical instruments as part of his religious revival program (Olearius 1656:302). Although these purges did not take any human lives, they may be regarded as the forerunners of the pogroms of more recent times.

The Quest for Authenticity

Even a superficial glance at Russian history will reveal a strong national preoccupation with *truth*. There are few terms that can compete with the word for truth in its influence on the Russian language: law, justice, righteousness, Orthodoxy, government, and many more expressions are closely related to the word *pravda*. And there are few western societies which have struggled as hard as the Russians to prove to themselves and the world that truth is not a relative concept changing with time and fashion, but rather a stable notion characterized by immutable standards. Russian history could be interpreted as a long series of events tied together by the preoccupation with Truth.

This quest began with the acceptance of Christianity. As in every other Christian nation, God, as the ultimate source of all meaning, played a central part in it. But, unlike in the West where, largely in consequence of the Renaissance, theologians searched for new approaches to God, Muscovite churchmen laid down rules against religious experimentation in an attempt to canonize their version of truth. Having appropriated Orthodoxy, the "truthful faith", holy Russia claimed to have found what others were still searching for. Its ideology was adapted not to a search for but to the preservation of *pravda*.

The religion embraced by the Muscovites as the source of all meaning directed their attention to the past. The birth and life of Christ were regarded as the most complete revelation of God and, therefore, truth. In order that they grasp the significance of the present, the church directed people to improve their understanding of the Christian past, which provided the key required to unlock the mysteries of the future. To improve their moral fibre, believers were instructed to learn from and imitate the conduct of Christ and the saints. Hence the past served as a model not only for proper thoughts and feelings, but also for the food, clothing, and daily habits of the Muscovites. For the average person, intimate knowledge of the early Christian era permitted the imitation of an entire life-style that was considered indispensable for salvation (Aleppo 1873; Olearius 1656).

The importance attached by old and new Russians to the past as the source of models worthy of emulation comes through in their expression for "education", *obrazovanie*. Deriving from *obraz*, which designates a figure, model, or prototype, education literally means the process of copying an example from the past (Billington 1970:38). *Obraz* has a second meaning, which is also relevant in this context: it can be used to refer to depictions of religious scenes, popularly known as icons. Originally developed as a pictorial substitute for the Bible and employed in the instruction of illiterates, icons enjoyed unprecedented popularity in Muscovy. Their presence in every public and private domain demonstrated the power of the past in a most detailed fashion. For it was largely through icons that the Orthodox verified the authenticity of their way of life, comparing it, as it were, with the divine prototypes of the early Christian era.

The tendency to define truth as a reflection of the past, which could not be improved upon but merely preserved in its original form, presented two formidable problems. Firstly, there had to be a consensus on how much of the early Christian culture required preservation, or, in other words, which traditions were essential and which were not. And, secondly, it was necessary to develop a reliable method for testing the authenticity of essential traditions in order to ensure that they did indeed preserve the original model laid down by Christ and His first followers.

Both tasks took on an urgency in the sixteenth century with Muscovy's territorial expansion and appropriation of the role formerly played by the Byzantine Empire. Religious customs in the many corners of the vast country were by no means uniform, and there were considerable discrepancies between traditions upheld by the Orthodox churches in Russia, Serbia, Greece, Asia, and Africa. Thus, in Muscovy men wore beards in imitation of Christ; in Ukraine they did not. In Novgorod crosses were made with four ends; in Moscow they had eight. In the Near East churchmen smoked opium; in Russia this was a crime. In Greece *alleluia* was repeated three times; in Muscovy only twice. Having gained cultural independence, holy Russia assumed responsibility for examining its traditions, authenticating the truly ancient ones, and standardizing the national church without the accustomed guidance from Constantinople.

The standardization of Muscovite religious customs began in the second half of the fifteenth century and lasted for almost two hundred years. It required, first of all, access to the entire written tradition of the Christian church, including the Bible and the voluminous patristic literature. The Bible was translated into Church Slavonic, the liturgical language of Russian Orthodoxy, by the end of the fifteenth century, but the writings of the Fathers of the Church remained largely inaccessible. Owing to their poor command of Greek and Latin, Muscovite theologians were compelled to rely on undated and unauthorized Slavonic excerpts from a variety of sources, many of dubious authenticity. By the second decade of the sixteenth century, it had become clear that the standardization of the national church depended on the *verification* of its most important link with the past: the entire written tradition (Hoesch 1975; Koch 1962).

The step of examining, revising, and complementing the very foundation of Russian Orthodoxy evoked strong fears. Because of widespread illiteracy, the written word had taken on a magical quality, a power unknown in literate societies. The written language, Church Slavonic, differed from spoken Russian in style and origin. It was a *lingua sacra*, a sacred medium believed to have been composed by God Himself in order to make people receptive to the Word of Truth (Matejka 1984). The elevated status of the written language stood in the way of genuine scholarship, which uses the word not as an incarnation of divinity but as a servant that can be manipulated and subjected. This attitude was not yet present in Muscovy.

The inability of Muscovite churchmen to authenticate the written tradition in accordance with accepted philological standards retarded the emancipation of the national church from Greek influence. Greek scholars were needed to help with the revision process, which did further the progress of the project but also generated friction between Russian and Greek correctors.[7] Finally, by the middle of the sixteenth century, several important liturgical and canonical works had been translated in their entirety, and a major church council had attempted to inject new energy into the standardization process. This latter step was taken by the so-called *Stoglav* Council, convened by Ivan the Terrible in 1551. Upset by the variety of religious customs upheld by his subjects, the immorality of the clergy, and the haphazard manner in which the church traditions were being examined, the tsar decided to end the confusion once and for all by compelling leading ecclesiastics to provide unequivocal answers to one hundred questions concerning Christian conduct (Kozhanchikov 1863). The result of this effort cannot be underestimated. For the first time in the history of Russian Orthodoxy, a binding national standard was supplied to guide the entire society in its quest for authenticity. The *Stoglav* outlined the proper conduct of liturgical services, and stipulated how to paint icons and how to behave at home and in church.

Still, however valuable these guidelines were, they did not solve the perennial problem of Russian Orthodoxy, namely the inability to separate the universal from the particular, and authentic from spurious traditions. The formulators of the *Stoglav* selected one custom over another without awaiting the conclusion of the ongoing standardization process and without always proving the wisdom of their choice. Furthermore, the decisions of a single national council could not regulate every detail of an ancient and complex religion. It wasn't enough to ordain that the liturgy be conducted in accordance with traditions confirmed by Basil the Great, Gregory the Theologian, John Chrysostomos, and Gregory the Great (Kozhanchikov 1863:65). The real challenge was the standardization of the various editions of these liturgies, copied over several centuries by semi-literate and careless scribes. The *Stoglav* admitted that there was a problem with literacy within the church (*ibid*.:43,91), but the suggested solution invited further problems. The council instructed educated churchmen to review liturgical books used in their parishes and to prohibit the reading of "wrong books" (*ibid*.:95). This order implied that the authentication and standardization of liturgical books had been completed, and that what remained to be done was the simple removal of "wrong books" from churches. This simplistic suggestion created a false impression of the state of Russian Orthodoxy in mid-sixteenth century.

The following one hundred years saw very few changes in the principles employed by the Muscovite church in defining and enforcing orthodoxy. While most of Europe was undergoing manifold types of religious reform, the eastern empire continued to seek truth in the past and to preserve it through highly formalistic means. As late as the mid-seventeenth century, God's word was regarded as a concrete text written down and preserved in the exact format in which it had been delivered. This text could not be modified in even the slightest detail, for perfection defied improvement (Olearius 1656:222)[8.] Lest they confuse the harmony of God's words, priests were barred from interpreting the divine text by way of sermons or discussions (Herberstein 1926:91; Olearius 1656:279). The only legitimate method for spreading the truth was its faithful repetition.[9] But which text was the authentic one? How much of the ritual performed every day in Muscovy's churches and homes adhered to genuinely ancient traditions? These questions remained unresolved. The *Stoglav* provided a mere breathing space, a lull before a storm unleashed in mid-seventeenth century which split Russia apart on the question of the authenticity of her religion.

The Raskol

Raskol, the schism of the Russian Orthodox church, arose out of the religious and social tensions which pervaded early seventeenth-century Muscovy. At its heart were conflicting views on how the standardization of liturgical traditions should be carried on, and in particular on the role played in this undertaking by the Greeks. But the theological debate itself was but a manifestation of Muscovy's search for a new identity. In spite of all the precautions taken by the xenophobic church and state, seventeenth-century Russia had been infected by the virus of western culture. Though lip service continued to be paid to the old supremacist ideology of holy Russia and Third Rome, the country's rapid modernization had shaken the archaic foundation and revealed many inconsistencies between normative and actual behaviour. The contradictions in the theory and practice of Muscovite society led to a deep cultural crisis of which the *raskol* was the first and longest-lasting symptom.

The schism erupted during the reign of Tsar Aleksei Mikhailovich (crowned in 1645, died in 1676), the second ruler of the Romanov dynasty. The tsar embodied the contradictions that plagued Muscovy at this time. With his one foot he stood in the eastern tradition of semi-divine kingship, leading him to expect and receive respect bordering on idolatry (Fuhrmann 1982:76,90). His other foot rested on a different foundation altogether, one that was being solidified by borrowings from the very West attacked by his church and army. The royal residence was equipped with a stage for theatrical performances as well as with musical instruments and secular paintings—all innovations considered anti-religious and proscribed outside the palace (Fuhrmann 1982). Despite protests from churchmen, Aleksei played cards and chess and hunted. He even went so far as to feed his falcons with specially bred pigeons—a grave infraction in a society which protected these birds as incarnations of the Holy Spirit (Fuhrmann 1982:104).

The conflict between worldly and spiritual pleasures by no means began with Tsar Aleksei; the court had always served as a magnet for new fashions, most of which originated in the West and hence were regarded as somewhat naughty. What seems to set Aleksei apart from his predecessors was his deliberate search for innovations and his determination to modernize Muscovy. This quest led to the establishment in 1649 of the country's first institution of higher learning, an academy entrusted with the task of studying and disseminating ideas developed by western humanists (Fuhrmann 1982:38). At a more applied level, the tsar set up a model farm near Moscow where he experimented with imported breeds of trees and animals (*ibid.*:119). And his fascination with things western conquered even the traditional fear of astronomy as a form of sorcery and prompted the tsar the appoint a German scientist his court astronomer (Olearius 1656:184-185). As if to underline the impact of the westernization process on Russia's future generations, Aleksei included Polish and Latin among the subjects studied by his children (Fuhrmann 1982:199).

One powerful institution which regarded the many changes that took place during Aleksei's reign with great alarm was the Russian Orthodox church. The pro-western sentiments disseminated by the royal court, the numerous foreign experts, and the new academy conflicted with the traditional view of the West as a source of spiritual decay, and generated fears that Muscovy was about to be "Latinized". In response to this and some other trends which threatened the role of the church as the leading cultural force, a group of clerics known as the Zealots of Piety set in motion a revitalization movement aimed at renewing traditional Russian Orthodoxy and renewing its purity. Beginning in the 1630s, the movement endeavoured to improve the moral and intellectual standards of the clergy, increase the prestige of the church, and fight the gradual secularization of Muscovite society by western influences (Lupinin 1984).

This loosely knit group of clerical moralists was joined in the 1640s by two men who were to become the manifest instigators of the *raskol*: Archimandrite Nikon (1605-1681) and Archpriest Avvakum (1620-1682). In 1649, Nikon ascended to the Metropolitan seat of Novgorod, which increased the Zealots' influence in the highest circles of the church hierarchy. Nikon's authority over the important see strengthened the position of the church in its fight against secularization, but the archbishop's dictatorial methods began to alienate members of the lower clergy, including some Zealots. When the Patriarch of Moscow died in 1652, Nikon no longer enjoyed the support of the Zealots' inner circle. In the meantime, however, he had gained the admiration of Tsar Aleksei, and with the tsar's help Nikon managed to be nominated for the vacant patriarchal seat (Lupinin 1984:87-90).

The events that followed Nikon's appointment in July of 1652 are extraordinarily complex and controversial. Indisputably the most contentious patriarch in the history of Russia, this relatively uneducated but fiercely ambitious man was determined to complete the standardization of liturgical texts which had been underway for over a century. Like his predecessors, he had to choose between Greece and Muscovy in determining the guardian of authenticity. Unlike his predecessors, Nikon turned his back on the ideology of holy Russia and returned to the Greek mother church, recognizing it as the supreme arbiter in questions affecting Orthodoxy. And this was the spark that ignited the flames of *raskol*.

Two hundred years after the fall of Constantinople, the Greeks had established a relatively peaceful coexistence with Roman Catholics. Deprived of political and cultural autonomy by the Turkish conquerors, they relied on western universities and presses for the preservation of the Byzantine heritage. In some parts of the Mediterranean, the former Greek-Latin animosity had receded to such an extent that joint Orthodox and Catholic masses were becoming common (Ware 1972:108).

The Roman Catholic influence was even stronger among Muscovy's Orthodox neighbours, the Ukrainians. The Union of Brest, signed in 1596, weakened the Ukrainian church and subjected many of its former members, as so-called Uniates, to Rome. The rest remained affiliated with Constantinople, but here too the Latin influence grew. Its most lasting expression came to be the celebrated *Orthodox Confession*, written in 1640 by the Metropolitan of Kiev, Peter Mogila. The document was based directly on Roman Catholic models, and it remains the most Latin treatise ever adopted by the Orthodox church (Ware 1972:107). Although both Greek and Ukrainian theologians continued to defend Orthodoxy as the sole true expression of the Christian faith, it was becoming increasingly difficult to reconcile the pro-western Greek/Ukrainian and the fiercely anti-western Muscovite positions.

This difficulty became apparent after the printing in 1648 of a religious work written several years earlier by an obscure Ukrainian monk. The *Kniga o vere* (*Book of Faith*) caused an uproar in Moscow by suggesting that the Florentine Union had never possessed any validity, and that the Greeks remained the leaders of Orthodoxy (Pascal 1938:150). A similar opinion was expressed in Peter Mogila's *Little Catechism*, published in Moscow a year later (*ibid.*:151). Although neither work explicitly attacked Russian Orthodoxy, the absence of any reference to Moscow's being the Third Rome was disturbing to Muscovite clerics. The impact was reinforced by the arrival in 1649 of the Patriarch of Jerusalem, Paisios, who rebuked his hosts for assuming that their practices were more orthodox than those of the Greek mother church (*ibid.*:203). To add insult to injury, the patriarchal visit coincided with the burning in Greece of several Muscovite pamphlets which proclaimed the Third Rome theory (*ibid.*:204).

One of the few Muscovite ecclesiastics who listened with interest to Paisios was the future patriarch Nikon. The Greek visitor seems to have struck a responsive chord in the Russian prelate by admitting that Muscovy could indeed rise to the desired position of leadership if its church standardized local practices with those adhered to in the rest of the Eastern commonwealth. Without such a reform, Paisios warned, Russia would forever remain a semi-barbaric province (Pascal 1938:203).

Acting on Nikon's request, the tsar appointed Arsenii Sukhanov, a learned monk, to accompany Paisios on his return journey and to investigate the state of Orthodoxy in Greece and other eastern lands. The envoy spent several years gathering impressions, and upon his return in 1653 filed a report, which expressed some serious reservations about Greek religious practices. The eastern clergy were criticized for using Latin vestments, for eating and inter-marrying with "Franks", and, above all, for having adopted the Roman Catholic baptism by effusion (Conybeare 1962:44; Pascal 1938:205-206). Sukhanov was dispatched anew in 1654 with the task of acquiring Greek manuscripts to be used in the correction of Slavonic liturgical texts. When he returned in 1655, he brought with him more than five hundred works collected at Mt. Athos and Constantinople (Stavrou & Weisensel 1986:50).

Sukhanov's critical assessment of the state of Greek Orthodoxy was not allowed to be made public without alterations ordered by the new Patriarch of Moscow, Nikon (Lupinin 1984:220). Ignoring the anti-Greek stance of his fellow Zealots and, indeed, most of the Russian church and people, Nikon em-

Apostle Andrew introducing *dvoeperstie.*
(Ikonenmuseum Recklinghausen)

barked on a campaign which must have appeared to his contemporaries as a frontal assault on some of the most cherished traditions of holy Russia. It began during Lent of 1653 when the patriarch sent a pastoral letter instructing all clergymen to make the sign of the cross with three fingers according to Greek custom (Avvakum 1974:407). This was in direct contradiction to the *Stoglav*, which, barely a century earlier, had decreed that the authentic form was *dvoeperstie*, that is, a sign made with two fingers (Kozhanchikov 1863). The belief that *dvoeperstie* alone guaranteed salvation had since then been raised to a major article of Russian Orthodoxy (Koch 1962:95-99), and the Greeks had been repeatedly chastised for rejecting it in favour of their *troeperstie* (Conybeare 1962:44; Pascal 1938:205-206).[10] The impact of Nikon's directive can be savoured from the following sketch provided by Archpriest Avvakum:

> We met together and took counsel. It was as if winter was of a mind to come; our hearts froze, our limbs shook. Neronov [another prominent Zealot] entrusted his church to me and shut himself up in the Miracle Monastery, and he spent a week praying in a cell, and one day a voice came from the icon of the Savior: "The hour of tribulation has come; it behooves you to suffer and be strong." (Avvakum 1974:407)

The refusal of many priests to adopt the new sign of the cross led to charges of sedition and a string of arrests. The ranks of the Zealots were decimated and their leaders defrocked and banished to remote monasteries. Among them was Avvakum, who was sent to Siberia in 1653 (Avvakum 1974:410). Having removed his most vocal opponents, the patriarch took firm control of the printing house and the group of correctors entrusted with the liturgical standardization. The composition of the team changed, with Ukrainian and Greek scholars replacing Russian ones (Zenkovsky 1970:100-101). By 1654, Nikon was in complete charge of the correction project.

Although the patriarch had silenced the Zealots, he still had to persuade the tsar and the bishops of the validity of his opinions. Of vital importance here was Nikon's alliance with the highest dignitaries of the Greek church, who were interested in restoring its influence in Muscovy and actively supported the patriarch's cause. One of these men was the Patriarch of Antioch, Macarius, who visited Moscow between 1654 and 1656 and was involved in many of Nikon's decisions affecting the religious reform. His nephew, the deacon Paul of Aleppo, wrote down impressions from

that visit, which provide a valuable insight into the early phase of
the schism.

According to this account, Nikon delayed the departure of the
eastern embassy by more than a year in order to seek the oriental
patriarch's advice on and support for his actions. Deacon Paul
noticed the extraordinary nature of such a request in a country
where Greek clergy had not even been allowed to celebrate mass
on account of their association with the Moslems (Aleppo
1873:97). While most Muscovites are said to have retained their
traditional suspicion, Patriarch Nikon is described as an admirer
of all things Greek. Prompted by his "natural disposition to love
the Greeks and their ecclesiastical ordinances and ceremonies"
(*ibid.*:109), Nikon apparently shocked his countrymen by a string
of highly unusual innovations, which began with the order that
church cantors sing in Greek rather than Slavonic (*ibid.*:140). A
while later, he caused an outrage by exchanging his own Russian
mitre for a Greek one. The voice of opposition rumbled,

> See how he has changed the dress of our bishops which
> they received by inspiration of the Holy Ghost from the
> time we became Christians! And does not the earth
> tremble at this his act, who, having hitherto dressed as
> a Muscovite, has made himself a Greek? (*ibid.*:272)

In due course, all Russian bishops were compelled to adopt
the modified and hated garb (*ibid.*).

In 1654, Nikon convened a synod to discuss the further stages
of the reform. He sought approval for his plan to correct liturgical
texts which had already been standardized under two of his
predecessors and, in exchange, promised to appeal to the
Ecumenical Patriarch to help solve the controversy surrounding
the sign of the cross and other ritual points affected by his changes
(Ammann 1950:273). Out of the assembled thirty-four church
leaders, only three refused to endorse the plan (Fuhrmann
1982:63).

Without awaiting Constantinople's reply, Nikon convened yet
another synod in the spring of 1655, which was to debate sugges-
tions made by the visiting Patriarch of Antioch. The tone for this
assembly was set by Nikon's welcoming words: "I am a Russian,

the son of a Russian; but my faith and religion are Greek" (Aleppo 1873:175). The ecclesiastics endorsed the changes made by the patriarch thus far, including the highly controversial *troeperstie* and the recognition of Roman Catholic baptism. Both innovations originated with Patriarch Macarius (*ibid.*:174-175; Ammann 1950:274-275).

Nikon now began to purge Slavonic texts of Muscovite "heresies" and to issue standardized editions of liturgical manuals. Despite his claim of having based the corrections on ancient Greek manuscripts, some sources indicate that out of the hundreds of parchments brought to Moscow by Sukhanov, only a handful were actually consulted by the correctors (Conybeare 1962:47; Lupinin 1984:135-136). One of the first "corrected" books, the all-important *Sluzhebnik* (Liturgikon), which determined the proper conduct of daily services, contained so many controversial changes that another outcry shook the church. By this time, however, Nikon had received a reply from Constantinople, which seemed to fortify his position. The Ecumenical Patriarch cautioned his junior colleague not to attach undue importance to "small matters" which did not touch "the dogmas of faith" (Palmer 1873:408-409). But he clearly supported *troeperstie* and urged Nikon to excommunicate dissenters who "keep to their own books, their own liturgy, and their own sign of the cross" (*ibid.*:410). As for the question of authentic models of Orthodoxy, Nikon was advised to follow the lead of Peter Mogila (*ibid.*:411).

Armed with this favourable verdict and supported by the Patriarch of Antioch, Nikon convened a third synod in the spring of 1656. The assembled prelates confirmed the validity of the conclusions reached the previous year, agreed to adopt the new editions of liturgical books, and anathematized the patriarch's opponents (Ammann 1950:275; Conybeare 1962:58). These "schismatics", or as they came to be known in Russian, *raskolniki*, were condemned for having "rebelled against the four [eastern] patriarchs, saying that they were fallen from their dignity and office, in consequence of the dominion of the Turks over them" (Aleppo 1873:325).

One of the more striking phenomena arising from the course of events between 1653 and 1656 was the apparent willingness of the higher clergy to help Nikon undermine the autonomy of the

Russian church. The question as to why virtually all the bishops lent their support to a reform which contradicted the ideology of their time cannot be easily answered. Some eyewitnesses, foreign as well as Russian, point out the despotic character of Nikon and his ability to intimidate opponents (Avvakum 1974; Olearius 1656:292). In the words of Paul of Aleppo, the patriarch exercised "uncontrolled authority", which led him to act as a "great butcher over the bishops" (Aleppo 1873:110). The uncertain fate of the only vocal critic among the bishops, the presumably martyred Paul of Kolomna, may have indeed served as a warning to other prelates.

The intimidation factor notwithstanding, it is likely that the patriarch enjoyed genuine support among some of the higher ecclesiastics. This support derived in part from Nikon's determination to broaden the powers of the church—an ambition which he realized during the turbulent 1650s (Lupinin 1984:90-91). In addition, Nikon retained the moralistic bent of the Zealots and the anti-western orientation of his predecessors. His opposition to western culture prompted him to burn organs and "Frankish" icons (Aleppo 1873:151; Olearius 1656:302), to impose harsh penalties for the use of tobacco (Olearius 1656:318), and to renew rules confining foreign residents of Moscow to a ghetto (ibid.). As Deacon Paul put it, the patriarch nurtured an "immense hatred against all heretics" (Aleppo 1873:130).

Although Nikon's "Muscovite traits"—despotism, clericalism, anti-Latinism, ritualism and dogmatism combined with charisma and genuine piety—may have endeared him to some sectors of the church, his Grecophile tendencies would have probably led to his downfall had it not been for the tsar's support. Tsar Aleksei liked Nikon from the time of their first meeting. Attracted by his "magnetic personality" (Fuhrmann 1982:43), the tsar came to refer to the patriarch as his "special friend" (ibid.)

Subsequent developments confirmed the trust Aleksei placed in the church leader. Even before Nikon accepted the patriarchal seat, his benefactor broke with tradition by promising not to interfere in the appointment of bishops and other ecclesiastical matters (Aleppo 1873:169; Lupinin 1984:90). The tsar surrendered further powers in 1654 when, as a reward for Nikon's help during a plague epidemic, he made him co-regent (Fuhrmann 1982:67).

Thus it was the patriarch's almost papal status that helped him clear the hurdles in the uncharted course of his reform.

The support rendered by the tsar was not entirely selfless. He felt flattered when the Patriarch of Jerusalem appealed to him in 1649 to become Orthodoxy's "new Moses" by taking greater interest in Muscovy's potential as a genuine rival of the Ottoman and Roman empires (Fuhrmann 1982:44). Aleksei's aspirations to gain recognition as one of Europe's great monarchs were expressed more openly after that appeal. He put a Latin inscription on the royal standard (Olearius 1656:41) and surrounded himself with portraits of Alexander the Great, Darius, Constantine the Great, and Julius Caesar (Fuhrmann 1982:200). These acts underlined the official theory according to which the Romanovs descended from the lineage of the Roman emperor Augustus (Aleppo 1873:121).

The tsar greeted any token recognition of his imperial status with almost infantile joy. For example, after reading a letter in which the German emperor addressed him as "the new Cesar [sic] of the empire of orthodoxy", the tsar is said to have been "delighted in his heart with this new title to an infinite degree" (Aleppo 1873:265). And he lost no time in placing an order for a carriage which, in his own words, was to be "like the one in which the kings of Spain and France and the Emperor go about" (Fuhrmann 1982:200).

The somewhat pathetic eagerness with which the autocratic tsar emulated the conduct of his enlightened western peers echoes the enthusiasm of Moscow's semi-literate patriarch for the mitre and sign of cross of his eastern colleagues. The dual quest for authenticity, in itself a truly Muscovite phenomenon, bears testimony to the importance of foreign models in mid-seventeenth-century Russia. Neither the secular nor the clerical ruler was content with playing a purely domestic role in a backward and contemptible country. The tsar ogled the status of an eastern emperor; the patriarch aspired to the position of an eastern pope. The achievement of either goal required a considerable dampening of Muscovy's xenophobic sentiments and a re-definition of Russian Orthodoxy as a cosmopolitan rather than a narrowly national ideology. The combined effect of secular and religious reform led to the disintegration of Muscovy as a homogenous

Archpriest Avvakum. (Museum of Ethnography, Moscow)

society and to its division into two mutually hostile camps: the reform-minded Nikonites and the fiercely traditionalist Old Believers.

The Old Believers

It has already been mentioned that the most vocal opponents of Nikon's reform were found among the members of the lower clergy, in particular those affiliated with the Zealots. The handful of clerics led by Archpriest Avvakum and several other priests and monks at first wielded little influence within the church and even less outside it. It is quite likely that their opposition would have been tempered had the patriarch employed gentle persuasion and patience in dealing with his critics. Instead, the Draconian punishment meted out to clerics who insisted on using the old books and rites alienated further segments of the church, including less radical opponents of the reform who had hoped for a compromise allowing the use of both types of books and ritual, that is, the pre-Nikonian as well as the "corrected" versions. The possibility of such a solution was destroyed by the council of 1656, which dictated that the controversial innovations *replaced* the old customs. The ensuing polarization contributed significantly to the growth of the ranks of clerics who openly disagreed with Nikon's position (Kostomarov 1871:482).

The spread of the schism was affected further by a serious conflict that erupted between the tsar and the patriarch in 1657. Angered by Nikon's interference in state affairs and his intransigent handling of the church reform, Aleksei branded his former "special friend" a "son of a bitch" and forced him to retire from public life (Fuhrmann 1982:138,141-145). While Nikon waited for the tsar to call him back—he spent his time building a spiritual retreat by the name of New Jerusalem outside the gates of Moscow—the persecution of the *raskolniki* was suspended and their leaders were released. Avvakum, whose uncompromising rejection of the reform had made him the chief spokesman for the Old Believers, returned from exile in 1662. The "Moscow thaw" led him to believe that he was about to be posted at the printing office as one of the official correctors—an appointment that could have neutralized the schism (Avvakum 1974:434).

Although the tsar and several influential courtiers were favourably disposed towards Avvakum and other Old Believers, the church hierarchy continued to treat them as schismatics who were expected to eventually embrace the changes carried out by Nikon. The future of the reform and of its instigator was to be resolved once and for all at a council held in Moscow between 1666 and 1667. It was attended by an impressive array of Russian and foreign bishops and presided over by two patriarchs, Makarius of Antioch and Paisios of Alexandria. The fate of Nikon, who was still nominally the head of the Russian church, was resolved quickly. According to the judgement, he "lived tyrannically, and not meekly as befits a prelate" and was given to "iniquity, rapacity, and tyranny" (Vernadsky 1972, 1:258). He was stripped of his position—Patriarch Makarius, his former advisor, personally defrocked him—and banished to a monastery to "lament his sins" (Lupinin 1984:166).

The reform itself, on the other hand, found approval. The eastern dignitaries attending the council took the position that the innovations implemented by Nikon had freed the Russian church of Muscovite idiosyncrasies which conflicted with universal Orthodox practices (Lupinin 1984:171). In order to prevent a return to pre-Nikonite traditions, the council nullified the *Stoglav* and condemned its signatories for having "reasoned inadvisedly, wilfully, without consulting the most holy ecumenical patriarchs" (Vernadsky 1972, 1:259). Having de facto concluded that the Russian church was incapable of autonomy, the synod terminated further textual corrections and ordered future contentions to be resolved "according to the practice of the Eastern [i.e., Greek] Church" (in Lupinin 1984:171).

With the ideology of holy Russia in shambles, the council dealt with its last defenders, the Old Believers, in a most predictable manner. They were given the choice of either recanting the Muscovite "heresies" or of facing excommunication and death. Members of the state church who helped these *raskolniki* in any manner, even by failing to report them to authorities, were to be flogged (Kostomarov 1871:491).

These harsh measures forced the Old Belief underground. Deprived of a legitimate place in late seventeenth-century Russia, the opponents of the reform underwent a gradual transformation from a relatively small clerical faction to a popular movement which combined religious and social dissent. The beginning of the *raskol* coincided with important economic and social changes which led to the enserfment of the peasantry (Masaryk 1919:30-35; Smith 1977). Prolonged military campaigns and widespread epidemics and famines all exacted a heavy toll on the lowest strata of society and fomented dissatisfaction which erupted occasionally into popular uprisings. The schism served as catalyst for the pent-up social unrest. By virtue of its association with the "good old times", the old faith came to be seen as a most powerful symbol of not only authentic Christianity, but also social justice (Kostomarov 1871:485). This perceived connection assured its popularity but also persuaded state authorities to draw an indelible parallel between *raskolniki* and political dissidents. Henceforth, they were to be persecuted as enemies of church *and* state.[11]

Despite the perception of the Old Believers as dangerous rebels, there are only a few documented instances of armed conflict involving the defence of the old faith itself. The best known of such incidents was triggered in 1667 by the refusal of the residents of the famous Solovetski Monastery to accept the liturgical reform. The militant monks stopped praying for the tsar and took up arms to defend themselves against troops dispatched from Moscow (Smirnov 1898:104-105). A defector from the monastery reported in 1674 that the monks spoke about the monarch "in words so violent that it is terrifying not only to write, but even to hear them" (in Fuhrmann 1982:180). This disconcerting message may have prompted the final onslaught in 1675, which led to a bloodbath and an aura of martyrdom for the defiant monks.

Armed resistance of the kind offered by the Solovetski monks was highly unusual for the early Old Believers.[12] A far more typical response to the persecution carried on by the state is exemplified by Avvakum with his unshakable faith in the tsar. Unlike Nikon, described by Avvakum as a "wolf and apostate" (Avvakum 1974:434), Tsar Aleksei continued to be regarded with the greatest respect as an autocrat "set over us by God" (*ibid.*). This attitude wasn't weakened even by the terrible ordeal endured by Avvakum and his closest associates during the banishment which followed their final refusal to renounce the old faith. Neither the killing of his beloved wife and two sons—nor the maiming of fellow Zealots before his very eyes (Avvakum 1974:445) undermined Avvakum's stance vis-à-vis the ruler. In what seems to have been his last letter before dying at the stake in 1682, the condemned archpriest wished the tsar "peace and salvation, and good health" (in Akademiya nauk SSSR 1927:705).

It is important to understand the attitude of Avvakum and his followers to the tsar in order to appreciate the limitations against which the early Old Believers tried to keep the flame of tradition alive. The movement that emerged in the 1670s and 1680s in defence of the old faith was, despite its influence on politically motivated dissenters, a reactionary force dedicated exclusively to

Differences between "old" and "new" texts summarized in *Pomorskie otvety.* (Andrei Denisov)

the restoration of pre-Nikonite Orthodoxy. Neither Avvakum nor any other influential schismatic intended to set up a counter-church or some other institution that would have challenged the legitimacy of the political order. The main goal of the civil disobedience displayed by the monks of Solovetski and other prominent figures was to persuade the tsar to turn back the clock by ordering a reinstatement of the old books, priests, and ritual.

Eucharistic stamps depicting a *krizh* (above) and a *krest* (below).
(Andrei Denisov)

The first systematic analysis of the changes carried out by Nikon, conducted in the early eighteenth century by an influential Old Believer, identified thirty-eight objectionable *textual* innovations (Chrysostomus 1957). Most of them were known only to a relatively small circle of well-versed spiritual leaders, but at least two played an important part among all Old Believers. Of the greatest significance was the "correction" of the spelling and pronunciation of the name of Jesus from *Isus* to *Iisus* (Chrysostomus 1957:105; Subbotin 1881:31-32,85,287). The new name was universally rejected and associated with the antichrist (Anonymous 1694:041). Similar resistance was evoked by the addition of a third *alleluia* before the frequently repeated phrase "Praise to thee, Lord" (*slava tebe Bozhe*). The new triple *alleluia* was compared with the Latin *filioque* and dismissed on similar grounds (Barskov 1912:56; Subbotin 1881:4-6).[13]

The impact of altered words notwithstanding, the single most offensive innovation was seen to be the replacement of *dvoeperstie* by the Greek *troeperstie*. The modification prompted speculations that the new symbol expressed faith in Satan, represented by the unholy trinity of the apocalyptic beast, the snake, and the antichrist (Hauptmann 1963:95-96; Smirnov 1898:44). This association was strengthened due to the connection made between *troeperstie* and the pinch of tobacco snuff. Henceforth, the Russian term for "pinch", *shchepotka*, came to be applied to the heterodox sign of the cross, and those who had adopted it became known as *shchepotniki*, "users of snuff" (Pleyer 1961:42; Subbotin 1881:167). In this way it proved possible to weave together spiritual and physical defilement in a most effective manner.

Nikon had changed not only the sign of the cross made spontaneously during prayers but also the shape of crosses painted on icons, stitched into vestments, erected on top of churches, and imprinted into eucharistic bread. For centuries, the Russian church had used two versions of the cross: the Latin form with a vertical and a horizontal bar, and the Eastern version with one vertical and three horizontal bears of unequal length. The Latin type, referred to as *krizh*, was accepted as valid but only in association with the Eastern *krest*, which alone could symbolize Christ's crucifixion and power (*Kniga o vere* 1648:68; Koncevicius 1927:92,161; Kozhanchikov 1863:56). Nikon broke this rule of precedence by directing that the *krizh* replace the *krest* as the symbol of the "life-giving cross" of crucifixion on eucharistic bread, leading to charges of heresy from the Old Believers (Smirnov 1898:196,206).

The defence of the eight-pointed *krest* was part of the wholesale opposition by the Old Believers to westernized iconography. They drew a parallel between the erosion of traditional standards in religious texts and in paintings, and Nikon was blamed on both counts. In Avvakum's words, "But as the Niconians copy the European books, so do they copy their icons" (in Andreyev 1961:43). Although this charge was not quite justified—the patriarch too opposed the introduction of western iconography (Andreyev 1961)—Nikon had become so firmly associated with the diffusion of heterodox innovations that he was held responsible for every departure from Orthodoxy. The stereotypical image was reinforced through reports of "eye-witnesses" who claimed that the patriarch had an icon and a cross (*krest*) stitched into the inner sole of his boots, crushing the holy symbols with each of his steps (Subbotin 1881:299).

The Old Believers objected to the anthropomorphism of the new iconography—Avvakum charged that "the swift dog, Nikon, the enemy, wishes to paint the icons as if the figures were alive

Mother of God with child painted in traditional style.
(Ikonenmuseum Recklinghausen)

as the foreigners do" (in Andreyev 1961:44)—and to heterodox symbols depicted in the westernized images, such as *troeperstie* and the *krizh* (*ibid.*:43). Such paintings were not only held to be inauthentic on account of being dissimilar (*nepodobnye*) to ancient prototypes; they were held to be outright harmful, because their use was seen to encourage the acceptance of a new, false, god: the antichrist (Subbotin 1881:82,87). Avvakum urged his followers

Mother of God with child painted in westernized style.
(Ikonenmuseum Recklinghausen)

to spit on such images just as they would spit on a heretic (Smirnov 1898:98), and trial proceedings indicate that such expressions
of displeasure were not infrequent (Lopukhin 1862; *Sviedenia*
1862).

The changes in the traditional "text" of Orthodoxy—its
spoken and written signs—were seen by the Old Believers as
destroying its very purpose, namely the ability and necessity of

believers to communicate with God and each other as Christians. To them, the icon was not just a nice picture but a reflection of Truth as defined by God. If people were allowed to distort this or any other divine symbol, then how could one maintain knowledge of Truth and its source?

The Old Believers recognized that the most threatening influence from the reformed church was its refusal to admit to having become topsy-turvy. Just as the antichrist pretended to be pious, post-Nikonite heterodoxy continued to lay claim to orthodoxy. This perceived eradication of boundaries separating order from chaos and right from wrong was depicted most astutely by Deacon Feodor Ivanov, a prolific early commentator on the schism who shared Avvakum's exile. In his essay on the antichrist, he blames him for having connected

> dishonesty with piety, curse with blessing, agony with generosity, mercy with tyranny, meekness with brutality,...triad with dyad, church with [Latin] temple, papists with priests, westerners with easterners,...holy relics with the corpses of heretics, sacred icons with godless pictures. (in Subbotin 1881:84-85, my translation)

Because of the cunning of the antichrist, Deacon Feodor continued;

> orthodoxy is appealed to, and the orthodox are being exterminated; heretics are damned, and the orthodox are treated as enemies; church holidays are celebrated, and their founders are called schismatics; idolatry is condemned, and depraved images are venerated; Roman impiety is cursed, and Christ's crucifixion on two pieces of wood [krizh] is accepted; clergymen are ordained, and priests are burned as enemies; the devil is renounced, and the snake is reckoned to be venerable. (ibid.:86-88, my translation)

The objections of the Old Believers to the reform carried out by Nikon and his successors were not at all original, nor were they meant to be. In its structure, justification, and vocabulary, the criticism voiced in the latter part of the seventeenth century was almost indistinguishable from earlier Muscovite attacks on the Latins, which in turn derived inspiration from Byzantine campaigns waged against the West. At its core was the ancient belief in authenticity and Truth as an absolute, concrete, and easily identifiable property, a position which made change in religious matters a most difficult problem. What was new in the position taken by the Old Believers was their willingness, borne out of despair rather than choice, to maintain orthodoxy outside the womb designed to protect and cherish it, namely the church. This was an unprecedented situation, one which required the preservation of the "text" of the old faith without the context on which it had traditionally depended. This meant that in order to be faithful to tradition, the Old Believers also had to depart from it. The task of resolving this seeming contradiction proved the most challenging undertaking faced by the early leaders.

For many adherents to the old faith, the new situation seemed so incomprehensible that they sought solace in radical apocalyptic beliefs which explained *raskol* as the first sign of the antichrist's impending arrival. The crises experienced by Russia during the second half of the seventeenth century inclined this period to give rise to numerous eschatological expectations, which were to have particularly strong and lasting reverberations among the Old Believers. According to the popular *Book of Faith*, Orthodoxy was to be attacked by the antichrist in 1666, fulfilling a prophecy made already in the Bible (Rev. 13:18; *Kniga o vere* 1648:270-273). It was difficult not to give any credence to this prediction. Foreshadowed by wars, plagues, unexpected eclipses of the sun, and, of course, Nikon's unprecedented reform, the fateful year began with the all-important church council, which was to determine the future course of Russian Orthodoxy. Two months into the council, the people of Moscow witnessed the sudden disappearance of the sun on a bright summer day, prompting fears of an unparalleled catastrophe (Akademiya nauk SSSR 1927). For many Russians, those fears were confirmed by the outcome of the council, and the country plunged into an apocalyptic mood that lasted for several years. Its reverberations are depicted in this sketch of rural life:

> In the autumn of 1668 the fields were neglected, no one ploughed or sowed, and at the beginning of...1669 the huts too were abandoned. Assembling in crowds people prayed, fasted, confessed their sins to each other, partook of the Holy Sacrament, and being prepared awaited with awe the Archangel's trumpet call. According to an ancient superstition the end of the world was to come at midnight; and so at nightfall the zealots of ancient piety, arraying themselves in white shirts and shrouds, lay down in coffins hollowed from the trunks of trees, and awaited the trumpet call. (Miliukov 1942:43)

Not all believers in the apocalypse were content to wait passively for the expected climax. Many thousands came to regard death by fire as a second baptism which would cleanse them of the antichrist's influence, and entire parishes chose collective self-immolation during the 1680s and 1690s (Akademiya nauk SSSR 1948, 2/2:336; Crummey 1970:56). This form of radical response was condemned at a meeting of Old Believer leaders in 1691 (Akademiya nauk SSSR 1948:336), but state officials continued to report sporadic resumptions of mass self-immolations until at least the 1750s (*Sobranie* 1858, 1:551).

The contrast between hope in the restoration of the old faith and deeply felt despair arising out of apocalyptic expectations set the perimeters for the early history of the Old Belief. United only by their opposition to Nikon's reform, its adherents expected either to have the walls of holy Russia reassembled or to face the end of the world. Life without traditional Orthodoxy seemed unimaginable. A plan for the preservation of Truth outside the established church did not yet exist. But by the late seventeenth century such a plan seemed more and more necessary. Despite apocalyptic signs all around, life went on—at least for the time being. Those who refused to succumb to despair or persecution faced the task of carving out an entirely new existence, suspended between the comforting memory of holy Russia and the threatening future of a society no longer perceived as Christian.

Popovtsy and Bezpopovtsy

A strategy for survival outside the official church emerged in the last decades of the seventeenth century. Its designers no longer lived in Moscow, the centre of Old Believer resistance throughout the 1650s and 1660s. Attempting to escape persecution, most leaders of the traditionalist movement gathered their followers and headed for isolated locations in the south and southwest. Their first colonies were founded along the river Kerzhenets—a tributary of the Volga—along the Don, and in the Starodub region north of Kiev. The Starodub settlement fuelled the first expansion beyond Russia when the Polish island Vietka—today in the Byelorussian SSR—was settled by Old Believers in the 1680s.

A parallel colonization took place in the north and northwest, particularly in the region between Novgorod and Pskov, and along the shore of the White Sea, in an area known as Pomorie. The defence of the old faith in this territory became not so much the responsibility of refugee from Moscow as of survivors of the siege of the Solovetski Monastery. The monks who had escaped the bloodbath dispersed into the northern wilderness and acted as the most dedicated propagators of the Old Belief.

Although these early centres of resistance maintained contact with one another, they possessed no form of common leadership nor any type of forum for discussing problems and strategies. As long as Avvakum was alive, his advice was sought and usually followed by many of the local leaders, but his death put an end to that. The only source of shared kinship remained anchored in resistance to the reform imposed by Nikon and his successors.

The thorniest problem faced by the fugitives surrounded the future of priesthood. According to Old Believer historiography, the anti-Nikonite movement received explicit support from only one bishop, namely the allegedly martyred Paul of Kolomna (Shchapov 1906:291). His disappearance circa 1656 meant that the decimated ranks of traditionalist priests could not be replenished as long as the ancient custom of allowing only bishops to ordain clergy was observed. Old Believer sources claim that only forty-three priests defied the anathemas decreed at the council of 1666-1667. Twelve of these are said to have founded the refugee settlements along the southern and western frontier, with the rest escaping to other parts of the country or, as in the case of Avvakum, dying as martyrs (*Malaya rodoslovna* 1920:1). Whatever the exact numbers might have been, the group of pre-Nikonite priests who left the church and survived persecution was very small, hardly sufficient to serve the thousands of widely dispersed adherents to the old faith.

Problems of logistics aside, these early shepherds agonized over a quandary which affected the very survival of what might be called "Old Orthodoxy". Assuming that the schism was not to be healed in the foreseeable future, and that life itself would go on for a while, to whom would future Old Believers turn once the surviving pre-Nikonite priests had died out? Who would baptize their children, administer communion, confirm marriages, hear confessions, and celebrate the mass? In short, who was to ensure that Old Orthodoxy survived despite its banishment?

In theory, the early leaders could have chosen one of three solutions. The most comprehensive strategy would have been to set up an independent church with bishops and priests of its own. This was in fact attempted later on, but the climate wasn't ripe for it in the seventeenth century. The second solution was the use of priests who had been ordained in the reformed church and then left it to join the Old Believers. The status of these clergymen, was, however, controversial because unlike the old priests, who had been ordained by pre-Nikonite bishops, these new ones had in a sense compromised themselves by receiving consecration from bishops whom the Old Believers dismissed as heterodox. Nevertheless, urged by Avvakum to adopt this strategy (Smirnov 1898:137-138), most of the southern and western communities came to rely on these fugitive priests, which earned them the designation "priestists" or, in Russian, *popovtsy*. This concession to necessity was rejected by the vast majority of the northern Old Believers, who opted for the third and most radical alternative: the total repudiation of all elements of the reformed church, including the new clergy. Determined to make do only with laity, this branch came to be known as *bezpopovtsy*, the "priestless ones".

The divergence of the Old Believers into the two factions of *popovtsy* and *bezpopovtsy* took place in the last years of the seventeenth century, at a time when the almost complete disappearance of pre-Nikonite clergy made urgent the design of a lasting model for spiritual survival. The official birth of the priestless wing was announced at two meetings held in Novgorod in 1692 and 1694. The assembled leaders defined the reformed church as defiled by the antichrist and called upon all Christians to refrain from using its sacraments and priests (Smirnov 1898:126,134; Vasilev 1694). Converts to Old Orthodoxy who had grown up in the official church were required to be baptized anew, and their marriages had to be dissolved (Smirnov 1898:127-128; Vasilev 1694). Although provisions were made for specially designated laymen to administer baptism, the designers of the priestless strategy did not dare to give these elders the power to sanctify marriages. Consequently, membership in the new congregations required universal celibacy, and future growth was expected to be generated exclusively by converts from the official church (Vasilev 1694).

The model embraced by the *bezpopovtsy* rested upon foundations that had been laid long before the schism. Due to the vastness and isolation of its territory, Pomorie and other parts of northern Russia had always been deprived of complete and regular contact with the church. Faced with an acute shortage of priests, the local population was accustomed to turn to pious laymen—mostly hermits and monks—who filled the spiritual vacuum with the help of abbreviated services and incomplete sacraments (Bolshakov 1950:70; Hauptmann 1984:478-480; Zenkovsky 1970:494-495). Thus the brand of Old Orthodoxy that took root here was understandably monastic and communalistic in orientation, shaped as it was by monks rather than priests (Crummey 1970; Scheffel 1991a).

The Demise of Muscovy

Despite the fragmentation and persecution experienced by the Old Believers in the late seventeenth century, their cause attracted ever more followers. Perhaps the single most important reason for the mass appeal of the traditionalists derived from the popular dissatisfaction with Russia's rapid westernization during the reign of Peter the Great, one of Tsar Aleksei's sons. Unlike his father, Peter did not intend merely to modernize Muscovy; he was determined to abolish it altogether and to erect in its stead a Russian empire constructed in accordance with western models. To realize this ambition, he subjugated the church to the state and replaced Russian hierarchs with westernized Ukrainians who helped the tsar transform the institution into a tool of his government. This shift assisted the Old Believers in their struggle with the official church to win recognition as the sole remaining guardians of Muscovite Orthodoxy, protecting the country against the onslaught of heretical ideas and customs imported from the West.

Foremost among the innovations legalized by Peter the Great and rejected by the Old Believers were those which affected appearance. In an unprecedented break with tradition, the tsar shaved his beard and insisted that his subjects, with the exception of clergy and peasants, follow suit. To add insult to injury, Peter also demanded that traditional Muscovite dress be exchanged for western types of clothing (Esipov 1863; Vernadsky 1972, 2:347). In a society which had adopted the eastern view of the beard as a symbol of Christian status and where as late as 1690 the church had condemned shaving and western fashions (Akademiya nauk SSSR 1941, 3/1:32), the new decree triggered considerable resistance. That resistance, however, came no longer from the official church—but from the Old Believers who, to the last man, refused to part with their beards. Their stubborn refusal led to the imposition of a special "beard tax" and to such a lasting association between beards and the old faith that as early as the 1720s, bearded men—condescendingly referred to as *borodachi*—were automatically suspected of schismatic tendencies (*Sobranie* 1858, 1:21).

But beards were by no means the only visible sign of traditionalist inclinations. The Old Believers attacked the entire gamut of western fashions, including raised heels, wigs and powder, neckties and scarves, long hair on men, and loose and uncovered hair of women (Andreev 1870:239; Uspenskii 1976:22-26; Zhuravlev 1831:135). Here too they were defending Muscovite and Byzantine norms and resisting a trend explicitly sanctioned by Peter the Great.

Peter's westernization campaign provided the Old Believers with an excellent opportunity for affirming the traditional association between outer and inner defilement. In their eyes, it was only natural that failure to observe the laws governing Christian appearance should lead to destruction of the body through self-abuse. This link seemed to be confirmed by the behaviour of the tsar himself: he was not only the first beardless ruler, but also the first smoker on Russia's throne. Peter flouted the Muscovite view of tobacco as a physical and spiritual poison, just as he mocked ancient dietary rules, such as the taboo on eating meat during Lent (Vernadsky 1972, 2:314,349). Again, the official church did nothing to counteract these quite explicit breaches of ecclesiastic norms. On the contrary, some of its highest dignitaries were suspected of snuffing tobacco in church and of eating unbled meat all year round (Markell 1862:3-8).

In addition to legalizing tobacco, Peter the Great introduced tea, coffee, potatoes, and a host of other exotic spices and foodstuffs. Many of these substances, especially tea and coffee, came to be equated by the Old Believers with tobacco and alcohol and were banned as pollutants. Often referred to as plants from beyond the sea (*zamorskiya ovoshchi*), these products demonstrated the bond between foreign customs and defilement first asserted by the Muscovites and then converted into a principle by the Old Believers. In order to affirm their disapproval and fear of these new sources of pollution, many Old Believers abstained not only from the substances themselves but also from food served by members of the official church and even the dishes it was served on.

Largely as a result of Peter the Great's westernization policies, the Old Believers of the early eighteenth century had won the battle with the official church for recognition as the champions of Old Orthodoxy. In their position on beards, clothing, diet, iconography, and ritual, the Old Believers came to be recognized as the rightful interpreters of *starina* (tradition). This popular opinion was to some extent shared by the reformed church. Unable to prove the greater authenticity of Nikon's liturgical changes, eighteenth-century theologians were quite willing to bury the hatchet and legalize *dvoeperstie*, double *alleluia*, the single "i" in the spelling of the name of Jesus, the "old books" outlawed by Nikon, in short, the entire platform of Old Orthodoxy. But this concession was not the victory the Old Believers had been fighting for. Rather, it stemmed from the official church's conviction that Old Orthodoxy itself had become irrelevant.

Under Nikon and his immediate successors, the battle between the two parties separated by the schism was fought according to a shared set of rules, which derived form the belief that the search for ritual authenticity was meaningful and necessary. In this sense, the term "Old Orthodoxy" could be claimed by both parties, because both of them evaluated orthodoxy with the help of models inherited from the past. The issue that separated them was not the recognition of this principle, but rather differences of opinion about the location of the cherished ancient models. This willingness to use the past as the source and measure of orthodoxy began to dissipate as a result of changes in the structure and composition of the official church carried out by Peter the Great. The Holy Synod—the new governing body that replaced the patriarch—infused the institution with indisputably western doctrines, which challenged the ritualism of Old Orthodoxy, Avvakum's as well as Nikon's, and dismissed it in favour of spirituality (Ammann 1950:375-88). Henceforth, arguments about the antiquity of various signs of the cross and spellings of God's name were seen as fruitless and irrelevant. What mattered was faith itself rather than the form of its expression.

This new spirit in Russian theology is well illustrated by one of the landmarks of *raskol* literature, *Oblichenie nepravdy raskolnicheskiia* (*Exposure of Schismatic Falsehood*). Written in the early 1740s by Archbishop Feofilakt Lopatinskii, a prominent member of the Holy Synod, the work was intended as the first official response of the reformed church to attacks levelled at it by the Old Believers (Chrysostomus 1957). In his opening remarks, the archbishop accuses the *raskolniki* of schismatic views not because they cling to the old books, but rather because they confuse dogma and ritual. In sharp contrast to earlier position statements, Nikon's innovations are not defended on grounds of authenticity; both versions of ritual are dismissed as trifling human conventions which are said to be

> not dogmas of the apostolic orthodox faith but outward
> acts [*vnieishnya chiny*] and rituals [*obriady*] of church
> conduct; not ordained by Christ, not by apostles, not by

ecumenical councils, but by shepherds desiring unity for their congregations. (Lopatinskii 1745:2, my translation)

The distinction made by Lopatinskii between ritual and dogma allowed him to denounce the Old Believers' reverence for icons, beards, crosses, and similar outward signs of faith as symptoms of "praying with the body rather than the spirit" (*ibid.*:11). These symptoms are presented as an unavoidable outcome of traditional Russian ignorance of theology and scholarship in general. Dismissing the Old Believers as "dull Russian bats trying to be eagles" (*ibid.*:78), the author concludes his indictment with a rhetorical question which leaves little doubt about his views that spiritual guidance was to be sought abroad rather than at home:

Do you know that other nations understand Greek better than you understand Russian; do you know that among the Latins and Germans all Greek texts...are not only read but printed so correctly and purely that even at the time of the authors' lives their publication wasn't better?(*ibid.*:77)

The diminished role of ritual in the ideology of the new synodal church led to the lifting of bans imposed in the past on the display and use of the pre-Nikonite books and ritual. The two-finger sign of the cross was legalized in 1763, and further important concessions to Old Orthodoxy were made during the next three decades (*Sobranie* 1858:599,708,729.759.771). Henceforth, the Old Believers, in their capacity as a *religious* minority, came to be regarded quite benevolently as old-fashioned and superstitious traditionalists.

But the tolerance of ritual pluralism did not lead to the legalization of the Old Belief as a social movement. In accordance with his enlightened views on religion, Peter the Great ended the persecution of the *raskolniki* as *heretics*, but he retained their classification as *criminals* (*Sobranie* 1858:99). The crime they were accused of was treason on account of their refusal to belong to the official church, which itself served as the long arm of the state. The unwillingness to participate in state-controlled ceremonies was no longer seen as an insult to God but still very much as an expression of contempt for the monarch.

Stripped of most civil rights, the Old Believers lived in a semi-official capacity until the early twentieth century. Neither explicitly persecuted nor expressly tolerated, their collective and personal security depended on the goodwill of local and state officials and, above all, on their own strength. In order to escape the unpredictability of this precarious existence, many members of the movement continued to reside in inaccessible frontier locations within and even outside Russia. By the end of the eighteenth century, Old Believer settlements could be found all the way from Ukraine to the Far East and North as well as in East Prussia, Austria, and the Ottoman Empire.

It was not until the early twentieth century that the Russian government legalized the Old Orthodox movement, prompted probably by its potential role as an ally of the conservative forces in their fight with the socialist opposition. The Old Belief was recognized as Orthodox, albeit with a "mistaken view...of the uncanonical nature of the Ruling Church" (in Curtiss 1940:320). In 1912, the former enemies were urged to unite with the official church in its struggle against their mutual foes: the atheists and the revolutionaries (*ibid.*). The numerical strength of the Old Believers approached at that time the twenty million mark (*ibid.*:137; Zenkovsky 1957:52). The October Revolution of 1917 interrupted the process of appeasement and triggered renewed persecution. As in the past, exile was chosen by some Old Believers, among them the founders of Berezovka.

Berezovka

Starting in the late nineteenth century, groups of Old Orthodox immigrants took up residence in the northeastern United States and Canada. Post-revolutionary chaos brought numerous refugees to North America, one group of which established what is now the oldest existing Old Orthodox congregation in Canada, near Hines Creek in northern Alberta (Scheffel 1989a). But the largest influx occurred during the 1960s when the United States admitted over a thousand Old Believers from China who arrived via South America. Soon after the settlement of this group in Oregon, some of its members branched off to Alaska, and still others decided to move to Alberta.

This plan was at first resisted by Canadian immigration officials, who opposed the admission of isolationist sectarians (Scheffel 1989a). Eventually, however, over one hundred Old Believers were admitted between 1973 and 1974. It was then that Berezovka came into being, making it one of the most recent outposts of Old Orthodoxy in North America. The arrival of additional immigrants during subsequent years has made the community the largest Old Believer settlement in Canada.

The Setting

Berezovka is situated approximately 250 kilometres northeast of Edmonton, at the boundary of sparsely populated farm land and the boreal forest. Its name derives from the clusters of birches—*berozi* in Russian—which line a shallow river along the banks of which the settlement stretches. The closest Canadian community is the medium-sized village of Josephville, which is located approximately fifteen kilometres away. It consists of several stores, a post office, a garage, and a large school where most of the Russian children are enrolled. The gravel road that connects Berezovka with Josephville joins a major highway here, which provides easy access to several towns nearby. These centres are visited whenever the Old Believers need farm supplies, spare parts for their vehicles, or the attention of a physician. Berezovka itself does not provide any services of this kind.

The land upon which the settlement is established was purchased from a local farmer who had used it for pasture. Step by step, most of the trees were cut down, the pasture made way for fields, and houses appeared along the river. One of the first buildings was a low, rectangular structure which serves as the church. Berezovka's founders put up the first ten or twelve houses, and subsequent settlers increased its size by another forty or so. Several families purchased isolated farms or acreages nearby.

"Little Russia", as Berezovka is known in the district, is an odd mixture of East and West. The homes are all perfectly ordinary frame structures constructed in accordance with North American models, and, increasingly, mobile homes inhabited by young couples without the means to build a house of their own. All dwellings have electricity, running water, flush toilets, and whatever appliances are deemed necessary. A car and a truck in the driveway add to the impression of predictability.

The ordinary quality of Berezovka's homes surprises every outsider. First-time visitors expect to see log buildings with carved and painted exteriors, petunias in the windows, and hand-hewn heavy furniture dominated by a massive stove. Such dwellings were in fact inhabited in the not-so-distant past. But today they are no longer considered appropriate by the younger generation, whose tastes have been influenced by North American culture. The new homes are larger, more easily kept clean, and evocative of the modern ethos of self-improvement to which the Old Believers are slowly falling prey. "Keeping up with the Joneses" has a double meaning here. It describes both the internal competition for status by means of flashy cars, trucks, homes, and other material possessions, as well as the rivalry between Berezovka and the surrounding society. Many of the new settlers believe themselves to be held in contempt by their Canadian neighbours, and large homes and powerful cars serve as easily understood cross-cultural symbols which are meant to dispel the negative stereotype. Therefore, cosy log cabins and troikas hurrying across the steppe have been relegated to the realm of folklore. They adorn the Old Believers' living rooms on huge tableaus celebrating peasant life in Russia, recalling a more heroic but also a somewhat barbaric age, which few people would want to return to.

Despite the gradual gentrification of its residents, Berezovka retains several features that lend it an unusual aura. Above all, it remains a village in the (East) European sense of the word. Unlike Josephville, which, akin to countless other rural communities, is being transformed into an outpost of urbanity, "Little Russia" exudes the views, smells, and sounds of the countryside. Instead of the strictly rectangular blocks guarding Canadian communities from spilling into the countryside, Berezovka possesses a single dirt road that hardly disturbs the landscape. The houses which line it sit on comfortably large lots and are surrounded with all the signs of rural life that have vanished from villages elsewhere. Across the muddy yards strewn with cow pies are barns filled with cattle, pigs, and poultry. The sounds and smells of the animals fill the air. Nature and culture seem to co-exist wherever one looks.

Local residents enjoy the pastoral quality of the settlement. When I first arrived, one of the community leaders took me to the large porch of his home, from which he embraced the view with both arms. He pointed out the fast-flowing river at our feet, fields golden with wheat, clusters of birches with their rustling leaves, and the nearby pasture dotted with cows. "It's just like in Russia", he exclaimed, and then added, "That's what made us choose this place." Then I was led to a huge enclosure where my host kept several dozen foxes. He opened the door to a small building containing fodder and pointed to a ladder reaching a platform above. Once on top of the platform, he carefully opened a tiny window which provided a view of the foxes below. I grasped then that the foxes were more than a source of income; they amused and intrigued the man, who, crouching in his observation tower, spent long hours marvelling at the games foxes play.

Although Berezovka is larger than several municipalities in the surrounding area, it remains unincorporated and indeed unrecognized by provincial and district authorities. Maps do not indicate its existence; road signs do not advertise its location. Far from competing with other communities for government attention and funding, the Old Believers deliberately distance themselves from the outside society. In spite of the familiarity of Berezovka's houses, no visitor fails to notice that "Little Russia" is very much a world on its own. And this impression is quickly confirmed by the appearance and demeanour of its residents.

The People

It is not difficult to spot an Old Believer, and the best place to do this is the Josephville school. Every morning the school bus from Berezovka disgorges a large crowd of girls and boys whose unusual appearance catches the eye of every passer-by. With their long, flaxen braids of uncut hair covered with a brightly-hued kerchief, blouses and dresses in all colours of the rainbow, and long aprons adorned with ribbons, the girls look like old-fashioned dolls. The boys' exterior is less striking, but with their also brightly coloured embroidered shirts and closely cropped hair they too stand out.

Old Believer parents do not take the appearance of their school-going children lightly. More than any other segment of the Russian community, the students serve as Berezovka's envoys to the outside world. Fearful lest a shadow should be cast over the entire group by the sloppy dress of a youngster, a mother spends long hours sewing, mending, and washing in order to impress the "Canadians" with the attention she bestows on her offspring. But the message of respectability must not detract from the message of "otherness" which the unusual appearance of the Old Believers underlines. The youngster at school signals the desire for acceptance through neatness and cleanliness; yet he or she also demands to be left alone in order to pursue goals that differ dramatically from those taught at school. And here the dilemma of the child parallels the predicament of all local Old Believers: how to achieve respectability without surrendering cultural otherness.

Old Believers past the school age are most likely to meet their Canadian neighbours in Josephville's one room post office. Like

Aleksandr Solzhenitsyn with Old Believers in Oregon.

everybody else, the Russians come here on their way to town in order to inspect their mailboxes, buy stamps, and peruse the community announcements posted on the door. Unlike everybody else, they show little desire to mingle and share news with the locals. The required business is attended to briskly, a civil hi or hello is exchanged with whoever else may be present, and the Old Believer walks off to the nearby co-op store to purchase some goods in the same efficient manner. The demeanour resembles that of a first-time visitor rather than of a local farmer who makes weekly visits to town.

The appearance of the adults also supports the impression of otherness. Unlike their Canadian counterparts, the Russian women cannot wear pants, short hair, T-shirts, or make-up. Even at the height of summer, their arms remain hidden under long-sleeved blouses, and a carefully tied kerchief covers most of their hair. The dresses and aprons are sewn at home using patterns, colours, and fabrics which seem strange to North American eyes.

Their purpose is clearly to conceal rather than divulge characteristics of the bodies draped in them. What is visible of the female frame is the unfashionable robustness which develops from multiple births and a lifetime of hard physical work.

The men are easily recognizable by their physique, which tends towards the gigantic. This impression is underlined by long, straggling beards which frame furrowed and weathered faces. The hair is closely cropped to the skull, with short bangs falling over the forehead. Instead of the standard baseball cap advertising a local farm-machinery dealer, older men prefer cotton hats in summer and huge fur hats in winter. The upper body is clothed in long-sleeved bright shirts with a stiff embroidered collar buttoned up to the neck. The Tolstoyan impression created by the men is completed by shabby coats and trousers of indeterminate shape and colour, usually purchased at the Army & Navy store in Edmonton. Blue jeans have been adopted by only a few young men.

Although the Old Believers do not alter their dress to suit outsiders, they do alter their designation. The first immigrants introduced themselves as "White Russians", a term associated with the fugitives who left Russia in the aftermath of the October Revolution. This is the name used almost exclusively by local authorities, teachers, and residents of the surrounding district. On the other hand, the term "Old Believers", and its synonym, "Old Ritualists", is employed by the people of Berezovka when they converse with Russian-speaking visitors. But by far the preferred self-designation is the Russian term for "Christians", *khristianini*. It makes clear the Old Believers' sense of religious superiority; for them, this name can refer only to the category of people whose views and practices coincide with their own. Everybody else, whether Roman Catholic, Hindu, Moslem, or agnostic, is cast into the much vaster class of *mirskie*, worldly people. The contrast and resulting tension between the two categories is heightened by the frequent use of the term *poganyi* as a colloquial synonym of *mirskii*. It is a derogatory designation which applies to explicitly un-Christian, "pagan" behaviour, especially transgressions of sexual and dietary purity rules.

The gap separating "Christians" and "pagans" cannot be bridged: the former are absolutely prohibited from sharing in meals, worship, or sexual relations with the latter. People from

TABLE 1
Correlates of the "Christian"/"pagan" dichotomy

Cultural Traits	"Christians"	"Pagans"
religious orientation	Christ	antichrist
sexual behaviour	chaste	promiscuous
food preferences	pure	impure
appearance	traditional	confusing
home environment	neat/clean	chaotic/dirty
work habits	diligent	lazy
education	applied	theoretical
language	Russian	foreign
conduct of children	disciplined	spoiled
sign of masculinity	forcefulness	meekness
sign of femininity	meekness	forcefulness
deviance	drinking	drugs
destiny	heaven	hell

the opposite camps do of course interact at school, in stores, and, to some extent, at work. The Old Believers treat their neighbours with civility, and shallow friendships do develop here and there, especially among young people. But there is a fine line between necessary and excessive contact with the *mirskie*, and those who cross it run the danger of eventual excommunication from the realm of local Christianity. The sin these unfortunates are accused of is called mixing up or *pomieshchanie*; it is one of the gravest infractions an Old Believer can be guilty of.

However, no one knows exactly where to draw the boundary between acceptable and unacceptable association with the worldly society. Everybody agrees that intimate physical contact, at the table or in bed, is a serious form of *pomieshchanie*, which must be punished. There is further agreement regarding the rejection of television, radio, and record players as powerful magnets of the forbidden outside world. But this does not disturb the many young couples who keep a portable TV set in the closet, activating it only in the presence of trustworthy friends when the monotony of a long winter night calls for some diversion (I still remember my shock when I first heard the faint voice of Barbara Frum behind a carefully closed door in a house that I visited one evening without prior notification). As everywhere else, the definition of deviance varies from one family to the next and between one year and the next. But even in the most liberal household, the separation between "Christians" and "pagans" is maintained. It is supported by stereotypes, outlined in table 1, which justify in an easily understood way the dangers of "mixing up".

The stereotypes which underlie the "Christian" view of the "pagan" world are permeated with the same ethnocentrism and xenophobia which shaped the earlier Muscovite mistrust of the West. Indeed, although daily experience with North American society is used as empirical evidence of their correctness, the convictions held by the Old Believers about *mirskie* are largely imparted by Byzantine and Russian religious propaganda, with which the people of Berezovka are well acquainted. The confines of holy Russia may have shrunk, but its ideology lives on. As in the past, this ideology hinges on three ancient suppositions: that Christianity cannot exist beyond the limits of Eastern Orthodoxy, that these limits are threatened by western culture, and that the most appropriate defence is social and spatial segregation. This triad infuses the people of Berezovka with their sense of purpose.

Unlike many western fundamentalist groups, the Old Believers do not search for converts. Theirs is an attitude to the world which goes back to Greek and Russian monasticism with its profound craving for solitude and separation from the surrounding society. Worldly people are treated with civility and charity when they seek help, but no missionary goes out into the countryside to save souls. The "world", or *mir*, is held to have fallen too far for salvation. Building on this ancient tradition, Berezovka resembles a monastic community whose residents regard the outside as a source of corruption that must be kept at bay. Such a view underlies the careful avoidance of *pomieshchanie*.

The aloofness of Berezovka's Old Believers inevitably has the effect of persuading their Canadian neighbours that they are held in contempt. To the extent that the newcomers are convinced of being God's chosen people, this impression is valid. The Old Believers cannot avoid feeling superior as long as they sustain their faith in an exclusive religion which is built on the notion of inequality. But that hardly exempts them from self-doubt, deep-seated insecurities, and the usual range of weaknesses affecting the average person. Like everybody else, the people of Berezovka confront the daily tasks of raising children, finding and keeping a job, running a household, and maintaining mental and physical balance. Like everybody else, they must cope with illnesses, deaths, disappointments, financial worries, and numerous other hardships. But few outsiders are allowed to catch a glimpse of the Old Believers' frail side. Banned from Berezovka and seduced by the uniformity of the Russians' appearance, an observer feels tempted to overlook their individuality and humanity. Instead of connecting a face with a name and a past, one delegates it to the amorphous class of "White Russians".

Many of the difficulties experienced but rarely verbalized by the Old Believers stem from their being recent immigrants. Despite their own immigrant past, surprisingly few Canadians appreciate the full implications of this status. Under the best of circumstances, the permanent abandonment of one's country of origin is a challenging experience, which often leads to a profound linguistic, cultural, and personal disorientation. Unable to comprehend the language, norms, and values of the host society, the immigrant faces the difficult task of constructing order out of apparent chaos. Not unlike a small child, he or she must absorb the meaning of countless clues in order to understand and be understood by other humans. Unlike a child, however, the immigrant is deprived of the loving and patient assistance provided by parents and relatives; the immigrant is alone and rootless.

To a certain degree, the self-imposed "ghetto" of Berezovka protects the Old Believers from the anonymity and confusion experienced by immigrants who arrive alone. However, the determination to maintain an insurmountable fence around Little Russia has thwarted or at least retarded the acquisition of knowledge which any immigrant needs for a reasonably successful coexistence with the host society. This observation applies primarily, though by no means exclusively, to old people and adult women—two categories of residents who have had neither any formal schooling in English nor much exposure to the dominant society through their daily work. For these people, English remains a poorly mastered language and Canada a foreign land whose institutions, geography, and culture are only vaguely familiar. The consequences can be traumatic: every phone call, every shopping trip, every physical examination at the doctor's office requires the assistance of an interpreter. Suffering from the combined handicaps of figurative deafness and dumbness, and functional illiteracy, many Old Believers experience culture shock every time they are compelled to leave the security of Berezovka. This can exacerbate their abruptness in dealings with strangers.

The stress from cultural marginality is not the only source of anguish which outside observers fail to appreciate. In spite of the tendency to appropriate Christianity as their exclusive property, many Old Believers are willing to concede that the piety displayed in Berezovka falls short of standards set by traditional Orthodoxy. They frankly admit that the settlement, far from being an oasis of spiritual growth, is saturated with worldly strife and competition. They also acknowledge feeling burdened by the ascetic self-denial imposed by their religion. It is not uncommon for people to express desire for carnal pleasures during long periods of fasts when sex and rich foods are proscribed. And instead of curbing their appetites, more than a few give in to their bodies' urges. The tension between the requirements of the soul and the needs of the body is a pronounced trait of the local culture.

The competition between spiritual and physical needs seems so marked here because Berezovka's Old Believers have very earthy, and indeed, "carnal" preferences. Daily work revolves around rich food, sufficient sleep, work in fresh air, and the warmth of human companionship. Natural body urges, such as belching and smacking during meals, or breaking wind are not suppressed. Normal speech is punctuated with vulgar expressions. Marriage occurs early and universally in order to allow young people to express their budding sexuality. Although these desires are satisfied within a wider context of ascetic-like prayers, fasts, wakes, and similar acknowledgements of a supra-human force, this religious dimension of life appears more as a control mechanism imposed by an external agent than as an internalized inhibition against carnal excess. An interesting display of this condition is the remarkable ease with which an Old Believer slides from the "spiritual" into the "carnal" state. A long church service inevitably ends with an elaborate meal and several cupfuls of potent fruit wine, which in turn leads to a prolonged nap. Not surprisingly, paradise is portrayed literally as a land of milk and honey.

Many people admit that their attention to bodily needs detracts from the ideals of monastic asceticism associated with Christian perfection. At the same time, virtually no effort is made to attain more ideal conditions either through a call for reform or a reassessment of the definition of piety. Instead, the inability to live up to traditional Orthodox expectations is accepted as inevitable. The imperfections are excused as unavoidable consequences of semi-literacy, hard physical work which calls for long periods of rest, and simple human frailty. In short, the people of Berezovka do not see themselves as saints or super-humans, but rather as simple peasants who, deprived of external guidance because of the *raskol*, are doing their best to preserve the most they can of Old Orthodoxy.

But although the gap between the ideal and the reality of Christian living seems to have always been a part of the historical experience of Berezovka's Old Believers, elders and young adults agree that it has been widening at an alarming pace since their arrival in North America more than twenty years ago. Few deny that what were formerly exceptional concessions to worldly society have become gradually incorporated into the local culture as its permanent ingredients. The role of material possessions is a case in point. Unlike in the past, it is claimed, when a man was judged on his diligence and devotion to God, social status today is measured increasingly in the materialistic terms defined by the surrounding society. Consequently, the argument goes, religious services are less well attended and shorter than in the past, reflecting the current generation's unwillingness to sacrifice personal comfort.

This verdict is not dismissed by younger residents as the fabrications of senile minds. They admit to being responsible for embracing many worldly values which their ancestors had fought against, and their justification is once again individual weakness. But unlike the traditional tension between spiritual and physical demands, which is accepted as an inevitable fact of life, its modern extension is seen as being caused not merely by human nature but above all by new values catering to that inborn weakness. That is, while the people of Berezovka blame themselves for bridging the gap between spirituality and carnality, North American society at large is held responsible for providing the incentive. This view seems to underlie the repulsion, combined with fascination, which characterizes the Old Believers' dealings with *mir*. The fruit that grows outside Berezovka's perimeters is still forbidden, but its appeal is becoming irresistible. This is the source of the main predicament and strain facing the local settlers.

TABLE 2					
Geographical Origins of Berezovka's Founders					
Arrival	*Age*	*Place of Birth*	*Arrival*	*Age*	*Place of Birth*
1973	21	Harbin [Manchuria]	1974	30	Manchuria
			1974	28	Harbin
1973	31	Harbin			
1973	29	Khabarovsk [Far East]	1974	21	Harbin
			1974	19	Harbin
1973	52	Primorie [Far East]			
1973	48	Primorie	1974	28	Harbin
			1974	26	Turkey
1973	18	Harbin			
1973	17	Hong Kong	1974	41	Primorie
			1974	41	Manchuria
1974	44	Primorie			
1974	44	Primorie	1974	42	Primorie
			1974	42	Harbin
1974	40	Primorie			
1974	40	China	1974	44	Primorie
			1974	45	Primorie
1974	25	Harbin			
1974	22	Istanbul	1974	25	Harbin
			1974	22	Harbin
1974	23	Turkey			
1974	17	Mirgin [Manchuria]	1975	47	Tomsk
			1975	46	Harbin
1974	27	Harbin			
1974	26	Singkiang	1975	29	Sinkiang
1974	32	Manchuria			
1974	29	Sinkiang			

Historical and Geographical Origins

Because of the still relatively short period of time spent by the Old Believers in Canada, their community life continues to be very much shaped by people born outside North America. A good impression of Berezovka's roots can be obtained by examining the geographical origins of its founders. The thirty-six adults who moved in between 1973 and 1975 are described in Table 2 according to their place of birth, age at time of arrival, and year of immigration to Canada. The married ones are listed in pairs.

The geographical origins of the founding generation provide a valuable clue to the make-up of the community. It is dominated by residents whose roots go back to the Russian and Chinese Far East, specifically to eastern Siberia, the Amur province, and northeastern Manchuria. Collectively, they refer to themselves as *Kharbintsy*, which expresses the fact that at some time most of them either lived in or passed through Harbin, the capital of Manchuria.

Numerically and politically far less influential are the so-called *Sintsiantsy*, whose ancestry extends to western Siberia and the Chinese province of Sinkiang. In Berezovka they are represented for the most part by women married to *Kharbintsy* and by a few men who live on the fringe of the community. The *Sintsiantsy* do, however, compose large congregations in Oregon and an isolated settlement in northwestern Alberta, which was founded concurrently with Berezovka.

Finally, there is the third and smallest local group, which consists of Old Believers born in Turkey, who are referred to, appropriately, as *Turchane*. This contingent has only a few hundred members in North America, and its representatives are perceived as somewhat removed cousins of the two "Chinese" factions.

To depict adequately the distant history of the three local groups would require a separate volume and several more years of thorough research. In a nutshell, it seems that all of them are to some degree associated with Old Orthodox fugitives who left European Russia in the course of the eighteenth and early nineteenth centuries. The ancestors of the *Turchane* appear to have fled to Dobrudja (in today's Romania) and from there to have moved on to Anatolia in successive waves (Biggins 1985; Call

1979; Kelsiev 1866). Prompted by epidemics, discrimination, and the threat of inbreeding, all of Turkey's Old Believers left during 1962 and 1963 for the Soviet Union (Shamaro 1964) and North America respectively. After an unsuccessful attempt at immigrating to Canada, all of the 224 *Turchane* who had chosen not to return to Russia were admitted to the United States (Piepkorn 1977; Scheffel 1989a). Most settled down in Oregon where they joined their co-religionists from China, and this state has remained their base to this day (Morris 1981).

Originating most likely in the Russo-Polish border region, the ancestors of the *Sintsiantsy* seem to have been forcibly resettled in Central Asia in the latter part of the eighteenth century. There they established several villages in the Altai Mountains, in the northeastern corner of Kazakhstan, along the Buhktarma River. This location earned them the designation *bukhtarminskie* Old Believers—a name made famous by a Soviet ethnographic expedition carried out in the 1920s (Blomkvist & Grinkova 1930). Beginning with the Russian Civil War and peaking after the collectivization campaign of the early 1930s, several fugitives from this and surrounding areas crossed the border into China and established residence in the neighbouring province of Sinkiang. Here they remained until the turmoil created by the Chinese communist revolution, which prompted another exodus in the 1950s, this time to the New World.

The fate of the *Kharbintsy* was dictated by the same historical events. Their ancestral region, the coastal strip north of Vladivostok known as Primorie, and the Amur River basin, had been settled by Old Believers in the second half of the eighteenth century, but new waves of migrants arrived in the course of the nineteenth and during the first years of the twentieth century. Here too, the Civil War and the collectivization campaign set the stage for defection to China, which inevitably led to Harbin—the capital of Manchuria and the Far Eastern centre of "White Russian" settlement after the Bolshevik victory. Like the *Sintsiantsy*, the *Kharbintsy* left China soon after the 1949 communist revolution.

This short account of the roots of Berezovka's founders is, admittedly, sketchy. Most of the older residents have had their lives disrupted by traumatic political upheavals which led to involuntary migrations, the violent deaths and deportations of close relatives, and other forms of family dislocation which have an adverse effect on their ability to reconstruct the distant past. Many of my informants were unable to remember the names and origins of all four grandparents, and family roots reaching as far back as the nineteenth century were guessed at only with considerable difficulty. Furthermore, as I show in subsequent chapters, the people of Berezovka display the universal tendency to adjust their past to the requirements of the present. For many this means that too thorough a search for family roots may reveal uncomfortable contradictions between one's assumed and real past. For these reasons, local residents tend not to dig beyond the last fifty or sixty years in establishing and maintaining their collective identities. If you lived in Turkey prior to your arrival in North America, you are automatically a member of the *Turchane*. Whether your roots there were short or long matters little. Similarly, the fact that you were born in western Siberia or that your father may have arrived from Moscow makes no difference to your status as a *Kharbinets*, which is established simply on account of your residence in Manchuria after the Revolution.

The simplified tri-partite classification conceals the staggeringly turbulent and varied collage of events experienced by Berezovka's elders in the last seventy-odd years. This applies primarily to the *Kharbintsy* and *Sintsiantsy*, who lived through revolutions, civil wars, foreign occupations, numerous migrations, and similar traumatic occasions which have marked their outlook on life. The following lengthy excerpts from interviews with older *Kharbintsy*—conducted in Russian and later translated into English—reveal something of that turbulent past and shed light on their complex origins. The first excerpt is from the biography of a man who is one of Berezovka's oldest residents.

> I was born in 1910 in the village Solovievo [Bukhtarma region]. My mother was native to Siberia, but my father had come from the western provinces. They both married at sixteen, and I was the first-born. Nine children followed; three of them died. When I was half-a-year old, we moved to Vladivostok to settle the coast of the Okhotsk Sea. My father was sent there to escape military service. That region was populated exclusively by Old

Believers—they were the first people there. We were supposed to fish and to trade fish for goods from Japan. But my father was not a fisherman, he was a farmer, and we returned to our old village one year later.

Father was then drafted to fight the German [sic] in Austria during the First World War. At that time, we still lived with my grandparents, their six sons and families. We had some twenty people living side by side in a single house. We all worked in the fields, on land owned by the tsar and allotted to individual households on the basis of need.

A family paid 50 kopeks a year for all the land it used. There were no taxes. Most people were neither rich nor poor, but quite a few had little to live on. It depends on the household head, how well he can manage things. Only the lazy ones were poor, just like today. The village had three churches, prayer homes just like here. There were no schools prior to 1917, and I learned to read and write by myself. Church Slavonic was taught by parents and an old man who instructed groups of children for free.

Father returned from Austria in 1917, but nobody knew about the revolution until it arrived in the village. We had no radio or newspapers. Late in that year, there was sporadic fighting between the Bolsheviks and Cossacks. Some of the Bolsheviks lived in Old Believer homes for two days. They behaved well and advised us not to accept any weapons from the Whites. Then they moved further east, because White resistance had been broken here. The Cossacks were leaving for China.

Between 1917 and 1920, life was as free as ever before. Changes were made only in 1920 when the Soviets set up a school—which the Old Believers refused to go to— and an administrative council modelled after Moscow. Then the churches were closed down, and we had to pray and baptize in secret, in the basement. Then the Reds started to *kulachit*—to rob. They divided the farmers into three categories: *biednaki* [poor ones], *sredniki* [in-between] and *kulaki* [rich ones]. If you were a *kulak*, they took all your food and locked it up. They started to disperse the population from east to west in order to mix up people. Parents lost children, and children became orphans. We were assessed as *sredniki*, and we immediately sold everything and moved east.

I was the first one to go, leaving with my uncle in early 1927. At first we travelled by sled to Semipalatinsk and then by train to Birobidjan in the Jewish Autonomous Republic, some three thousand kilometres away, near Khabarovsk. This area was still the same as before, and the Cossacks lived as if the tsar were still in charge. From Bira we walked two hundred kilometres to Amur River, sleeping in Old Believer villages or with Cossacks. The rest of the family arrived in the spring by steamboat. Together with some fifty other Old Believers we founded a small village on the Amur—we had all come from different regions. The railway remained in tsarist hands; the Communists controlled it only up to the Irtysh. The countryside was empty, with just a few villages of Cossacks.

I moved for a while to the Jewish region where I got work. Jews were arriving by steamboat from all parts of the country, even from Palestine. They didn't like it too much because of the cold, and many left later on. Some couldn't even speak any Russian. I worked for them and then returned to our settlement in 1930. By then, our people had already left for the northern taiga, driven out by two great floods in 1928 and 1929, and by the arrival of the Communists, who forced them to work without pay. I returned to the Jews and told father to make preparations for leaving Russia.

Father made a cabin on top of our sled, and the whole family escaped across the Amur in the winter of 1931. Altogether we were sixteen families, all originally from Kazakhstan. Many of these people still live together here in North America. In China there was freedom, only the language was unintelligible. But Old Believers knew their way around, because they used to smuggle food from China, and they knew Russian women who had married

Chinese men. We arrived in a large village, fortified by walls against attacks by bandits known as *xunxuzi*. Soldiers led us the next morning to the closest town, situated on Sungari River, which empties into the Amur. Here we spent the rest of the winter in the house of a rich Chinese.

In the spring of 1931, we left by steamboat for Harbin, some six hundred kilometres upstream. There we were met by officials helping refugees. The city had about half-a-million residents, and perhaps one third of them were Russians. We found sponsors and received tsarist passports. Even the currency was still in gold, using tsarist coins. The immigration authorities allotted work to all the refugees in exchange for pay or board. I supplied families with milk. Everything was directed by Russian officials and police, and the centre of the city was closed to the Chinese. This was mainly because the Chinese Eastern Railway was controlled by Russians, but that changed when the Japanese invaded Manchuria.

Our group left Harbin in 1934 and moved two hundred kilometres east to an important railway station. The line was then in Japanese hands, but Russian officials and workers continued to run the trains. I worked there with my brother for the next while, hunting big game and supplying the station with meat. Then, in 1935, we heard about a settlement founded by other Old Believers in the vicinity of Mutankiang, approximately one hundred and fifty kilometres east of Harbin. At first, there were three villages, later on five. We moved there. Some of us left at once, others remained in the station and joined us later.

This account provides a good illustration of the chequered origins of Berezovka's founders. Here we have a man who belonged to the *bukhtarminskie* Old Believers but who, instead of fleeing south to Sinkiang, went east and joined the *Kharbintsy* to eventually become one of them. As his story makes clear, such exceptions occurred rather frequently. The east Manchurian villages established by the Old Believers in the 1930s did indeed

White Russians from Manchuria arrive in Alberta in 1924.
(Wetaskiwin City Archives)

have a Far Eastern core, but quite a few of their residents came from a mixture of backgrounds. The five settlements—called Romanovka, Kolumbo, Selen-khe, Chipigu, and Mediany— probably did not exceed five hundred souls. There were much larger Old Believer communities in the northwestern border region known as *Trekhrechie*, but those were dominated by the *popovtsy*, whom the *Kharbintsy* regarded as distant cousins (Scheffel 1989b).

The time spent in China is recalled fondly. The Japanese occupation of Manchuria changed little for the Old Believers, who were left in peace to live as they deemed appropriate. They had access to excellent soil, which provided abundant crops of wheat, and to vast wilderness teeming with limitless numbers of game animals. These two resources determined the annual economic cycle: the summers were spent in the villages with agricultural activities as the main focus, and then, as the winter approached, the men formed small groups of hunters and disappeared into the bush. Although some animals, such as the wild boar, were hunted for meat, the Old Believers specialized in animals whose body parts could be sold to the Chinese tradesmen as medical remedies. This applied particularly to the Far Eastern elk, called *zubr* by the Russians, which supplied highly valued antlers that were ground up and sold by the ounce to native pharmacists. An even more precious animal was the Siberian tiger, which government officials in Harbin paid very good money for. Younger tigers were apparently sold for a huge profit to foreign zoos. The favourable conditions encountered in Manchuria are described in this excerpt from an interview with a *Kharbinka* born in 1933:

> I was born in Mongolia. I remember a little, there were Cossacks, Tungus, and Mongols there. Then we moved to our own people, father's relatives, farmers who lived there before. Here we lived well. Father wasn't much of a hunter, he was a carpenter, a cooper, a housebuilder, he made carriages and sleighs, he made boots, tin dishes and wooden ones. He could do all this.
>
> The Russians always lived in their own settlements. The Chinese had their own, and the Russians had their own. They didn't want to speak Chinese. They all knew the language well but didn't care to speak it, not like now when everyone speaks English. People were living, they would go hunting, they would go quite far and make arrangements: "Let's live where there is game!" And they would gather, look over the place, and if it was suitable for a settlement, they would pack up and go there, they would build, cut timber—they could cut all the timber they needed. The Chinese would mill the lumber—they would hire Chinese for that.
>
> One could hunt wherever one wanted and kill whatever game was needed. They could sell it. They would live here for a while, then move to an even better place, further away. There, they would build again, and the old place was then occupied by the Chinese. Before the war, as far as I can remember, we were children and liked everything. What did children need? Everybody would gather at home, it was warm, we weren't hungry, we had

cows and milk and meat. Anything that was planted grew
well, no matter what you would put in the ground.

Life changed with the outbreak of war between Japan and
the Soviet Union in August 1945. It lasted for barely a month,
but its outcome had serious consequences for the Old Believers.
After bloody skirmishes, their settlements were occupied by the
Red Army, which treated the émigrés as enemies of the Soviet
regime. The Japanese had used some of the Russian men as scouts
along the border, and a few may have actually fought against the
Red Army. This prompted the forced repatriation of dozens of
men and adolescent boys. Most of them were never seen again.
The events leading up to this calamity are recalled in the following
account by the same woman quoted above:

The war stared quickly, or rather suddenly. One day we
noticed war planes flying, and we saw fires here and
there. We were in the field cutting the wheat. Father
said, "Go, fetch me some water!" So I went to a spring,
and a woman was harvesting nearby. And we saw the
Soviet advance unit—three soldiers on horseback. They
rode up to us and asked, "Are you Russians?" And the
woman said, "We are." So we talked a little, and when
I returned, father asked about the encounter. I explained, and he immediately put down the scythe and
told mother, "Take good care of the children, I won't
survive this, things don't look good. Whatever happens,
be together." So we went home, and by then the troops
were riding in. They had already occupied the cities and
were now covering the villages. They started to alter the
railway tracks to match Soviet trains.
I was a young girl. I saw how people were hiding during
the fighting with the Japanese in our village. There was
a skirmish under the mountain. I saw how many dead
there were. The Russians, the victors, picked up their
soldiers' bodies. The Japanese were left laying around.
Here the dogs would tear up pieces, here there would
be a head or a skull, a hand or a knee may be sticking
out of the ground. The summer was over, and we would

go to the woods looking for mushrooms. We would see corpses here and there, all decayed. Lots of people died.

The repatriation of a considerable number of able-bodied men was not only an emotional trauma for the remaining Old Believers. It was also a serious blow to the local economy, and led to several years of food shortages. Further hardships were felt in consequence of the Chinese communist revolution, which threatened the Russian fugitives once again with collectivization and curtailment of their cherished freedom. Some of the changes undergone by the Old Believers are alluded to in the continuation of the above narrative.

[After the war] the Chinese demanded that we take Chinese citizenship and be like them—have all their rights and be punished like them if we do anything wrong. They clamped down on cutting timber, if they find green wood in your house, you go to jail. Or if you kill some game, you will be held liable. Everything became stricter. You got prosecuted for everything, everything became organized. If you kill anything, you have to hand it in to the Hunters' Union, to the authorities, and they'll pay you something, but there were no more independent hunters. They started to chase everyone into collective farms. The Chinese really tortured their own people. They forced them to carry lumber, pull the plough—twenty people would pull it; nineteen hitched, and one would walk behind. They would move so slowly! And they would plough all the fields, you couldn't see the end of them, everything would be black. These were all the people who had been convicted of being against the regime. They would carry wood in the winter, so much of it, so much! They would be loaded up the sledge like a truck, and they would pull and pull. Some were sick, at the end of their strength, one would fall, couldn't walk any more. Soldiers would shove him aside, and he would die right there. The same with ploughing: if he runs out of strength, they'd push him out of the way, they would beat him, and if he can't get up, they would drag him aside, and he would die right there.

Well, our people would never live like that. The Russians cannot live like the Chinese. Whatever they would order, we would be doing it their way, the Chinese way. How could we live like that?

My father (and many other men) was forced to return to Russia, where he died. But many went back voluntarily. My husband's sister went, she didn't want to, but her husband went, and she couldn't stay behind. Many went to Russia on their own. The consul [from Harbin] would go around, trying to talk people into returning. He would go from house to house, saying, "Please, come to Russia, things are good there. Here, on foreign soil, things won't be so good." So some did go back.

The majority of the *Kharbintsy*, however, remained in Manchuria and applied in 1952 for exit visas to emigrate to a western country. This plan encountered resistance from Soviet authorities, who considered the Old Believers Soviet citizens and expected them to return to the USSR. The resistance was apparently overcome with the help of the United Nations, and approximately five hundred of the *Kharbintsy* managed to arrive in Hong Kong in the course of 1957. It was in Hong Kong that they met the *Sintsiantsy*, and the two groups decided to co-ordinate their exodus to an appropriate location abroad.

The stay in Hong Kong dragged on as the Old Believers negotiated with several countries and organizations in an effort to find a new home. In the end, instead of moving collectively to the same location, small groups of families and friends seceded from the main body of the émigrés and left for Australia, New Zealand, Paraguay, Argentina, or Bolivia on their own. But the majority stayed together and eventually managed to obtain the necessary permits for large-scale group settlement in Brazil. Financially supported by the World Council of Churches, they travelled in several parties by ship to Rio de Janeiro and then to Ponta Grossa in the state Parana.

Although the move to Brazil was undertaken by both groups, the *Kharbintsy* and the *Sintsiantsy* travelled separately and established their own communities. The former founded three settlements within the same area, while the latter chose a neighbouring district some twenty kilometres away. With time, members of the two groups began to intermarry, but both factions preserved their autonomy. For all the migrants, the move to Brazil represented a radical break with the lifestyle to which they had grown accustomed in China. Starting with the journey from China to South America and ending with the climate, geography, and culture of Brazil, everything experienced during the late 1950s was entirely new. One of the more surprising encounters, recalled in the following account, brought the Old Believers face to face with blacks.

We met blacks for the first time in Africa. There were also some in Hong Kong, but here [in Mombasa] it was different. The men landed first and they knew about these black people, but they didn't tell us anything. So we went, and we got into town, they were running around, and I was walking, carrying my little son in my arms. So there we are walking, looking, everything was so different, so interesting. And all the people who looked after the city, they were all in skirts, everybody wore skirts, soldiers on guard duty were in skirts. They weren't eating with a spoon but with their hands from the bowl into their mouths.

So we were walking, and our little girls saw these blacks, and they started crying so hard that I couldn't pull them away. They didn't even want to look. "The devil!" they shouted, and "This is the devil, this is the devil!" And then I looked and saw this one running towards us. First I didn't notice, but then I heard the noise, that was him running, and everything was rattling. I looked up—he was *so* close! So I turned around to run, but there was a store right there with a large window, so I ran right into the glass, but it didn't break. Then we walked around a bit, and these blacks were sitting around with their music, all over the place, and wherever they went, they took their music along. I don't know why they like music so much.

And then they started loading up the ship, and we were observing them. They work, they work, and then they sit down in the hold—you know how deep it can be—and they look up. The sailors would bring them cookies or candy, they'd throw down a box, as if they were dealing with a pack of dogs, and they would grab it like animals. It was scary to look at them; it was horrible. They would come on board after we had eaten and eat in an awful hurry from the garbage. They were very hungry in Africa.

The living conditions in Parana were trying. The settlers were plagued by crop failures, tropical diseases, corrupt officials, and a host of other seemingly insurmountable problems. Although their lot improved within a few years as they grew accustomed to the new environment, many had become persuaded that North America offered much better opportunities than Brazil. In 1964, with the help of the Tolstoy Foundation of New York, over thirteen hundred *Kharbintsy* and *Sintsiantsy* applied for admission to the United States and Canada. Ottawa replied with an almost unconditional rejection (Scheffel 1989a), but Washington approved the request, which triggered yet another exodus, this time to Oregon.

By 1970, the stream of migrants from Brazil to the United States had largely dried up, and the Willamette Valley area of Oregon was inhabited by some twelve hundred *Kharbintsy*, six hundred *Sintsiantsy*, and between two and three hundred *Turchane* (Hall 1970:13-15). Although the new economic conditions were superior to those left behind in Brazil, another problem surfaced in the form of acculturation. For the first time in their history, the Old Believers proved unable to maintain a safe buffer zone between themselves and their worldly neighbours. Instead of isolated villages, they found densely populated rural towns where space and privacy were rare commodities. Far from establishing separate settlements, the new arrivals were compelled to move into crowded apartments, townhouses, and trailers where the conduct of traditional economic, social, and ritual activities proved next to impossible. With these changed conditions of daily life, the core values and norms established by previous generations came to be threatened (Morris 1981; Sabey 1969; Smithson 1976; Wigowsky 1982). The following excerpt from an interview with a woman who now resides in Berezovka sums up her impressions of life in Oregon:

> But when we came to America, the children started going to school right away. During this time they would get hold of bad books, and they would come back from school with nothing to do. There were no settlements in Oregon. You can't buy suitable land for setting up a community. The Turks have one of sorts, but it's in the city just the same. You can't keep much of anything. The children step out the door, and they are in the city. One step, and they are in the store. So our people made up their minds to leave when we started to hear about drugs. People became apprehensive and began to look for a place to go to. We had come from far away, but it was still crowded.

The final leg of the journey from the Old to the New World involved only a fraction of the Old Believers. It was spearheaded by a group of tradition-minded and adaptable *kharbintsy* dissatisfied with the life in Oregon who, as early as 1968, began to stake out a wilderness settlement on Alaska's Kenai Peninsula (Reardon 1972). They founded a large village, Nikolaevsk, and several smaller communities dispersed throughout a rugged and inaccessible region (Basargin 1984). A parallel effort in Canada led to the establishment of Berezovka and a smaller settlement of *Sintsiantsy* in northwestern Alberta.

This short historical overview demonstrates the context in which Berezovka was born. Intended as a refuge from the rapidly changing main community in Oregon, the frontier settlements in Alberta and Alaska remain nevertheless dependent on the former. The source of the dependence can be grasped when one compares the size of the parent community with that of its offshoots. While Oregon accommodates around five thousand Old Believers, the combined population of the "colonies" founded in Alaska and Alberta is still well below two thousand. Because of strictly enforced religious endogamy and a wide definition of incest, the settlers on the "frontier" would be at a loss for suitable marriage partners if it were not for their recourse to the large, albeit culturally adulterated, pool of their co-religionists in Oregon.

The dependence on Oregon determines to a considerable degree Berezovka's relations with the outside world. Especially in the warm summer months, when weddings traditionally take place, much visiting goes on between the Canadian and the American outposts of Old Orthodoxy. While these contacts are a source of pleasure and amusement, they can also lead to friction as the more conservative *Kanadtsy* are exposed to new fads embraced by their more liberal-minded cousins in the south. Attempts at increasing Berezovka's size through a massive influx of traditionalists from Oregon have been thwarted by Canadian immigration policies, and it appears unlikely that the American influence will diminish.

Although Oregon and Alaska are the two centres of Old Belief which maintain the most extensive relations with Berezovka, permanent contacts also exist with several communities that are still located in South America. The distance between the continents makes visits rare, but not impossible. Occasional inter-continental marriages do take place, and some people travel to Brazil to see their relatives once every few years. Finally, sporadic contact, for the most part through letters rather than visits, exists with family members in the Soviet Union and Australia.

Community and Family

Community Organization

It should now be clear that the driving force behind the migrations undertaken by Berezovka's founders during the last sixty years has been the search for autonomy and freedom. Old Believers place tremendous value on the notion of freedom, and they assess entire countries, epochs, and national characters on the basis of how much freedom, or *vol'nost'*, they stand for. It is their unquestioned assumption that Russians require more freedom to thrive than other peoples, especially the regimented Chinese and Germans, but one must be careful to take into account the context in which this freedom is defined. As it is understood locally, *vol'nost'* applies to what may be called "freedom of action", examples of which are unhampered hunting, lack of government interference in local affairs, and absence of building restrictions. Significantly, this realm does not include "freedom of thought" as it is understood in a liberal democracy. An Old Believer is not free to think what he or she wants nor to read whatever may seem interesting. Such tendencies are referred to as *volnodumstvo* (freethinking), and correlated with agnosticism. The mind, which is associated with the soul, belongs to God and must be receptive to the Holy Spirit. The body, on the other hand, is under direct personal control, and it is through this entity that one enjoys liberty. Even the cherished freedom of action is, of course, curtailed, owing to God's demand for *physical* sacrifice by means of fasts, sexual abstinence, prayers, and similar demonstrations of obedience. But this sacrifice is limited to the religious realm, where it serves as a measure of individual piety. Secular authorities cannot expect to be treated in the same manner as God.

It is useful to relate the distinction between freedom of action and freedom of thought to the distinction between Berezovka's political and religious organization. Unlike the latter (described in greater detail below), which is well-defined and rarely challenged, the former, civil authority structure, is fragmented, acephalous, and bordering on anarchy. It rests with the heads of individual households, who enjoy unrestricted autonomy in the running of their affairs. The house manager (*khozyain*), assisted by his wife (*khozyaika*), has undisputed authority over all members of the household, and this right is guarded with great determination against any outside interference. Even the religious leader, who may have to become involved from time to time in internal affairs that impinge on spiritual matters, is extremely careful not to create the impression of curtailing the autonomy of the family.

The political structure of Berezovka revolves around the household heads. Each of them automatically becomes member of the *sobor*, which is an informal council responsible for the adjudication of religious issues and the election of church officials known collectively as elders (*stariki*). With the increased contact between the Old Believers and outside authorities following their exodus from China, there has been a tendency to use the *sobor* as an advisory body in not only religious but also civil matters, which affect the entire community. Its members elect annually a mayor (*starosta*) and a village secretary (*sekretar*) who may be called upon by outside agencies which need to deal with a "community representative". However, the office of the mayor has merely an advisory role, and any binding agreement requires the assent of *all* household heads. In practice, then, the mayor limits his involvement to calling public meetings (*sobranie*) to discuss a given issue, such as local education, which is used as an example below. Should the participants agree on a course of action, something that happens rather rarely, their resolution is still not binding for the community at large. Even when it is supported by most residents, any collective action remains voluntary and may be opted out of by the families of dissenting *sobor* members. This is entirely misunderstood by federal and provincial government officials, who expect to encounter the kind of well-defined authority associated with Hutterite colonies (Scheffel 1989c).

One of the primary reasons for the inability to arrive at a community-wide consensus in other than spiritual matters is the unwillingness of most residents to cooperate politically with un-related people. Moulded by geography and recent history, Berezovka's social structure cannot be divorced from the realm of kinship. The web of kinship underlies virtually all important factions and determines who will cooperate with whom.

The most divisive influence stems from the separate back-grounds of the three local groups—the *Kharbintsy*, *Sintsiantsy*, and *Turchane*. Unlike in Oregon, where these segments constitute separate congregations, and, at least in the case of the "Turks", a separate community, Berezovka unites them in a single parish and community. This conglomeration could only have been ac-complished in the expectation of the two weaker groups' subor-dination of their interests to those who regard themselves as the founders of the settlement, namely the *Kharbintsy*. Although the linguistic and folkloristic distinctions separating the three contin-gents have been waning under the impact of inter-marriage and daily contact, both of Berezovka's minorities have retained the awareness of distinct identities. This may be at least partly caused by the heavy-handed insistence of some of its leaders on Berezovka's being the property of the Manchurian group, with members of the other two parties tolerated as mere guests.

The tensions deriving from the tri-partite division are further magnified by distinctions within the separate "tribes". Although virtually all the members of a given local group are interrelated by multiple links, only relatively close kinsmen can determine with certainty the nature of these bonds. And since consanguinity coin-cides to a considerable degree with historical residence patterns, one can detect a second level of "local groups" which goes back to the divisions that existed among the *Kharbintsy* in Manchuria and, to some extent, Brazil. Although these boundaries are not always clearly drawn, it can happen that a person expresses dis-approval of a neighbour's action and concludes, "After all, *these* people used to live in a different village in China!" Of course, there are many other issues which, as anywhere else, can give rise to animosity and factionalism. But the point being made here is that whether conflict develops out of jealousy, fear, anger, or envy, the lines drawn by the combatants will most likely coincide with the existing boundaries separating close kinsmen from distant ones and strangers.

The inability of Berezovka's residents to overcome divisions deriving from their "kinship polity" (Fortes 1949) was demonstrated most poignantly in a crisis triggered by the introduction of Russian-language instruction at the school in Josephville. Since their arrival in Alberta, the Old Believers have been worried about the gradual erosion of their children's ability to retain the mother tongue. From time to time, the option of a private school or at least of a Russian curriculum at the Josephville school would be brought up at a meeting, but political ignorance and fragmented community support prevented any real action from taking place. Eventually, my presence in Berezovka served as a catalyst for exploring the issue jointly with the provincial department of education. Under pressure from Edmonton, the local school board finally budged and agreed to experiment with limited Russian-language instruction for the Old Believer children. Ostensibly as a sign of cultural tolerance, the school board made the Old Believers responsible for locating a certified teacher who was to design and carry out an appropriate curriculum.

The first step, after this landmark decision, was taken by some Old Believers living on farms outside the village whose children do not attend the school in Josephville. They distanced themselves from the project, declaring it the responsibility of the "villagers". The latter began scouting for a suitable candidate, and, with my help, a list of qualified persons was drawn up. When they arrived for interviews, I had to take them from house to house, searching for spokesmen able to communicate to the candidates what kind of education the community was interested in. Only a few elders were located, and their comments made it clear that a consensus as to the type of curriculum desired did not exist and probably would never do so.

At this stage, when the chance of finding an acceptable teacher was becoming dimmer and dimmer, one of the junior *Kharbintsy* elders arrived with an acquaintance by the name of Yuri R. A middle-aged Soviet refugee, Yuri sported a wild untrimmed beard, a huge cross around his neck, and an Ontario teaching certificate. Within a few days, he had met with the school board officials and all the elders, displayed Russian-language books and other instructional tools, and persuaded everybody of his ability to set up a viable program. In the meantime, I had completed my field work, and Yuri, by now a teacher at the Josephville school, moved into my former quarters.

Several months into his very successful teaching career, Yuri bought a house built and formerly occupied by a *Turchan*. At this point, several voices were raised against his presence in what was considered Old Believer territory. The opposition gathered momentum after Yuri was seen taking notes during a religious service, which gave rise to fears of his being a spy. This suspicion was fanned by the previous owner of Yuri's house, who had become entangled in a legal suit stemming from an alleged breach of contract. The former owner received assistance from another *Turchan* and from several in-laws. This opposition party physically assaulted Yuri, vandalized his home, and began to intimidate the teacher's supporters, all of them core *Kharbintsy*. The explosive situation began to spill over into religious services, which were disrupted by shouting and verbal attacks as the community threatened to fall apart. Prompted by Yuri's enemies' refusal to allow their children to attend the Josephville school as long as he remained on its staff, the school board discontinued the Russian program and dismissed its teacher.

During several visits between the end of my field work and the winter of 1986, I was able to appreciate the degree of animosity generated by this affair. After Yuri's dismissal, several families continued to support him by paying for his services as a private tutor. With time, however, this group grew smaller and smaller, eventually including only the closest relatives of the teacher's initial sponsor. For these people and their less courageous allies, the decline of the "teacher party" is seen as a clear sign of the harmful influence upon Berezovka of the "Turkish bandits".

Kinship and the Family

The Old Believers distinguish between natural kinship, which is based on biology and coincides with the incest boundary, and spiritual kinship, which is shared by all Christians who uphold the tenets of Orthodoxy as defined in Berezovka. Both of these realms come to the foreground in the expression most often employed to describe relatives, namely the word *nashi*, which can be translated as our people. Depending on its use, this term designates the perceived unity between the residents of Berezovka and the early Christians, as well as the importance of ties based on close consanguinity.

The centre of *nashi* in the emotional and social sense is not so much the nuclear family as the extended household built upon agnatic ties between married siblings and their parents. This household, sometimes referred to as *dvor*, is the result of the ten-

One of Berezovka's founding couples (centre) with family.

dency of married children, especially sons, to establish their post-marital residence in the immediate vicinity of the parental home. The process out of which it grows starts with the marriage of the first, usually the eldest, son. Instead of moving away, he and his wife stay on for one, two, or even more years, occupying a single room in the parental residence and helping out with the running of the household. Such a unit, known in the anthropological litera-ture as the "patriarchal extended family" (Murdock 1949:34), is called locally simply a large family (*bolshaya semya*). It is in a constant process of segmentation (*dielenie*) called forth by the separation of older sons and the incorporation of younger sons and their wives. Unlike in the not so distant past, when parents shared their residence with several married sons concurrently, the growing need for comfort and privacy prompts most young men today to establish a separate home soon after the birth of the first child. Still, the new residence, today most likely a trailer, is usually located in the immediate vicinity of the parental home, which con-tinues to serve as the focal point for several nuclear families. These clusters of agnatically related residences form the political, economic, and emotional heart of the community.

TABLE 3

Berezovka's Family Groups and the Corresponding Number of Nuclear Families. The groups are listed alphabetically.

Family Group	Number of Nuclear Families		Family Group
#1 [T]	1	4	#11 [X]
2 [X]	5	8	12 [X]
3 [S]	3	5	13 [X]
4 [X]	8	5	14 [X]
5 [X]	6	3	15 [S]
6 [S]	2	2	16 [X]
7 [X]	4	7	17 [X]
8 [T]	1	1	18 [X]
9 [X]	2	2	19 [X]
10 [?]	1		

T = *Turchane* X = *Kharbintsy* S = *Sintsiantsy*

The importance of agnatic ties is born out of Berezovka's history and its present make-up. The founders of the community arrived between 1973 and 1975 in eleven family clusters, which were dominated by groups of married brothers and their wives and offspring. Today, the four hundred or so people who live here belong to roughly seventy nuclear families—around fifty in Berezovka proper, and some twenty on farms in the vicinity—which still represent only nineteen family names. With a very few exceptions, each nuclear family is embedded in an extended network of closely related kinsmen whose core consists of married brothers scattered around the parental residence. The largest of these "clans", depicted schematically in figure 1, comprise three generations and eight nuclear families with a total membership in excess of fifty adults and children. However, just as Berezovka is part of a much larger network of Old Believers, so also these agnatic clans extend beyond Alberta into Oregon, Alaska, and South America.

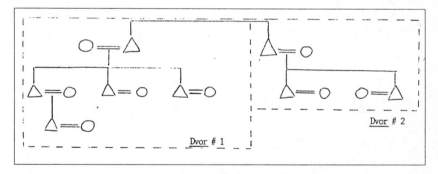

Figure 1. A family group or "clan" founded by two brothers and consisting of two extended households and eight nuclear families.

The world view shaped by the local residential arrangements coincides to a large extent with the salient features of peasantry as defined by George Foster (1965) in his famous essay. It is based on suspiciousness and the belief that only the most immediate relatives can be trusted. Anybody outside the realm of *nashi* in the narrow sense is a potential enemy. This expectation influences the socialization of children, who are encouraged to play with siblings and first cousins rather than with unrelated peers. It also influences the choice of partners in the economic co-operation of adults. And it is this distrust of the world beyond the *dvor* which hampers community-wide political action.

Because the people of Berezovka regard the ties established by kinship as the most enduring assurance of solidarity, great care is taken in maintaining and extending the universe of relatives. Kin are gained through consanguinity (*rodstvo*), affinity (*svoistvo*), and godparenthood (*kumstvo*). The boundaries of the kindred, which comprises all real *nashi*, are drawn in accordance with canon law and delineate the circle of people who are excluded from sexual relations and marriage. The rules adhered to in Berezovka extend to the seventh degree of consanguinity and the sixth degree of affinity and godparenthood. These degrees are reckoned in steps (*stepen*) that separate two relatives from their closest common ancestor. For example, full siblings are separated by two steps—each is one step away from the parent—first cousins by four, second cousins by six, and so on. The eighth degree coincides with third cousinship, and this is the closest type of consanguinity tolerated in marriage.

As can be gathered from figure 2, the terms applied to consanguines reveal properties of the Eskimo system of cousin ter-

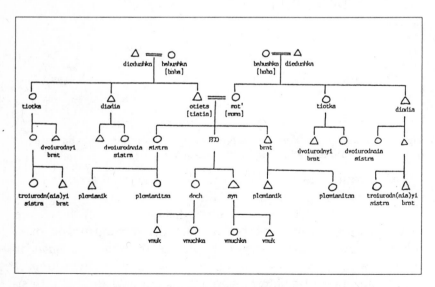

Figure 2. Consanguinous kinship terminology, with terms of address in brackets.

minology. They are almost identical with modern Russian usage, which goes back to the eighteenth century (Friedrich 1963). One interesting archaism is the retention of the word *nianka* as a term of address for the oldest sister. It derives from the verb *nianchit*, which means to nurse. This usage reflects the position of the oldest sister as a surrogate mother for her younger siblings. *Nianka* is the only expression that serves as a kin term of address between members of the same generation. In all other instances, one prefers to exchange personal names among siblings and cousins.

The affinal terminology contains a number of archaic designations, which are, however, intelligible to speakers of modern Russian. The bifurcation that used to distinguish pre-modern Russian terms from their English counterparts (Friedrich 1964) has been largely retained, placing the local terminology between that of medieval and modern Russian. Many of the affinal designations double up as terms of address between members of the same generation, who rarely resort to personal names. Of particular importance are the terms *svat* and *svata*, which literally mean matchmaker. In theory, they should be reserved for use by the two sets of parents who are bound through the marriage of their children. In practice, they serve as generic terms of reference and address for affines in general. The intricacies of the terminological system are outlined in figure 3.

The richness of the affinal terminology expresses a complex pattern of interaction between relatives by marriage, and a differentiation of several roles within this category. The importance of in-laws derives in no small measure from Berezovka's strictly enforced patrilocal residence pattern already alluded to above. Within the cluster of agnatically related families that comprise a *dvor* or a family group, in-laws occupy an intermediate position somewhere between *nashi* in the narrow sense and potentially dangerous outsiders. Akin to the famous Slav *Zadruga* (Halpern 1967; Pesheva 1971), the prototypical affine is the daughter-in-law who, as the bride of the son who is destined to stay within the parental "compound", invades the closely knit household, bringing with her a host of strange ideas and habits. The bride, usually between fifteen and seventeen years of age and probably from Oregon or Alaska, must be socialized into the subculture of her husband's parental home. The "breaking in" of the newcomer becomes the responsibility of the mother-in-law (*sviokorovka*), who represents, at least in theory, the interests of her son. The tensions that invariably build up between the young woman and her parents-in-law must at all costs be contained, because the future independence of the newlyweds cannot be attained without the goodwill of the groom's parents. The ideal meekness of the daughter-in-law resounds in the artificial sweetness of the terms

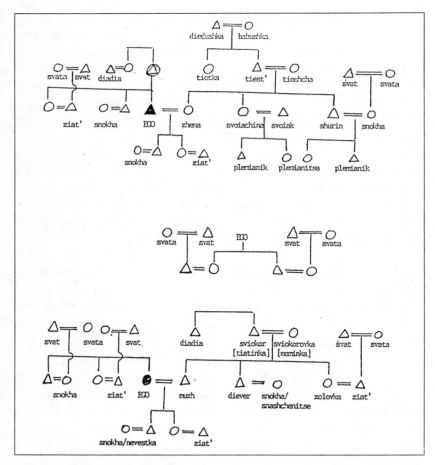

Figure 3. Affinal kinship terminology.

maminka and *tiatinka* which she employs in addressing her parents-in-law.

The bride is also under the command of her husband's oldest unmarried sister, the *nianka*, who acts as her mother's right hand. The term by which she is referred to by the bride is *zolovka*— loosely translated, the evil one—and it expresses the conflicts that are expected to dominate this relationship. On the other hand, the name for the husband's brother's wife, *snashchenitse*, derives from the verb *snosit'* and indicates mutual solidarity. Similar to the co-wives in a polygamous household, the three, four, or even five daughters-in-law that live side by side in Berezovka's extended families find each other's company of great significance for their ability to pass through the first years of marriage as peacefully as possible. Each of them separated from friends and relatives and exposed to a foreign environment, these young women may at times come to regard one another as true sisters. Often, the *zolovka* establishes a good relationship with this informal support group and receives from its members her first reliable advice on matters pertaining to sexuality and marriage.

Although the realm of natural kinship does not extend beyond affines, there are several ways in which the Old Believers bestow the status of *nashi* upon technically unrelated people who, due to their cultural affinity, deserve to be reckoned among "our people". The most evocative of these methods is the use of diminutive forms of kin terms to address unrelated older people. The designations *diedushka* (grandfather) and *babushka* (grandmother) are used for members of the grandparental generation, while *diadushka* (uncle) and *tiotka* (aunt) serve to address members of the parental generation.

A second widely employed technique rests upon the distinction that exists in Russian between the intimate pronoun *ty*, which is exchanged between relatives and close friends, and the formal pronoun *vy*, which serves to address strangers. The distinction, which corresponds to that between the English "thou" and "you", allows to delineate the realm of spiritual *nashi* simply by addressing all Old Believers with the intimate pronoun, and all *mirskie* with the formal and distancing pronoun. The usage is explained in a religious proverb which goes something like: "*Thou* God art one, but *you* demons are many." The appeal to the supranatural sphere underlines the ideological roots of the local kinship system. Whatever its use and abuse in daily life, kinship serves to unite the believers in Christ and set them off from the pagans. This idea is expressed very nicely in the institution of godparenthood, which is the principal method for incorporating a complete outsider into the local network of kinship. It is described further on in conjunction with baptism.

The Economy

Ever since their arrival in Alberta, the "White Russians" have been suspected of eroding the livelihood of neighbouring Canadian farmers. This suspicion derives from the widely held belief that the newcomers practice a communal economy, which generates a profit of such magnitude that it will eventually lead to a take-over of the entire district. Such fears are based on clichés that seek to establish a connection between the Old Believers and the Hutterites. It is not hard to understand why such a link would be presumed. The Hutterites are well known in Alberta, and although the closest colony is some eighty kilometres away, local farmers are familiar with the controversies surrounding the existence of such settlements. The "White Russians" seem to fit the mould of communal agriculturalists. Like the Hutterites, they speak a foreign language, dress unusually, stick together, and segregate themselves in mysterious communities rarely visited by outsiders. And also like the Hutterites, they seem to be doing rather well while other farmers are suffering from high interest rates, low yields, and little demand for their crops. In the face of such realities, it is easy to jump to the conclusion that the Russians too practice a communal economy, and that they too are a threat to the independent family farm. The local propensity to refer to Berezovka as the "Russian *colony*" is a reflection of the popularity of such views.

The people of Josephville are not alone in lumping the Old Believers into the category of communal farmers on the basis of mere presumptions. During the founding years of Berezovka in the early 1970s, federal immigration officials expected the settlers to start a *colony*, and this belief seems to have played a part in the subsequent curtailment of the number of Old Believers allowed to immigrate to Canada (Scheffel 1989a). This type of official prejudice was still widespread at the time of my field work, when some social workers refused to consider "White Russian" applicants for social benefits in the belief that it was up to the *colony* to assist needy members.

The people of Berezovka do not practise a communal economy, and the settlement does no constitute a *colony* in the economic sense. In fact, as has already been alluded to in previous sections, local Old Believers consider the idea of communalism irreconcilable with their strongly felt need for individual freedom, and they have no sympathy whatsoever for regimes that stifle private initiative and free enterprise. Indeed, their very presence in Canada can be attributed to their resistance to the collectivization of agriculture in the Soviet Union, and later on, China.

Berezovka's economy reflects the isolated life-style embraced by its founders. The members of the older generation possess all the skills one would expect to find in a society moulded by the frontier. The men are well versed in hunting, fishing, and trapping. They know how to construct homes and how to go about transforming complete wilderness into fertile fields and gardens. The women have an excellent knowledge of domesticated and wild plants, cooking, weaving, and spinning. Although homes nowadays are equipped with modern appliances, indoor plumbing, and running water, the memory of a less comfortable era lives on in the pride all residents display in home-grown food, hand-made clothing, and many other achievements of an essentially domestic economy. The value placed on autarky parallels the desire for cultural autonomy. Both sustain independence and ensure the continuation of a life-style based on the avoidance of *pomiesh-chanie*.

The basic features of the domestic economy were established in Russia and China. They involve the pursuit of a number of seasonally determined activities, which necessitate the woman's remaining at home while the man engages in a semi-nomadic existence far away from the village. In the past, subsistence farming and gardening were combined with commercial hunting and fishing. While women and children remained at home in charge of livestock and crops, small bands of men combed the taiga in search of game. The hunters would return to the village for brief periods of time during religious holidays and to help with especially demanding agricultural tasks, such as harvesting. Although most men settled down to full-time farming with advancing age, the life-style of the nomadic hunter remains firmly associated with masculinity, and with the craving of many men for freedom from domestic responsibilities, and indeed from village life itself. Today hunting is no longer the source of cash, but the traditional economic pluralism has survived intact. The woman continues to

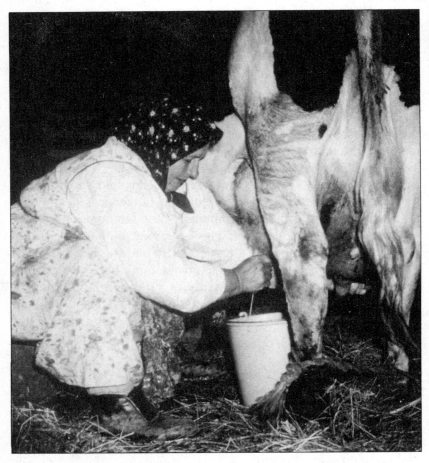

Women are responsible for daily sustenance. (Detmar Schmoll)

be responsible for daily subsistence, which most commonly takes the form of gardening, livestock keeping, and the gathering of wild mushrooms and berries. While the husband does help out with some of these pursuits, his primary specialization is seasonal work in the forest industry. Like hunting in the past, the planting of trees in the summer and felling in the winter are male activities which provide most of the cash required by a family. Women and older girls may occasionally spend a week or two in the bush, joining their husbands and fathers during the tree-planting season. But their limited exposure to the world outside the village does not affect the basic division of labour between the sexes, which demands that women occupy the traditional position of the nourishing housewife while the man takes on the role of the official provider and mediator between the household and *mir*. This asymmetry is justified by means of religious and biological explanations which portray the woman as an intellectually, morally, and physically weaker creature. Men express disdain for home and village life with its crowded and noisy quarters, domestic squabbles, and tensions between neighbours. They try to escape it as much as possible, craving the freedom of the bush and the camaraderie with male friends.

Both men and women subscribe to a notion of labour which in its essential features resembles the "Protestant work ethic" of introductory sociology textbooks. It is governed by a strong resistance to idleness, sloth, and any behaviour that smacks of wasting time or energy. This observation should not imply that recreational activities are frowned upon or altogether avoided. The Old Believers, as has already been indicated, greatly enjoy a nap after an elaborate meal, more than a few drinks at a wedding celebration, the telling of stories, and similar forms of relaxation. But these activities are separated from the realm of work, which is expected to be governed by exclusively rational considerations. A man felling trees in the bush does enjoy the fresh air, the pleasant sights, and the interesting sounds afforded by his work environment. But he would rarely think of stopping his chain-saw in order to dwell on such aesthetic factors. Only after the completion of the daily task would he allow himself to sit down, eat a meal, and take in the beauty of his surroundings. Work and play should be as strictly segregated as "Christians" and "pagans".

In several respects, the local work ethic is related to religious discipline, and it can be said that both, work and piety, are taught simultaneously, by means of similar techniques. Of special significance are the twin requirements of adaptability and endurance. As soon as a child can walk, he or she is introduced to this double expectation through a combination of religious and secular training. Rebuked with the omnipresent dictum of *nado privyknut'* (one must get used to it), the infant accepts the weaning from the mother's breast, the sparse diet during Lent, and attendance at church services that start early in the morning and last for several hours. As he or she grows older, the child is introduced to simple tasks in the household, a process which culminates with the first trip to the bush. Here too, *nado privyknut'* often remains the only explanation provided by the adults.

Concurrently, the child is introduced to the necessity of not only attending but completing the painfully long prayer sessions and the tediously exhausting task of tree planting. *Nado zakonchit'* (one must finish) is a most important command which governs religious and economic activities alike. Those who leave the church before the end of the service commit a sin, which the congregation takes note of. Those who walk away from a project prior to its completion earn a reputation for laziness, and they will be hard pressed to find work again with a local contractor. The echo of the demand for completion can be heard all over Berezovka as returning work crews are asked the ubiquitous question: *zakonchili*—did you finish? Those who fail to pass this "examination" face ridicule in addition to financial loss.

Equipped with patience and endurance, children are expected to complete the transition from play to work during early puberty. Girls have by then been exposed to most female tasks and are often given entire responsibility for the milking of cows, feeding of chickens, supervision of younger siblings, and preparation of simple meals. Boys are finally allowed to join their fathers and brothers not just in the planting of trees during summer, but also in the far harsher setting of the winter camp. This transition from the warmth and security of the home environment to the cold and danger of the frozen bush constitutes a significant rite of passage. Here, the young man is initiated into the male subculture with its glorification of strength, mobility, independence and a strong disdain for the safe and monotonous domain of women, or *baby* as they are referred to condescendingly.

Depending on the season, the terrain, and the size of the territory, the forest work is carried out by crews of ten to thirty hired hands under the supervision of a contractor or subcontractor (*kontraktchik*) who is responsible to provincial forestry officials. This man and his immediate assistants are usually close relatives or friends. The bulk of the crew consists of Old Believers, with an occasional handful of hired outsiders. Unlike the planting of trees, which requires no expensive tools, the felling operations in the winter are highly mechanized, and each participant is expected to use his own equipment. This tends to influence the division of labour: older and affluent men with their own skidder—a powerful tractor used for moving and cleaning logs—occupy the more lucrative and prestigious positions, while young rookies, armed with merely a basic chain saw, play an essential but subordinate role. The acquisition of a skidder frees a man to become a *kontraktchik* himself and to hire his own crew. Although this is the dream of most young men, such a purchase, combined with the responsibility of fulfilling a contract, involves so many financial risks that only a few men ever achieve this coveted status.

Even a rookie felling trees for the first time finds the forestry work lucrative enough to consider it as a life-long career. Seduced by the independence, comradeship, and financial rewards which go along with this activity, he is anxious to leave school as soon as possible in order to become part of the "real", adult world. This desire is encouraged by parents, as they receive the bulk of the wages earned by sons and daughters who have not yet married. More than subtle pressure is also exercised by other adults who are aware of the limits the bush imposes on adolescents' ability to engage in deviant behaviour during their potentially most rebellious years. Girls too are encouraged to look for paid work either in the tree-planting business or on the farm of a Canadian neighbour. But these jobs are not expected to go on past the summer, and consequently girls are more likely to complete elementary education than are their brothers.

Although it would be wrong to suggest that children are seen merely as a source of cheap labour and cash income—allegations made by some observers—it is true that the Old Believers tend to associate large families with economic prosperity and political power. At the macro level, people predict good fortunes for populous countries based simply on the sheer number of their inhabitants. At the micro level, numerous offspring are welcomed, and childless couples are greatly pitied in the belief that old age without the support of a large family can only bring about destitution and misery. Once again, religious tenets support this implicit economic population policy by prohibiting any interference in procreation. Although some young couples tend to take the biblical dictum "Be fruitful and multiply" with a grain of salt, most families are certainly much larger than the norm encountered in rural North America. According to the only systematic examination of their demography, the Old Believers surpass even the extremely fertile Hutterites (Hall 1970).

Berezovka's demographic profile reflects the fertility-friendly views of its residents as well as the frontier character of the new settlement. Out of the 121 immigrants who arrived here between 1973 and 1975, only one was older than fifty. The bulk, fifty-nine persons, or almost fifty per cent of the newcomers, were children below ten years of age. Of the seventeen founding couples, only three—the youngest ones—arrived without children. The remaining fourteen had an average of 5.5 children. The average age of the founding population was only slightly above fifteen years.[14]

Since the arrival of the first settlers almost twenty years ago, Berezovka has tripled in size, and its demographic profile has changed from that of a frontier community which attracted young and adaptable pioneers to one of a more sedate settlement. The founding couples have reached middle age, many of their numerous children have begun bearing children of their own, and in some cases elderly relatives have arrived from abroad. Although Little Russia remains strikingly young in comparison with other rural communities, the average age of its residents has increased significantly, and their needs have changed. Of great importance has been the pressure felt by aging parents to generate enough assets to make a significant contribution to each of their many children as they reach maturity and set up households of their own. The parental duty to make such a contribution (*pridanoe*) in the form of cash, land, or livestock is taken very seriously. However, in view of the rising expectations of the young generation, the fulfilment of this norm can lead to impoverishment of the parents.

Given the harsh conditions of the work in the bush, most men find it impossible to sustain such work by the time they reach advanced middle age. Drained by the expectations of their children and unable to provide more than a meagre income from farming, they sooner or later come to depend on social assistance administered by the very society they are taught to avoid. Their sons, in turn, are slowly coming to the realization that the life-style glorified by the older generation has unforeseen repercussions, such as the ever-present threat of industrial accidents, which have cost the lives of several men. At this point, the traditional semi-nomadic economy still absorbs the bulk of Berezovka's adolescents. But a few have chosen to return to school, several have joined the construction industry, and two or three are even enrolled in university. More will probably follow such non-traditional paths in the near future, a fact which can be expected to have far-reaching consequences for their values and beliefs.

Orthodoxy and its Interpretation

Despite the tensions and conflicts that rock Berezovka more or less permanently, it survives as a community because its residents share a purpose of such momentous significance that its defence overrides all the petty divisions created by history, geography, and kinship. This purpose is born out of the drive to lead a truly Christian lifestyle whose boundaries are so removed from the dominant North American culture that its perpetuation requires a determined effort by the entire community. As long as this sense of purpose endures, Berezovka and its sister congregations can be expected to weather the obstacles described in the previous chapter.

Local Old Believers see themselves as the last guardians of the path that leads to absolute truth and perfection. Since this path was opened up by God, the Old Believers regard their struggle against religious pluralism, heresy, and agnosticism as a manifest destiny whose source is self-evident. Betrayed and abandoned by everybody else, they alone remain God's allies in the eternal war between truth and falsehood, orthodoxy and heterodoxy, Christ and antichrist. But this undeniably ethnocentric claim must not be interpreted as suggesting that the Old Believers regard themselves as the keepers of truth and perfection. Such an exalted role is attributed only to God.

This chapter examines the manner in which the people of Berezovka go about defining their orthodoxy. Instead of raising all the issues related to this central characteristic of their culture, I focus on a single theme which surfaces over and over again in subsequent chapters. It pertains to the manner in which the Old Believers bridge the gap between the past and the present. According to their perception, orthodoxy, as an absolute and unchanging path to truth, has remained the same since its initial formulation by Christ, the apostles, and the Fathers of the Church. The formative period is seen as having been completed by the Seventh Ecumenical Council held in 787. Since then, time has, theologically speaking, stood still. From a purely historical point of view, the last twelve hundred years count only as a chronicle of the expanding influence of heterodoxy, culminating in the seventeenth-century *raskol* and the subsequent persecution and isolation of the Old Believers. Orthodox Christianity has, despite the rapidly shrinking number of its adherents, withstood the onslaught.

The question that emerges here is how the people of Berezovka establish the connection between themselves and the early Christians—a connection that is crucial for the legitimation of their exclusive claim to orthodoxy. Do they make a direct link with Palestine and Greece or do they use Muscovy as a shorter and more convenient bridge? And, in view of the dramatic impact of the seventeenth-century schism on the availability of acceptable clergy, how do the local Old Believers fill the vacuum left behind by their secession from the official church, with its responsibility for maintaining and interpreting the orthodox tradition? In short, how do the people of Berezovka reconcile the need for continuity with the equally pressing task of adapting to significant changes resulting from ravages of the very same time whose passage they have a tendency to deny?

The tension between timelessness as a condition associated with the preservation of orthodoxy, and change as a precondition for heterodoxy, can be usefully correlated with the commonly made distinction between *sacred* and *profane* elements. In the eyes of the Old Believers, sacred things are timeless and thus suitable for expressing orthodoxy, while profane things change and therefore threaten orthodoxy. Whether we look at the separation, described in this chapter, between Church Slavonic and Russian, written and oral tradition, or the religious and secular calendar, we discover important parallels between sacredness, orthodoxy, rigidity, and a cyclical view of time on the one hand, and between profanity, heterodoxy, flexibility, and a linear perception of time— as a source of change rather than stability—on the other. This tension underlies the very core of Berezovka's religion not only because of the relentless struggle with the surrounding worldly society—which is propelled by the desire for change—but also because the seed of heterodoxy is planted within Berezovka as part of its own secular and therefore changeable culture. The formidable challenge faced by the Old Believers in their defence of orthodoxy can be described as an endless effort at protecting the ancient boundaries which separate, both outside and inside the home, the realms of eternity and temporariness.

Written Tradition

As in other Christian denominations, the source of orthodoxy is God, and its vehicle is the divinely inspired word. However, unlike in many churches, where orthodoxy is often seen as part of an unfolding tradition, the Old Believers regard it as a completed system of timeless prescriptive rules referred to appropriately as the law (*zakon*). The entire collection of these universal rules is enshrined in old books (*starie knigi*), which share the following properties. They must be seen as divinely inspired, they must be of pre-Nikonian date, and they must be written in the liturgical language of Russian Orthodoxy known as Old or Church Slavonic.

Church Slavonic—a combination of several dialects formalized by Greek missionaries to the Slavs—is the only language used in Berezovka to address God, and its acquisition by all Old Believers is a prerequisite for membership in the congregation. Russian—which is also indispensable but only at the level of human communication—and Church Slavonic are taught in different ways, with different goals in mind. The former is the discourse of socialization, which emphasizes the spoken word. The instruction is informal, pronunciation tends to vary according to the speaker's geographical origins, and where some writing skills have been achieved, they differ significantly from standardized Russian.

This lack of uniformity is not tolerated in the use of Church Slavonic. The instruction, which begins around the age of five, is formal; it stresses reading skills, and its goal is the elimination of idiosyncrasies. The teaching process usually takes place at home, with all the children of the household seated at the kitchen table.

Depending on age and aptitude, each pupil receives a Church Slavonic text, either a primer or a book of prayers, and recites an appointed passage aloud along with the other participants. The instructor walks around the group, points out errors, demands repetition, and punishes inattention. There is no attempt at interpreting or summarizing the recited passages; rather, the goal of the sessions is to familiarize the students with clusters of words and to facilitate their repetition as rapidly and as uniformly as possible.

A lesson in Church Slavonic.

The insistence on Church Slavonic derives from the importance placed on receiving God's word in its original, orthodox version. Although it is conceded that the language was codified by Greek missionaries to the Slavs, its actual design is attributed to God. The exalted origin of the liturgical language makes it immune to change, since, as the logic goes, how can perfection be improved? Any deviation from what the Old Believers consider the ancient standard of Church Slavonic is regarded as a dangerous source of confusion which inevitably leads to heresy. It is this crime which the people of Berezovka see as the foundation of all other Christian churches, including official Russian Orthodoxy. In consequence of their "modernization" of the written tradition, they are believed to have lost access to the "law" in its orthodox manifestation. Instead of pure words and sentences, those which promise salvation, the reformed churches are said to make use of false texts which are the result of the mixing up (*pomeshchanie*) of sacred and profane elements. Examples of such charges are supplied further below.

Since the corpus of "old books" treasured in Berezovka is extensive, I must limit my description to a mere outline of the more widely used works. An exalted position belongs to the Bible, which serves as the anchor of the entire written tradition. As in other Christian denominations, it provides the ultimate justification for laws and rules formulated elsewhere. Surprisingly, however, the Bible is almost invisible in Berezovka. The church has a copy, which, on account of its sacredness, I wasn't permitted to examine; most families, however, seem to survive without one. I cannot say whether the dearth is due to difficulties arising from transcribing and copying existing versions or by the reliance on various compilations of excerpts from the Bible, which makes the entire book itself dispensable. As we will soon see, the latter speculation is not without foundation.

The core of the written tradition consists of the class of service books (*sluzhebnye knigi*), which are all claimed to be copies of editions employed in the pre-Nikonian Orthodox Church. These are the euchologion (*trebnik*), which contains the complete text of the mass and the sacraments; the liturgikon (*sluzhebnik*), which lists the three liturgies used by the Orthodox Church; the horologion (*chasovnik*), with a guide to all holy days; the psalter (*psaltyr*), which contains psalms and rules pertaining to the ritual conduct of individual believers; and, finally, the typikon (*ustav*), with a description of daily prayers and fasts.

While most of the service books are employed only in the conduct of public devotion, the psalter and the *ustav* are widely read works that are found in every household. The copy of the latter which I examined in some detail is entitled simply *ustav* and

Ѿ КРЕ́СНОМЪ ЗНА́МЕНЇИ .
Ка́кѡ зна́ме
своѐ кр҃то́шб
страхомъ сто
новати лицѐ
ра́знѡ , й со́
а́ти во ст҃є́й
бж҃їи цр҃кви, пи́шет сты́и
і҃ѡа́нъ зла́ . сн҃це! (про а҃пр н҃і).
Мно́зи о́убѡ невѣ́гласи маха́ю
ще по лицꙋ́ своемꙋ́ рꙋко́ю ,
твора́ще креста́тсѧ , всꙋ́е трꙋ́
жа́ютсѧ , зане́же неисправлѧ́ют
и́стово кр҃та́ на лицы́ своѐмъ,
томꙋ бо маха́нїю бѣ́си ра́дꙋют
сѧ . А́ е́иже кто̀ кр҃ти́тсѧ и́сто

к҃в

Dvoeperstie illustrated in the *azbuchik*.

is dated to the year 7,325 since the creation of the world, which translates as A.D. 1817. It was printed in Vilnius, an important centre of doctrinal *bezpopovtsy*, and the preface describes it as a collection of rules assembled from "many church books." The tome consists of three long sections. The first one, called "About Fasts", enumerates the purity precautions required during fasts, particularly with respect to the number and composition of meals.

The second one describes the various types of prayers to be said at specified times during ordinary as well as holy days. The last section takes up the topic of religious holidays and explains their significance and the manner in which they must be celebrated.

The psalter which I had an opportunity to scrutinize is un-dated. It begins with the heading "About the sign of the cross", which introduces the history and the power of this age-old symbol in the fight with the devil and heretics. Several ancient sources are adduced to confirm the orthodoxy of *dvoeperstie*, and to describe the sign itself. What follows is a short section on the "four-fold prayer", consisting of the words "Lord, Jesus Christ, Son of God", which should accompany the making of the sign of the cross. This formula is said to preserve from illness and to chase away demons. The last part, entitled "About the psalter", is said to have been extracted from the psalter of Basil the Great (330?-379), a work compared to "a great sea, which never loses water." Freely translated, several of the poetic sentences in this section read as follows:

> Not a single day are you allowed to omit the reading of the psalter...it opens your eyes, and makes you under-stand God's law. The writing of the psalter was prompted by John Chrysostomos who showed how the singing of psalms frightens demons and chases away darkness. The psalter shines like the sun, purifies like water, burns like fire...The singing of psalms is similar to the eating of honey...It consoles old men, beautifies young ones, it helped Jesus Christ Himself; the psalms are the mouth for the laws of the prophets.

The actual psalms follow in the last and longest section, ar-ranged under these headings: "Psalms of David", including those "suppressed by the Jews"; "Psalms of Asafok"; "Collected Psalms"; "Canon of Irmos"; and "Canon for the Dead", also at-tributed to Irmos.

In addition to the service books, the people of Berezovka pos-sess a number of exegetical works, which range from collections of Byzantine canon law to apologetics authored by Old Believers. The most basic of these texts is the primer (*azbuchik*), which in-

troduces children to the liturgical language and the religious traditions of Old Orthodoxy. The fifty-page-long hand-written booklet
that I examined begins with an outline of Church Slavonic, concentrating on the names of the letter combinations, and the rules
of punctuation and pronunciation. The remaining space contains
the text of the Ten Commandments, confession of faith, and the
ten or so prayers that must be said throughout the day. The last
few pages of the primer introduce the reader to a short outline
of Christian morals and, taken directly from the psalter, to instruc-
tions for making the sign of the cross. A large sketch of the correct
position of the fingers fills the last page.

More advanced readers find the principles of their faith confirmed in several classics of Old Russian Orthodoxy. The most
important of these is the *kormchaia kniga*, which can be translated
as the *Rudder* or *Pilot Book*. Based on the Greek *Nomokanon*,
the *kormchaia* constitutes the corpus of Orthodox canon law as
it came to be understood in Russia. The copy to which I gained
access in Berezovka was a 1914 reprint of the 1650 edition com-
missioned by Patriarch Iosif. The introduction summarizes the history of the schism between eastern and western Christendom,
attributing it to heresies of the Roman Catholic Church. They are
said to consist of the Latin confession of faith containing the *filioque*, the use of unleavened bread in the Eucharist, the notion of
purgatory, shaving by priests, modified holy days, incestuous relations between affines, and the consumption of impure food. These
reasons are enumerated as an explanation for the excommunication of the Latins by Greek patriarchs, who are said to consider
western Christians as "great enemies of the Greeks and of the
Orthodox Church."

The next section of the *kormchaia* lists a large number of rules
attributed to anonymous "holy apostles". The directives vary from
the prohibition of various sexual sins—such as the mutilation of
one's penis or the rape of a virgin—to definitions of defiling
categories of food. Great attention is paid to the necessity of correct baptism by means of a triple immersion, and of avoiding any
intimate contact with pagans and heretics.

The bulk of the manual is taken up with a myriad of rules and
recommendations issued by the seven ecumenical councils and by
several regional synods held during the first Christian millennium.

The issues discussed at these gatherings seem to have been copied in an almost verbatim manner, without any type of commentary. They concern all aspects of private and public life, in particular theological issues, sexuality, and community organization.

The volume concludes with a number of short treatises written by obscure or anonymous authors which are concerned with the various "heresies" attributed to western Christians. Thus a "Studdite monk Nikita" chastises the Latins for serving communion without salt and yeast; someone else proves with the example of Moses that trimmed beards constitute a sin, and yet another author speaks out against Christian men letting their hair grow long like women. The final section is a lengthy diatribe against the Germans and other Latins for their perverted customs.

The topic of Western apostasy looms large in another influential work, the *Book of the Only True Orthodox Faith* (*kniga o vere edinoi istinnoi pravoslavnoi*). Written in Kiev in the 1620s, the *Book of Faith* came out in Moscow in 1648 and became something of a bestseller. My copy, a reprint of the 1648 edition, begins with these words: "Lord, force us to remain within the bounds of sacred laws, and do not, Christ, abandon the East for the West."

The first part provides an overview of the history of Christianity in Russia, beginning with the exploits of the elusive Apostle Andrew—claimed by legend to have planted the Christian seed in eastern Europe—and ending with the conversion of Prince Vladimir and his marriage to the sister of the Emperor of Byzantium. Then follows a long analysis of Latin departures from orthodoxy, including the addition of the *filioque* to the creed, the absence of yeast from the host, the custom of reserving wine for the clergy, and similar sacramental inaccuracies. This section concludes with a full exposition on the significance of the correct sign of the cross, and an explanation of the theological basis of iconography.

The second part elaborates on the postulated heresies of the Roman Catholics and explains why the Florentine Union cannot be recognized as valid. The Greeks are said to have retained the orthodox faith, unlike the Ukrainian uniates, who are condemned on the same grounds as their Latin patrons. After a brief exposition of the western error of baptizing by sprinkling rather than immersion, the author offers a powerful apocalyptic vision of the near future. The antichrist is predicted to appear in the year 1666 in order to attack orthodox Christians and try to seduce them into joining the apostate Latins.

A third influential work, which I could not examine in detail, is *The Book of Cyril of Jerusalem* (*kniga Kiriliia Ierusalemskogo*), usually referred to as *Kirilova kniga*. It seems to have first appeared in Moscow in 1644, but its source may have been a Ukrainian text published in Vilnius in 1596 (Akademiya nauk *SSSR* 1948, 2/2:326). Attributed to anonymous "Church Fathers", this treatise is yet another compilation of western heresies, embedded in a strongly eschatological context. Unlike the *Book of Faith*, the *Book of Cyril* is critical of the Greek claim to orthodoxy. This seems to have occasioned its burning by the Greeks in 1650 (Pascal 1938:204).

These three works supply a powerful array of weapons defending many—though not all—local practices and beliefs, which cannot be justified on the basis of liturgical texts alone. Whenever I wanted an answer to a question starting with "What is the source of...", or "How do you know that your view on this is correct?", I would be told that the *kormchaia* or *kniga o vere* confirms the validity of the opinion in question. Never, though, was I helped in my search with an exact reference. My informant knew that the answer was validated somewhere in the mentioned work and did not bother aiding me further.

Various Old Believers' reluctance and, at times, inability to supply an exact connection between a contemporary opinion and its ancient source struck me as unusual in a people who profess to live for the maintenance of orthodoxy. Equally surprising, though not entirely unexpected in view of their Muscovite ancestry, is the Old Believers' reliance on compendia that contain mere *excerpts* from the "law" so jealously guarded in Berezovka. Often, the authors of these works remain anonymous, and some are attributed to saints and scholars whose very existence is disputable.

The lack of discrimination involved in evaluating the "old books" that form the backbone of the local culture extends all the way to the process by which they are disseminated. With the exception of a relatively small number of manuscripts, the books employed in Berezovka are copies of works manufactured in semi-legal print-shops in nineteenth-century Russia. They are mass-produced by two private companies in Portland and Ponta Grossa, which fill orders placed by individuals and groups of families. Far from undergoing a "quality check" after delivery in Berezovka, the tomes are simply shelved side by side with other "old books" in the expectation that the anonymous printers employed a correct edition of the original work.

It was more or less by chance that I discovered that many local Old Believers find it difficult to determine authoritatively which of the several Church Slavonic editions of liturgical books are orthodox and why. This was evidenced when I exhibited an eighteenth-century Nikonian edition of the *ustav* to several of my informants and witnessed the difficulties they had deciding whether the work was authentic or not. It took the examiners a long time to decipher the prominently displayed year of publication, and then, instead of looking for the spelling of one of the several contentious words changed by Nikon, they threw up their arms and gave up. The reason for their inability to authenticate the book might be the manner in which Church Slavonic is studied and used: the goal of its instruction is not the student's acquisition of literacy in the analytical sense, which would provide him or her with a tool for critical scrutiny and comparison. An Old Believer is furnished with passive knowledge of the language, favouring declamation at the expense of examination.

The obstacles that block access to the pre-Nikonian past are even more pronounced along the path linking the people of Berezovka with the founders of the Old Belief. It will have been noticed that the entire written tradition reviewed thus far dates back to a time when orthodoxy enjoyed the protection of a powerful state church in Byzantium or, later on, Muscovy. Consequently, while that tradition defines and defends orthodoxy, it fails to offer a suitable strategy for Christians deprived of a church and all the spiritual gifts associated therewith. This serious lacuna has consequences for the local Old Believers' self-perception and self-definition. Ultimately, it threatens the all-important belief in Berezovka as a bastion of God's chosen people.

The emphasis on conditions prevailing prior to the *raskol* can perhaps be seen as an understandable attempt at fuelling Berezovka's sense of importance with undiluted orthodoxy. But it may also be interpreted as an unconscious or semi-conscious endeavour to mask the divergent traditions of the three local groups and the inability of their members to justify or at least explain these variations. Local residents, being of different origins, find it difficult to appeal to the authority of any of the founding fathers of the Old Belief without facing contradictions between past and present definitions of orthodoxy.

This observation applies primarily to the general unwillingness to claim affiliation with either of the two mighty branches of the movement, the priestly *popovtsy* or the priestless *bezpopovtsy*. The man claimed by the former as their spiritual father, the famous archpriest Avvakum, is known to every adult of Berezovka, a few of whom have actually read his autobiographical account of the first years of the schism. Avvakum is very highly regarded as the most influential defender of the old faith and as one of its first martyrs. But his numerous theological writings are regarded with scepticism because of the archpriest's apparent support for self-immolation and, more markedly, because of his insistence on the use of priests as an unconditional prerequisite for the continuation of orthodoxy. The people of Berezovka, on the other hand, profess an unconditional resistance to any form of suicide and, at least under present conditions, priesthood.

Similar contradictions surface in respect to the second most important Old Orthodox theologian, Andrei Denisov, author of the famous *Pomorskie otvety* of 1723. Denisov, who is acknowledged as the earliest and best apologist of principles adhered to by the doctrinal *bezpopovtsy*, is not as familiar to the local people as Avvakum, but his position on several key issues is known to the better-educated elders. Although there are remarkable similarities between the religious practice adhered to in Berezovka and Denisov's emergency solution for a church without clergy, he too is dismissed as a potential authority figure. The bone of contention is seen primarily in Denisov's demand for celibacy which derives from his rejection of post-Nikonian priests.

The attitude of the local Old Believers to Avvakum and Denisov reveals a great deal about their own view on the key problem facing the traditionalists since their separation from the official church more than three centuries ago: the question of clergy. Their reluctance to be affiliated even in purely historical terms with either of the two branches makes their classification difficult to determine in a spectrum which is built upon the opposition between the *popovtsy* and the *bezpopovtsy*. The people of Berezovka, along with most of their North and South American relatives, are neither doctrinal *popovtsy* nor convinced *bezpopovtsy*. Their neutral position is built upon the recognition of the *possible* existence of an orthodox church hierarchy somewhere in the world, which, if found, would enable them to resume all those pre-Nikonian traditions which they are currently deprived of for lack of priests. However, as all known churches are considered heterodox, most locals are skeptical about the likelihood of ever abandoning the present position.

Despite the current unwillingness to become affiliated with a known hierarchy which would renew the supply of orthodox priests, there are several indications of Berezovka's closer proximity to the priestly than the priestless camp. Some older residents admit to having lived at one point or another in communities of *popovtsy*, and written sources suggest that the *Turchane* as well as the *Sintsiantsy* had been influenced by priestly traditions prior to their exodus to China and later to North America (Blomkvist & Grinkova 1930; Shamaro 1964). Such influence can still be detected in the Turkish congregation in Oregon (Morris 1981).

The *Kharbintsy*, too, recall a past shaped by association with the priestly branch. That past is illuminated by an exceptional piece of evidence which sheds light on the thorny issue of the clergy and its role in the collective history of most—though not all—*Kharbintsy*. The evidence in question consists of a manuscript written in 1920 which is entitled *malaya rodoslovna (Short Genealogy)*.

This highly interesting book is composed in the style of a hagiography that begins with the arrest of Paul of Kolomna, the sole Russian bishop openly opposed to Nikon's reform. Bishop Paul is portrayed as the guarantor of the apostolic succession of dissident Old Orthodox priests. He is said to have approved their resistance to the reform and to have assured them that even in the absence of a church hierarchy, Christ's priesthood would continue forever and His body and blood be preserved until the end of the world (pp. 4-6). The group of early leaders affiliated with Bishop Paul is claimed to have comprised twenty priests, among them Avvakum. This core was soon joined by another twenty-three, all of them ordained by pre-Nikonian bishops (pp. 8-10). These forty-three founding fathers of the *popovtsy* are alleged to have carried the seed of resistance into all corners of the country.

The ranks of the "old" clergy eventually had to be expanded by "new" priests, ordained by bishops who had accepted the reform and thus lost their orthodox status. These members of the clergy, however, are claimed to have retained their legitimacy by deserting the official church to join the Old Believers. Here they were corrected (*ispravlenie*) through a second chrismation, which in turn entitled them to act as "correctors" of future fugitive priests. In such manner, the apostolic succession of orthodox priesthood continued despite the lack of a church hierarchy.

According to *malaya rodoslovna*, the mechanism for renewing the supply of clergy broke down in the eighteenth century in consequence of the Latinization of the official church by its new governing body, the Holy Synod. The bishops appointed by this body are said to have been recruited among Ukrainian theologians who had been baptized by sprinkling rather than immersion—an innovation strongly disapproved of by the Old Believers. Faced with the prospect of admitting clergy ordained by bishops lacking Christian status, the ancestors of the *Kharbintsy* resolved not to employ priests who had belonged to the synodal church. Instead, they came to rely on clergy affiliated with the Georgian Orthodox Church, whose roots could be traced back to the last Patriarch of Moscow, Adrian (pp. 22-23).

The Georgian connection flourished until the 1830s when this source too dried up as a result of the forced incorporation of the Georgian Church into its Russian counterpart. Around this time, one of the last members of this branch, a priest-monk Antonii, seems to have found his way to the Lake Baikal region inhabited by the direct ancestors of several prominent *Kharbintsy* (p. 25; Iosif 1985:1,5). It is unclear whether or not this congregation was served by another priest after Antonii's death, but it seems that by 1867 there were only lay monks carrying out the duties of spiritual leaders in a de facto priestless parish (pp. 26-27). This impression is reinforced by an outside observer who claims that, starting in the 1850s, presumably after Antonii's death, the *popovtsy* inhabiting the Lake Baikal area placed the responsibility for spiritual leadership in the hands of lay pastors called *ustavchiki* (Anonymous 1865). Significantly, both versions agree in their attributing of this shift, not so much to a complete lack of priests, but rather to the refusal of the local *popovtsy* to employ clergy whose orthodoxy appeared questionable (Iosif 1985:45; *malaya rodoslovna*:23-24).

The priestly past of the *Kharbintsy* is not denied in Berezovka. While the details of its nature are subject to individual interpretation, some elders are willing to concede that the remnants of sacraments used in Berezovka do in fact derive from post-Nikonian priests. At the same time, however, virtually everybody rejects the suggestion that the institution of priesthood could be resuscitated using techniques employed by their ancestors. In this respect, the local parish resembles a branch of Old Belief whose members are known as the *chasovennye* (Scheffel 1991b). Without being formally affiliated with one another, *chasovennye* communities shared priestly origins as well as a reluctance to remain faithful to them once the status of the available clergy had become suspect. Such congregations of conservative *popovtsy* did then adopt customs usually associated with the *bezpopovtsy* without, however, necessarily embracing the doctrinal foundation of the priestless branch with its unconditional rejection of priesthood.

Oral Tradition

The people of Berezovka love to tell stories. Every adult of reasonably advanced age possesses a huge inventory of proverbs, parables, legends, and historical accounts. The telling of stories is, in fact, the only legitimate leisure activity. Parents entertain children with descriptions of life in China, adults reminisce about shared experiences, and elders edify young and old alike with biblical stories and parables. Although many of the narratives are meant to entertain, the stated purpose of the entire oral tradition is edification by means of accounts whose truthfulness should not be questioned. This applies above all to religious themes, including miracles experienced by Christian martyrs and sufferings endured by the Old Believers. Anything told about the Christian past is classified as part of history rather than mythology.

The appeal to historical accuracy notwithstanding, the truth underlying the oral tradition is not of the same standard as the truth expected of the written tradition. Unlike the latter, which is believed to be divinely inspired and thus absolutely correct, oral accounts are mere human interpretations of events that do not always make common sense and are therefore subject to some degree of error. This distinction parallels the differentiation between Russian and Church Slavonic: just as the former, profane, speech is not expected to approach the accuracy and meaning of the liturgical language, so also accounts told in Russian are not subjected to the same expectation of perfection as the Church Slavonic sacred texts. The oral historian is not a copyist, but rather a fallible translator. Because the written account of a given event is somewhere preserved, its oral interpretation can assume a number of versions, which are not entirely interchangeable. Different speakers may therefore develop their individual renderings of history without being accused of distortion.

What is important about all this is that because the codified history of the local Old Believers ends with the *raskol* and the demise of Old Orthodoxy as Russia's official ideology, their interpretation of the post-Nikonian past cannot be maintained within a larger and universal context of written and therefore truthful history. The result is a vast number of traditions developing out of the three groups' very different pasts; each offers a unique perspective on the post-Nikonian era, but none provides an authoritative model of Old Orthodoxy during its banishment. The question of clergy is a case in point. Unable to align themselves with either of the two branches, the people of Berezovka find it difficult to explain their position vis-à-vis the *popovtsy* or the *bezpopovtsy*. The short and sketchy *malaya rodoslovna* simply cannot measure up to the refined theology of priestly and priestless historiographers. Deprived of an adequate explanation of their place in the history of post-Nikonian Old Orthodoxy, local Old Believers tend to gloss over the history of their ancestors' adaptation to the conditions created by the schism. Instead, their oral tradition dwells on the long period between the birth of Christ and the eruption of the *raskol* on the one hand, and on events experienced since the emigration from Russia on the other. The two-and-a-half centuries separating these epochs are talked about less often and with much greater risk of disagreement.

The conditions leading to the schism are interpreted in a highly idiosyncratic manner, which can best be demonstrated with a few excerpts from accounts provided by informants. The following snippets are based on conversations with an older woman who was asked to describe the events that preceded and followed the *raskol*. The narrative has been translated from Russian, and the text has been edited to eliminate unnecessary repetition.

> There were many years, the Christian belief endured for a thousand years, unwavering. Then Patriarch Nikon changed it; he was seduced by a woman who wanted to test him. She told him, "If you cut off your beard, I will be able to be with you." But when he obliged, she said, "What kind of patriarch are you, one that got seduced by a woman; you abandoned your rank and violated the law. You are not a good man." So he got ashamed and wondered how he could show himself to the people. He came to church and fed the pigeons so that they ate grain from his ear. So he tied himself up so that nobody could see what had happened to him, and he said, "The Holy Spirit told me that beards must be shaved off, that's what God proclaimed, and I have shaven mine already." And then people got horrified, and those who were staunch Christians didn't follow him. But the weak ones who thought that if God had said that, then it should be done, began to shave. But the Christians were against it. So then he started to change books. But the righteous holy fathers didn't want to do it, so they were being tortured, they were burned, they were executed in all sorts of ways. At this time, Archpriest Avvakum emerged. He fought them, he was for truth, he was calling councils; many hundreds of people would come, from all countries, nothing would keep them; neither mountains, nor sea, nor spaces, nor rivers, nothing. As they said, they would flock together like eagles to these councils, in deserts, in caves where they lived, everyone would gather to the council by the strength of God, as the Lord ordained.

> And they were passing resolutions. All those who fol-
> lowed him [Nikon] are called Nikonites, and those who
> remained Christian, of the ancient belief, these are
> Christians, and this is what we are maintaining.

This account contains a number of highly interesting features.
The informant interprets the Russian schism within the context
of the earlier persecution of Christians by the Romans, and as
part of the schism between Byzantium and Rome. Thus the *raskol*
seems to have erupted around the year 1000—the approximate
date of the first serious conflict between the Christian East and
West—and Patriarch Nikon is given the role usually assigned to
Roman popes. He shaves his beard (there is no historical evidence
supporting this idea) and claims divine inspiration for a "heresy"
attributed by the Greeks to their Latin rivals.

Then the first Old Believers become merged with early desert
hermits, and an internal Russian affair is extended to "all
countries". Nikon's opponents are no longer peasants and members of the lower clergy but rather "righteous holy fathers", with
Avvakum acting as the convener of fictitious Church councils. This
tendency to interpret the *raskol* as a continuation of the eternal
struggle between the Christians and the pagans is perfectly con-
gruent with the Old Believers' view of themselves as the last Christians. For those who may question the relation between the first
and the last guardians of orthodoxy, this type of oral history fur-
nishes the proof.

The same informant supplied another powerful motif that surfaces in local views of the past, namely the belief in Nikon's com-
plicity with the devil. Like a sorcerer (*charodei*), the faithless
patriarch is said to have made a pact with Satan, thus preparing
the way for the rule of the antichrist. Attention should be paid
to the association made in the following account between the
polar opposites of right and left and God and Satan.

> Actually, Nikon's mind was possessed by the devil. Satan
> himself, you know. And he went to see Satan. His right
> hand was a deacon, something like a patriarch's servant.
> His name was John. He was God-fearing, and God was
> near to him, and he was near to God. So this deacon

entered his [Nikon's] cell and saw that Nikon was soul-
less, he lay there like a corpse. So John became afraid,
he ran out and was ready to shout that the patriarch had
died. But then he sees him walking! The body was rest-
ing, but the soul came out and said: "What's with you,
John, why are you so flustered as if you were afraid?"—
"Well, I was afraid when I came in and saw you soul-
less," replied John. And Nikon spoke, "Don't tell
anyone." And John looked into his boots and saw that
in one of them there was a picture of the Mother of
God and in the other—of crucified Christ! So Nikon was
trampling these pictures in his boots. And he said, "Don't
tell anyone. I went to see Satan, and we were about to
make an agreement. And he told me to baptize in the
name of Satan. I explained that I cannot do this, but
when I baptize in future, I will do it with the left hand,
the Satan's side."

When a child is baptized in the font, the priest places it
onto the right hand of the godparent who must stand to
his right. But the Nikonians started handing the child
onto the left arm...Then they started changing other
things, and so on. They started to say, "It's the same the
two-finger sign of the cross or the three-finger sign"; but
it is not the same...And there was a council, there was
Arius, he was also a Christian, and he said that the three-
finger sign is correct, and all who were on his side agreed,
but those who were Christians said it wasn't right. And
so it went that they started torturing the Christians, and
the Christians started to have strength, and the
Nikonians punished them, and so it went on and on.
They went along their path, and we went on our own.
They had their churches and started to baptize their way,
to warm the water. First, they also baptized with full immersion, but then they made more and more changes;
finally, they just placed the child in the font and poured
some water over its head. But now, I don't know. Perhaps they just drip a little water.

Tales of the post-Nikonian period usually deal with either of two complementary themes. One pertains to changes forced upon ordinary people in order to escalate their alienation from orthodoxy, and the other is concerned with tribulations experienced by the Old Believers. The first topic is usually rendered fairly accurately, as the following example shows.

> Afterwards, Peter [the Great] came. He had been travelling in foreign countries, and he brought back tobacco and coffee and started to oppress people. Older people who didn't smoke and didn't drink, he simply began to compel them. His servants would catch them and shave them and force them to drink coffee; and he forced women to cut their hair and to wear different clothes. And people would run away, they would hide in the mountains, and they would say that the antichrist had come already. They called him [Peter] the beard-shaver [*britous*], that's what they called him...people were so afraid of him. Already when he was growing up, he behaved like a hooligan.
> And he decided to build the city of St. Petersburg. He would chase people there, and they would carry lumber on their backs and run, and everything was built there in water and mud. They were saying, "It is too hard, we can't, people are hurting!" To no avail; no sooner did some die than they sent others. And so this St. Petersburg stands on top of human bones. So many people perished there, in the water, in the mud, with little food, that's how people died there. Still, they built the city, it is a beautiful city, but a great number of people died there.

The second theme, dealing with the fate of the Old Believers, sheds some light on how the people of Berezovka explain their mixed identity, that is, their position somewhere between doctrinal *popovtsy* and *bezpopovtsy*. The problem of priesthood is addressed in the following excerpt.

[The Nikonites] were trying to destroy all priests. As soon as they would see one that keeps Christian beliefs, they would either deport him, or put him in jail where he would fester, or kill him right there and then; that's how they were exterminating them. And we also had priests and the rest, but then all this started to disappear...There was a priest in Austria who had been blessed by righteous priests, and so people travelled there. In those days, you didn't just hop into a car and go—so when the people arrived there, he had already died. What to do? What can a deceased person do? So they selected a man and had him ordained with the dead priest's hand. And now they say about the "Austrians" [*Avstriitsy*] that they were blessed by a dead hand. But our people would not accept that. If you elected a priest [in the past], the people may say, "ordain this one", but then others would ask, "What kind of a person is this man?" So he would pray, he may perhaps not eat or drink for a week, and the Lord would reveal that this person is not worthy of being a priest, and that another one should be appointed. But here, when they bless with a dead man's hand, who knows, maybe he shouldn't have blessed that man at all? Maybe he would have found him unsuitable. And that's when our people left and went their own way.

And so Pavel Kolominski [Bishop Paul of Kolomna] was held under arrest already, and Christians would go secretly and ask him for guidance: "What shall we do, we are orphans, we have neither priest nor patriarch, we have nothing. How must we live?" But he is sitting in a jail, a prisoner, what can he do? So he blessed them [*blagoslovil*] and said, "My blessing will be upon you and your offspring." And so, now we follow this. As he blessed, so we now also bless one person in council, and so it goes on, when this person passes away, they bless another one, and in this way we have to gather and meet as long as we have the strength, and to teach our children to the extent of our strength to follow the right path, so as not to fail.

This narrative is memorable for the manner in which it depicts the events leading up to the final rejection of priesthood. It suggests that the impulse stemmed from doubts about the legitimacy of the "new" clergy, and this is a faithful rendition of the written tradition. But the two sources diverge when it comes to the dating and justification of this fateful departure from orthodoxy. The oral history implies that it occurred immediately after the schism when Paul of Kolomna was still alive, whereas the written version dates the loss of priesthood to the middle of the nineteenth century. This discrepancy is of some importance, since the oral account shifts the responsibility for approving an unprecedented and highly controversial innovation to a respected bishop. In this manner, the priestless strategy adopted by the ancestors of the people of Berezovka appears ordained and sanctified by Russia's last orthodox bishop.

Although most of the local oral tradition interprets the past, a very prominent place is assigned to eschatological narratives which speculate about the end of the world. The Old Believers have always been susceptible to apocalyptic thought, and the people of Berezovka are no exception. As in other locations, its main theme is shaped by a strong fear of the antichrist, the embodiment of Satan and hence the main rival of Christ.

The antichrist doctrine permeates every aspect of public and private life. Every conversation inevitably ends with the observation that the time of reckoning is near, and every world event is interpreted in accordance with this belief. It is difficult to provide a coherent summary of the doctrine, for there is no real agreement on who the antichrist will be or when he will arrive. In spite of one's informant's assurance that "it is all told in the Bible, in the books, everything is written", most people do not adhere to a literal interpretation of any written sources. Instead, they take a few passages from the Book of Revelation, a few from the prophecy of Isaiah, some more from the pre-Nikonian works reviewed in the previous section, and even from the *Awake!* booklets obtained somewhere from Jehovah's Witnesses. These sources are then combined in such a way as to explain contemporary political events as unquestionable indicators of the antichrist's readiness to invade the world. What follows is one informant's summary of the apocalyptic vision.

The Lord did not reveal to the angels [when the end will come], but He said that we should be ready at any hour. But He also said that if there be good people on earth, He will increase time; if not, He will decrease it. That's what He said, and nobody knows when this day will arrive. But when the antichrist comes, he will reign three years and half-a-year, and then time will come to an end. [Antichrist] will be reigning in Rome. He will be like a king. First, he will be such as to love everyone; he will behave like a Christian, go to church, build churches, give alms and protect the beggars, do everything after the manner of a sorcerer. He will do everything this way, but it won't be God helping him but the demons [*biesy*]. Demons will walk around as if they were people. And he will do things resembling miracles...He will do everything in a sly manner, and all people will say, "Has there ever been a king like this one? No, so this must be God and King!"
And when everyone will bow to him, then he will turn around and become evil, and then there will be hunger, and he will say that only those who venerate him may receive food and drink...And thus he will reign three years and a half. Then Eliah and Enoch will come and unmask him: "You are the antichrist, and things are not right!" And he will have them killed. And they will be killed and thrown on a haystack, somewhere in a village. They will lie there for three days..., and then the Lord will tell them, "Arise and go", and they will get up...That's when everybody will be at war, and they will annihilate each other, and the seven cities shall gather into one city. That means that if we had seven cities before, most of them will perish, and only one city will remain.

Although Rome is frequently mentioned as the antichrist's future capital, I heard rumours about several men from Oregon who, during a visit to the Holy Land, claimed to have observed the construction of the antichrist's temple in Jerusalem. Yet another version identifies Geneva and Brussels as the most likely capitals on account of their association with the United Nations organization.

What all these locations have in common are cosmopolitanism and internationalism, traits attributed to Babylon or to any other society that evokes an impression of chaos. It is the melting (*slivanie*) of distinctions and the mixing up (*pomeshchanie*) of values and beliefs which generates the climate required by the antichrist. The association of Rome with Babylon has deep roots in the ideology of eastern Christendom, and the promotion of an "international government" by the United Nations is seen as proof of its "Babylonian" tendencies.

The fear of the antichrist has important repercussions for daily life. First of all, it inhibits formal participation in politics, because any type of census, registration, or survey is regarded as a highly suspicious activity that could harm the Old Believers in their future fight with the antichrist. The people of Berezovka believe themselves to be particularly threatened because of their outspoken defence of Christian principles, and population surveys and other quantitative assessments of their strength and distribution are seen as potential weapons that could be used against them. Similar reasons underlie the local opposition to tattoos, skin stamps, and similar methods that could be employed in the antichrist's attempt at "marking" people. An adolescent girl who had visited a discotheque in Edmonton caused a great uproar displaying the stamp on her hand she had received instead of a ticket. For days afterwards, the village was abuzz with rumours that the antichrist's allies were preparing the ground by making people accept innocent-looking marks. Similar fears were expressed in response to the news that the United Nations had introduced a super-computer to store information on all people of the world.

Although nobody dares to question the antichrist doctrine itself, there is not consensus as to its chronology. Some informants provided exact forecasts, ranging from eight to thirty years, but most people concede that the final decision about when the antichrist is to appear remains up to God. Hence no contradiction is seen between expecting the antichrist at any time, and working hard to ensure care-free old age. When I joined some Old Believers during the tree-planting season in the bush, my foreman revealed to me that the seedlings we were planting by the hundreds would never reach maturity, because the end of the world was imminent. But when asked why then he engaged in such a futile activity, he replied, with a broad grin, "As long as there are people silly enough to pay good money for useless work, we will happily take it!"

This answer shows how the apocalyptic beliefs can reinforce one's feeling of superiority. Indeed, as the keepers of secret knowledge, the people of Berezovka feel able to assign meaning to otherwise puzzling phenomena, such as the ongoing environmental destruction or the arms race. This helps them to compensate for the disorientation and culture shock experienced outside their own community. The chaos which seems to surround them can be explained, and they believe they hold the key that fits the lock of meaning.

In spite of the functional integration of the antichrist doctrine into the local belief system, people do express a very real fear of the destruction of this world, with a wish to postpone it. Since God is assumed to grant an extension as long as there should be a sufficient number of Christians, the Old Believers are interested in increasing their numbers. The strategy which they follow does not involve any organized effort at converting outsiders, for the idea of "naturalized" rather than "natural" Old Believers is not at all popular. Instead, it entails a very informal search for "lost tribes" of ancient Christians believed to be scattered throughout certain isolated parts of the globe.

Having acted as a resource person, I can vividly recall some of the peculiarities that struck me in this search. The local spiritual leader had explained to me that according to oral tradition, there was an organized orthodox Church, including its own hierarchy and all, somewhere in the mountains of northern India, with possible branches elsewhere. He spoke of several persons he had met who confirmed this belief, and I was to provide assistance in establishing more concrete evidence. Our search was conducted with the help of richly illustrated anthropology and geography textbooks. We would leaf through photographs depicting the earth's inhabitants, and the elder would look for signs of Christian status. Once, he pointed out a bearded Serb, declaring, "He could be one of us!" I was then charged with the task of locating this man and writing to him.

On another occasion, I discovered a sizable community of Old Believers in Poland, and the photographic and written evidence was scrutinized with great interest by several elders. People displayed curiosity about this congregation, and the more adventurous ones were already talking of invitations and visits. The plan failed to progress very far, and talk about the Polish Old Believers soon died down. It seems that all the local people wanted was a flicker of hope that the tradition of the "lost tribes" had a firm basis. Had someone indeed proceeded to try to verify the available evidence, the likely discovery of "errors" among the foreign Christians would have cast a shadow over the tradition and indeed over Berezovka's own future. By clinging to the belief that Orthodoxy extends beyond the narrow boundary of the few hundred *nashi* known personally to the local Old Believers, people manage to postpone the assumed finality of the world. The importance of such a flicker of hope comes through in the following sketch of the extent of Christianity in the modern world:

> Some [Christians] survived somewhere in the desert. In Russia, there are some Christian monasteries...There are some in Brazil, in Bolivia, in Uruguay, just a handful here and there. I don't know about the others, maybe these are somewhere, but we don't hear about them. And there may be Christians in Poland, but we haven't seen them yet, only heard of them...There were Christians in Siam, but we didn't know them either. Maybe there are Christians in other places. Maybe they don't know about us, and we don't know about them. The Lord only knows. As the Lord said, "If there were two or three righteous people, I will extend the time..., but if there be no more Christians, then it will be the end of time." So, there must be more people somewhere, good, righteous people.

Ritual Calendar

The people of Berezovka subscribe to a chronology which is in several respects at odds with the western standard. Time is reckoned from the year of creation—determined as 5,508 years before

---

TABLE 4

Major Holidays in Berezovka

Fixed Dates

September 8	The Nativity of the Mother of God
September 14	The Exaltation of the Life-giving Cross
October 1	The Protecting Veil of the Mother of God
November 21	The Presenation of the Mother of God in the Temple.
December 6	St. Nicholas the Wonderworker
December 25	The Nativity of Christ
January 1	The Circumcision of Christ
January 6	The Baptism of Christ (Epiphany)
February 2	The Presentation of Our Lord in the Temple (Candlemas)
March 25	The Annunciation of the Mother of God (Lady Day)
May 8	St. John the Theologian [**Bogoslov**]
June 24	The Nativity of St. John the Baptist
June 29	St. Peter and St. Paul
August 6	The Transfiguration of Jesus Christ
August 15	The Falling Asleep of the Mother of God (Assumption)
August 29	The Beheading of St. John the Baptist

Movable Dates

	Palm Sunday
Easter	Easter Sunday (followed by Easter Week)
Ascencion	40 days after Easter

Christ's birth—the ritual year commences on the first of September, and it is kept track of with the Julian calendar, which means that Berezovka's time is some two weeks behind that of most other Christians. These discrepancies are taken quite seriously, as they seem to confirm Satan's success in confusing the "pagans" about the real passage of time. Since the latter are ahead of the orthodox calendar, their religious holidays supposedly cannot coincide with the occasions that they are meant to commemorate, and this deprives them of the opportunity to close the gap between the past and the present. This postulated deficiency allows the Old Believers to claim that the continuity required for the preservation of orthodoxy simply cannot exist anywhere without the use of the calendar employed in Berezovka.

In the past, the Old Believers depended on several techniques which ensured that they could always determine the correct day of the year without any help from the surrounding society. Older residents showed me complex astronomical charts attached to the *ustav*, which forecast essential holidays in blocks of sixty years. A somewhat rougher method relied on the human hand with its numerous lines and bones. A skilled person could read the correct year, month, and day from this simple tool, which is no longer adequately understood today. Such techniques guaranteed that even a person separated from the "social time" of a community was able to offer appropriate daily prayers.

The concern for keeping correct time has an exclusively religious basis. In their profane activities, people are, for the most part, propelled by pressure stemming from concrete chores that have to be completed, rather than from the abstract notion of "lack of time". One doesn't say, "The cutting of the hay must be finished by tonight"; rather, the cutting of hay continues until it is completed, whether it be today, tomorrow, or the day after. People become oblivious to the markers separating day from night and mornings from afternoons, unless a religious event effects a transition from secular to sacred time.

Corresponding with the shift from secular to sacred time are changes in the daily lives of the Old Believers; at such times, transformations from private and informal types of behaviour give way to public and formal ones. For example, on ordinary days, family members rise at different times, depending on the nature and amount of work that demands their attention. With the exception of small children, everybody eats alone in the morning and often also at night. Prayers are said privately, and the degree of social interaction can be minimal. This is in sharp contrast with the practice observed during holidays, when the entire family cooperates in the discharge of religious duties and social pleasantries. Everybody rises at the same time, prayers are offered as a group, and, following the church service in the village chapel, all family members and invited guests partake of a formal meal.

The people of Berezovka distinguish between three kinds of sacred occasions. The least significant ones, which are celebrated privately at home, are referred to as *malye prazdniki*, meaning "minor holidays". More important ones, *srednie* or "middle holidays", may be commemorated publicly, but attendance is not compulsory. The last and most authoritative class comprises *groznye*, that is, "formidable holidays" (table 4). These events must be celebrated publicly, and all parishioners are expected to attend. In addition to the major holidays outlined below, this category includes also every Sunday. This means that a formal religious service must be celebrated on at least eighty days in any given year.

The description of the ritual calendar would be incomplete without the inclusion of an extremely important component of Berezovka's annual cycle; the locally observed religious fasts. Every week, fasts are held on Wednesday and Friday in commemoration of Christ's trial and crucifixion. In addition, there are four blocks of fasts dedicated to the celebration of Easter, Christmas, Assumption, and the apostles Peter and Paul. In order of importance, these blocks consist of the seven weeks of Lent (*velikii post*), the six weeks between St. Philip's and Christmas (*Filipovka*), the two weeks preceding Assumption (*uspenskii post*), and one or more weeks prior to St. Peter's and St. Paul's Day (*post sviatykh apostolei*). The exact length of the last fast varies with the date of All Saints, since it comprises the period between the two holidays.

In view of the large number of days dedicated in Berezovka to fasts, it is not surprising that the annual cycle is often thought of as revolving around the contrast between fasts (*posty*) and fast-free periods (*miasoyed*). This distinction, which is more fully explained in subsequent chapters, influences the daily life of the Old Believers to such an extent that it is hardly an exaggeration to suggest that the passage of sacred time is felt as much in the stomach as it is in the heart.

Symbols of Orthodoxy: The Church

The acephalous authority pattern characterizing Berezovka's political domain is contrasted with a well-defined and binding power structure in the religious realm. Here too, decisions are taken collectively by the members of the *sobor*, striving to preserve the spirit of unanimity or, as it is called locally, *sobornost*. However, unlike secular deliberation, the conclusions of which community members may choose to disregard, decisions reached concerning the conduct of religious affairs must be heeded by the entire congregation. Dissenters face temporary or even permanent excommunication (*otluchenie*), the latter of which can amount to genuine banishment and the loss of Christian status.

The counterpart of the *starosta* in spiritual matters is the *nastavnik* or *nastoyatel* (preceptor). He oversees the performance of religious services, shapes the debates of the *sobor*, and tries to fill, as well as possible, the void created by the absence of a priest. The *nastavnik* remains, however, a layman whose authority is bestowed by the council. When a man gains a reputation for exceptional piety, knowledge of orthodox history and dogma, organizational abilities, and interpersonal skills, he may be elected to this prestigious position. The length of his service, which is carried out without remuneration, depends on age, health, and community satisfaction. A good spiritual leader should display charisma and independence, but he must not forget his accountability to the *sobor*. Should he act too autocratically, a *nastavnik* faces deposition and replacement by a more suitable elder.

Since Berezovka is part of a larger network of Old Believer congregations, its *nastavnik* and *sobor* are expected to co-ordinate their decisions with those of their counterparts in Oregon and

Alaska. But because each parish is required to heed the same tradition, the need for interregional synodal meetings arises infrequently, usually only when important customs are threatened by conditions encountered in a new environment. Apart from such exceptional occasions, each congregation manages its affairs autonomously, relying on its own council and *nastavnik*.

Besides the *nastavnik*, the elders of the *sobor* select a number of other religious specialists for several essential tasks. Because the spiritual leader may be ill or absent for long periods of time, the congregation has one or more deputies (*zamestitel*) to take over his duties if necessary. Another important office is that of the *ustavchik*, who ensures that every public service is performed exactly in accordance with liturgical tradition. Another official, referred to as the *zastavlianchik*, selects suitable readers of publicly chanted passages, and the principal cantor (*pervyi pevets*) determines the correct manner of congregational singing. These men shape the conduct of Berezovka's religious services and play a

Berezovka's chapel.

leading role in the decisions of the *sobor*. They are expected to be thoroughly familiar with the core of the written tradition as it pertains to the maintenance of orthodoxy.

In addition to these public officials, there is a large number of men and women who are selected by individual believers as their confessors and private counsellors. Every adult member of the congregation is entitled and expected to select a trustworthy and pious person to be consulted in matters that burden one's conscience. A woman may choose either a spiritual father (*dukhovnyi otets*) or a spiritual mother (*dukovnaya mat'*). A man, on the other hand, is restricted to a male confessor, because women are not expected to give advice to men. Children are supposed to consult their parents in all matters pertaining to religion.

Public Devotion

An average Old Believer spends a considerable part of his or her life in public religious services. Whether the occasion is an ordinary Sunday or a major holy day, the structure of the service remains the same. All work ceases in the afternoon prior to the commemorated day, and families, segregated by age and sex, undergo the ritual cleansing in the steam bath (*bania*) attached to every *dvor*. In the early evening hours, the congregation assembles in the local chapel for the vespers (*vechernaia*), a relatively short service that lasts up to two hours. The parishioners go home and rest, without eating, until early morning, when they return for the far longer matins (*utrenia*), which last for five or six hours. Major celebrations require an extension of this norm by up to three hours. It is expected that parishioners attend both parts of what is regarded as a single service (*sluzhba*).

The building which accommodates the congregation is a modest-looking frame structure that bears little resemblance to an Orthodox church. The sole external sign of its function is a silver cupola topped with a cross—which was erected only a short while before my research was conducted, in response to local jokes about praying in a barn. The chapel has no bell, which, I was told by the *nastavnik*, may not be installed without the blessing of a priest. The building lacks the status of a proper church (*tserkov*) and is officially designated as a chapel (*molenna*). But most people slip and call it *tserkov* instead.

One enters through the western door, which leads into a cloak room where heavy garments are hung up along the walls (figure 4 [1]). Adjoining this vestibule is a semi-enclosed area (2) reserved for women and impure visitors, including temporarily excommunicated members of the congregation. Women in good standing may proceed all the way to the imaginary dotted line, but only along the northern, or left, wall, which is considered the female side. The central space (3) is used by men and boys in good standing, giving them the best view of the ritual that unfolds along the eastern wall. The dotted line in the east separates common from "sacred" ground. The latter is occupied by a long desk (*chetnyi naloi*) (4), a small table called *pristol* (5), and a low bookcase (6) containing liturgical books. A lectern (7) is employed from time to time to support hymnals and may be moved to different parts of the central area (3).

The chapel lacks a proper altar, which is normally situated in a sanctuary adjoining the eastern wall. Similarly, there is no

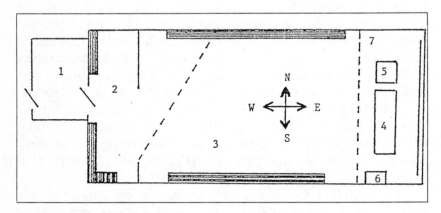

Figure 4. Berezovka's chapel.

iconostasis in the traditional sense, which would adorn the wall between the sanctuary and the public room (3). Instead, the icons are placed upon a board that lines the eastern wall. The small *pristol* (5) substitutes for a proper altar in supporting a covered book of gospels, a standing cross (*krest*), and a censer (*katsei*). As if it were a real sanctuary, the eastern section is reserved for religious specialists responsible for the ritual conduct.

The entire room is decorated with large embroidered square pieces of cloth, bearing flowers and symbols of orthodoxy, such as crosses and sacred monograms. Several long chains of decorations like those used on North American Christmas trees are suspended from the ceiling. Although the chapel is ventilated through four windows on the northern and southern walls, it retains a heavy smell of incense mixed with perspiration and beeswax. During a well-attended service, the building may hold as many as two hundred people.

The Old Believers are not expected to arrive at the chapel at a prearranged time. When I inquired prior to my first visit about the beginning of the matins, an elder told me vaguely to come "early in the morning". Pressed further, he mentioned two o'clock as an appropriate time. Having followed his advice, I found myself alone, waiting in front of a dark and locked chapel. About one hour later, the *nastavnik* and two other elders, dressed in the long black coats (*kaftan*) worn by some men during ritual occasions, unlocked the door and disappeared into the building. A few minutes later, I could see flickers of candlelight through the windows and hear the tones of a chanted prayer. Gradually, elderly men and women, followed by families and young couples, began to arrive. By six o'clock or so, the majority of the congregation was together. On important days, there is a tendency to start the service very early in the morning, and the "arriving time" may be considerably shorter. But there is no obvious desire to formally stipulate a point at which everybody is expected to congregate.

The flexibility of attendance is facilitated by the flexibility of the service. After entering the chapel proper, the worshipper carries out a number of prostrations (*zemnye poklony*) accompanied by numerous signs of the cross. He or she then bows to the congregation, whose members reply in kind, and takes up position somewhere in the main part of the chapel. Looking from the entrance, there is a clear concentration of female parishioners at the back and on the left side, while men congregate along the right wall and at the front. This arrangement agrees with local views which correlate the female sex with the left and the west, and the male sex with the right and the east. All participants are

expected to remain standing throughout the duration of the service, but, if overcome with fatigue, one may rest on benches that
line three of the four walls. The absence of pews or chairs encourages a lot of movement: small children are frequently sent
from one parent to another, and people step outside to breathe
some fresh air or to make use of the outhouses located to the
west of the chapel. The impression of commotion is emphasized
by the constant chatter of adolescents "hidden" in the cloak
room—and periodically reintegrated by an elder—and by the loud
banging of the door. Still, the tumultuous environment, which
resembles that of an Old Believer home, does not seem to detract
from the parishioners' ability to carry out their duties to God; the
necessary tasks are fulfilled conscientiously and imposingly.

The structure of the service is determined by the *ustav*, which
makes a distinction between the liturgy conducted by a priest and
that conducted by a layman. The latter, employed in Berezovka,
consists of four basic components that can be elaborated upon or
repeated, depending on the occasion. The longest part is allocated
to the chanting of "canons" (*kanuny*) by men selected by the *zastavlianchik* in accordance with their literacy and ability to
withstand this strenuous activity. I was not allowed to examine the
text of these canons, and can say little about them. Their content
is varied, ranging from expositions on the significance of Sunday
to commemorations of the deeds of the particular saint or martyr
who is being remembered on the day of the service. Each canon
is read by a separate man from a separate book placed on the
chetnyi naloi by the *nastavnik*. Shorter passages may be chanted
by boys who have mastered the liturgical language and the appropriate text.

The recitation of canons is interrupted repeatedly by prayers
said by the entire congregation. Most of them are taken from the
psalter and are known by heart. The prayer is concluded with the
request *Gospodi pomilui* (Lord, have mercy), which may be
repeated up to a hundred times. The counting is aided by a rosary
(*lestovka*) made of cloth and clutched in the right hand of every
worshipper. This rather long and stiff tool is also used in hitting
ill-behaved children during the service. The recitation ends with
prostrations and signs of the cross. A square flat pillow of colour-

ful fabric (*podrushnik*) is placed upon the floor in order to guard the forehead from contact with the ground.

The third component consists of the singing of hymns (*dukhovnye stikhi*) from special song books written in notes (*kriuki*) known as *znamenie* (sign). The reading of this old notation system requires special training which is passed on by the first cantor (*pervyi pievets*) and his assistant. The cantor is responsible for choosing an appropriate voice (*golos*) out of a scale of eight. The hymnal is placed upon a lectern and surrounded by a small group of men and boys. The rest of the congregation may join in, depending on their knowledge of the particular hymn.

The fourth and final component is the reading of an appropriate edifying passage known as *pouchenie* (instruction). This is usually a gospel on resurrection, but other biblical accounts may also be chosen. It is performed by the *ustavchik* or the *nastavnik*, with everybody else seated; heads are bowed and eyes closed. When asked why one cannot stand during this part of the service, informants underlined the *direct* contact with God through the Bible, which requires that the book be placed *above* the congregation. A prohibition on entering or leaving the chapel while the *pouchenie* is in progress contributes even further to the solemnity of this occasion.

Once these four components have been carried out, it is up to the *nastavnik* to decide upon the extent of elaboration and repetition. His decision depends on the importance of the commemorated event as well as on quite mundane considerations. For example, when there is a wedding ceremony to be performed later on in the morning, the service can easily be shortened by two hours, giving people more time to celebrate outside the chapel. Some of my older informants complained about what they saw as a tendency in recent times to abbreviate more and more services.

The Old Believers do not go to church in order to learn something new from a sermon, nor do they go in the expectation of being challenged to modify their behaviour. Even the short *pouchenie*, which has the most pronounced moralistic tendency of all the four components, is interpreted as a voice from heaven that remains external to the listener and does not require the kind of self-examination aimed at by sermons delivered in Protestant and Roman Catholic churches. Informants found it hard to summarize the content of the "instruction" or the canons recited during the service. They knew, of course, that the devotion was held in honour of a certain event or saint, but there was no need felt to analyze what exactly was done and why.

The chapel is considered to be a middle ground between earth and heaven. Although it is conceded to be less sacred than a real church with relics, bells, and altar, the building is more elevated than an ordinary home. This high status is reflected in the scrupulous avoidance of defiling acts, such as the penetration by animals or impure persons into the sanctuary. In accordance with the purity beliefs outlined in the next chapter, menstruating women are barred from attending religious services for fear of offending God. Similarly, visiting outsiders defiled by their consumption of impure substances such as tobacco, unbled meat, coffee, and tea may not venture past the western partition that separates "Christians" from temporary and permanent "pagans".

The insistence on outer, that is, material, purity is intertwined with the one activity which takes up most of the time spent in the chapel, namely the recitation of prayers and canons. With a few minor exceptions, all prayers in Berezovka, private and public, are audible. This custom has its genesis in the desire to express as forcefully as possible one's allegiance to God and renunciation of the devil. The cosmic rivals are believed to listen in on the prayers through the intercession of saints and demons (*biesy*) respectively, and their conclusion as to the status of the person influences his or her future after death. As my informants put it, depending on the nature of the prayer, either the angels or the demons "frolic" (*raduyutsia*).

As can be expected, a Christian prayer embodies all the standards of correctness observed in the realm of the liturgical Church Slavonic language. The incorporation of any linguistic deviation— such as words or accents borrowed from Russian or any other natural language—is held to transform the prayer into a tool of the devil and must immediately be rectified, often at the insistence of the congregation. I recall my amazement when confronted for the first time with this convention. An elder chanting a canon had mispronounced a word, and several voices supplied the correct version and demanded that he repeat the entire sentence. In this manner, the church service enforces conformity and reveals gaps in the knowledge of individual participants.

The insistence on ritual orthodoxy precludes the active participation of non-"Christians". Whenever I found myself in the midst of a religious event, my hosts consistently admonished me not to pray with them. This prohibition applied not only to prayers in the strict sense (*molitva*), but also to their extension, the multiple prostrations (*poklony*). For fear of undoing the worshippers' efforts at communicating with God, I was instructed to remain standing, with arms folded, behind them.

Despite a high regard for the divinely inspired word, few elders feel confident enough to explain exactly how their prayers differ from those employed in the official Orthodox Church. Of the numerous "corrections" instituted by Nikon, only three were known to my informants. Everybody is aware of Nikon's substitution of *Iisus* for *Isus* (Jesus) and of *Nikolai* for *Nikola* (Nicholas). The third modification pertains to the heresy of the triple *alleluia*. Unlike in official Orthodoxy, where *alleluia* is repeated three times and then followed by its Slavonic equivalent *slava tebe Bozhe*, in Berezovka the repetition occurs only twice.

The Old Believers are not allowed to visit the churches of other denominations for fear of defilement. They consider these institutions to be playgrounds of demons where God cannot dwell, and few seem to be at all intrigued by the prospect of seeing such environments personally. The stereotype of a "pagan" church is a Roman Catholic cathedral equipped with a huge organ, nicknamed "devil's pipes". The use of instrumental music is seen as a major result of the mixing of sacred and profane elements in heterodox religious settings.

A final aspect that deserves to be mentioned in this context is the link between devotion and discipline. I have already pointed out the parallel between religious and secular socialization of children. Here, I wish to emphasize the local view of church attendance as a demonstration of one's willingness and ability to withstand fatigue. My informants stressed the importance of sweating and aching during the service. The pain felt as a result of the endless vigil reminds the worshipper of Christ's sacrifice, which is, after all, recalled every Sunday. But it also evokes fear of God and of the punishment meted out to sinners. As I heard so many times, faith alone was not a sufficient proof of Christian status. Faith must be demonstrated, and what better evidence than visible adherence to God's law of ritual orthodoxy?

Because of the connection between endurance and piety, an Old Believer must participate in public services. Absence from two consecutive occasions leads to temporary excommunication, and even work in the bush at the other end of the province is not considered a sufficient excuse. Despite the apparent flexibility of one's arrival in the chapel, the congregation takes note of who comes when and modifies its assessment of the piety of all residents accordingly. At some point, one's marital prospects and standing among the elders may be influenced by the degree of endurance shown in church.

Sacramentals

Communication between God and the worshippers is facilitated not only by prayers, but also by several other acts and objects of unusual power, which I refer to as "sacramentals". The Old Believers designate this domain with the term *sviatost*; it can be loosely translated as "holiness" or "sacredness". Although *sviatost'* is distinguished from sacraments (*tainstvo*), the dividing line is thin. A most important factor is the dependence of sacraments on sacramentals, which underlies local attitudes to the spiritual gifts dispensed by the official Orthodox church. Since its sacramentals are considered heterodox, the sacraments administered by that church are claimed to be invalid.

My description starts with the sign of the cross, which the people of Berezovka single out as *the* symbol of orthodox Christianity. As soon as a child has learned to exercise some control over his or her body, he or she is introduced to the correct signing of the cross, a gesture performed on a countless number of occasions. In executing this sign, one joins the thumb, the ring and the little fingers of the right hand to denote the Trinity. The index and the middle finger are held erect side by side, with the latter slightly bent. This configuration symbolizes the double nature of Christ and His descent from heaven to earth. The hand then touches the forehead, navel, and both shoulders from right to left.

By touching the head, one affirms Christ's supremacy over the Church and over every believer. The pointing to the stomach is interpreted as professing His descent to earth and immaculate conception. The right shoulder signifies Christ's seat to the right of God the Father, and the touching of the left shoulder indicates one's belief in the final judgement and the casting of sinners into hell.

It can easily be seen that the sign of the cross serves as a simplified summary of Christian dogma. Understandably, then, any modification appears as an attack on orthodoxy and evokes accusations of heresy. This charge is made against all so-called Christians whose sign of the cross deviates from the norm observed in Berezovka. In short, the dichotomy of orthodoxy and heterodoxy is encapsulated in the dichotomy of the correct and the incorrect sign of the cross. The former is believed to derive from God; the latter is associated with the devil.

Any version of the wrong sign is seen as a derivative of the Latin-inspired three-finger sign introduced by Nikon. The confusion resulting from the substitution is seen as being related to the patriarch's alleged pact with Satan and his desire to make people submit to the antichrist: the new sign is believed to demonstrate that association. Although the Nikonites continued to affirm the Trinity, they did so by joining the thumb and the first two fingers while holding the ring and the little fingers concealed inside the palm. The Old Believers interpret this configuration as an attempt at denying the divinity of Christ and at replacing holy with unholy trinity. The latter is seen as consisting of the apocalyptic beast, snake, and antichrist, represented also by the three numerals 666.

The view that the Nikonites and other pseudo-Christians sign themselves with a symbol of the devil is further strengthened by the association of *troeperstie* with tobacco snuffing; as will be shown further below, tobacco is considered a strongly polluting substance believed to have been introduced, through Satan's influence, as a profane version of incense.

A most important class of sacramentals consists of icons. An icon (*ikona, obraz*) is defined locally as any painted or cast-iron representation of a holy figure or theme that is executed in accordance with orthodox iconographic views and methods. Al-

St. Luke painting the Mother of God.
(Ikonenmuseum Recklinghausen)

though the parallel between the painted and written traditions is not perfect, it is apparent that the rules governing pictorial designs are essentially the same as those observed in the copying of words. Both types of images are attributed to God, and both are protected from any kind of intervention which would threaten the full transmission of the original "text". This insistence on regarding major symbols of orthodoxy as faithful copies of divine prototypes may be designated the *iconic principle.*

My informants linked the appearance of icons directly to God. The oldest examples of holy images are associated with depictions of early Christian scenes surfacing miraculously without any human intervention. Encouraged by these expressions of God's desire to enshrine pictorial representations, prominent early Christians are believed to have taken up iconography in an attempt to instruct people and to facilitate their communication with God. The Old Believers single out St. Luke as the author of the first picture of the Mother of God painted by a human.

The Old Believers acknowledge that most orthodox icons found in the world today, including all those kept in Berezovka, cannot be attributed directly to God or to saintly iconographers. Instead, they are the work of ordinary artists who have conscientiously copied all the details required to preserve continuity with the divine originals. But this fact does not detract from their value. Just as "old books" are not evaluated on the basis of the age of the paper, so too "old images" may be of recent origin. Their status depends primarily on the faithfulness of the depiction.

Local residents accuse Nikon and his followers of having destroyed the perfect overlap between the prototype and its copy. The innovations enumerated by my informants concern the blurring of the boundary between sacred and secular paintings and the modification of a number of traditional symbols. For example, the depiction of holy figures in post-Nikonite art is claimed to emphasize physical rather than spiritual qualities; that is, instead of concentrating on the face, the new artists are said to be preoccupied with the body and its movement. Consequently, one is confronted with a picture of restlessness and flexibility, while old artists conveyed an image of stability and stasis. The culmination of this heterodox trend is identified in the depiction of nakedness, which is held to suggest that saints are merely made of flesh and bone, just like anyone else.

The rejection of naturalism is especially strong in the case of the representation of crucified Christ. Although the statements supplied by my informants were not entirely unequivocal, the dominant opinion was that Christ did not suffer during crucifixion. When I enquired as to the nature of His sacrifice, I was told that

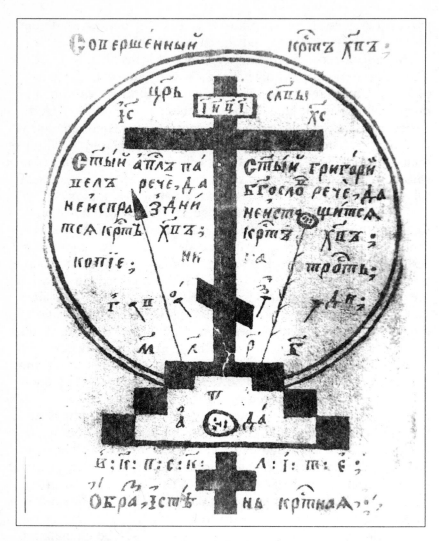

A seventeenth-century drawing of the krest.

He felt betrayed and suffered mentally but not physically. To suggest otherwise would, I was given to understand, amount to denying His divinity. This is exactly what the Old Believers see in new depictions of the scene, those in which Christ's body is twisted, covered in blood, eyes shut or filled with resignation. When I displayed a famous Baroque painting of the crucifixion, a woman glanced at it and exclaimed with distaste, "This is not our Christ!"

Because the Old Believers are opposed to three-dimensional carvings, their "crucifix" is either painted or, more commonly, made of cast-iron, which allows a slight projection of the body above the cross. This image, referred to as *raspiatie*, must employ a cross with eight points (*vosmikonechnyi krest*) which is considered to be the only correct copy of the life-giving cross of crucifixion. The four-pointed version (*krizh*) is associated with pre-Christian times and may be used only in conjunction with but not as a substitute for the *krest*. One of the major heresies attributed to Nikon is his betrayal of this tradition.

The insistence on the superiority of the *krest* over the *krizh* is fortified with numerous legends and symbolic associations. The three horizontal bars of the former are said to represent the three-dimensional, universal, realm of Christ's rule, expressed in the selection of three types of wood for the original construction. The trees used in this endeavour are believed to have grown from three seeds placed in Adam's mouth just before his death. The seeds had been fetched by Adam's son Seth from the vicinity of the tree of life in the Garden of Eden, and their growth ensured a tangible connection between fallen and risen man. In accordance with this belief, Adam's skull must be depicted beneath the crucified Christ, waiting to be cleansed by the latter's blood. Thus, while the horizontal axis of the cross expresses spatial universality, the vertical axis links the past with the future.

Although all of its properties need not be discussed, there are several more details of the *raspiatie* mentioned by the Old Believers as important Christian symbols. Starting at the top, there is an image of Christ the King (see [1] in figure 5) making the two-finger sign of the cross. Underneath Him are two angels with trumpets (2) announcing the Second Coming, separated by a barely recognizable depiction of a dove above the head of the crucified. In crosses used by doctrinal *bezpopovtsy*—in local terminology referred to as *Pomortsy*—the dove is missing. This seemingly insignificant difference is emphasized in Berezovka as evidence of the heterodoxy of priestless Old Believers. The dove signifies the Holy Spirit and its protection over the Old Orthodox church. Its absence expresses resignation over the loss of the church and clergy.

A further important distinction between a local and a priest-less cross can be seen in the inscription or "title" (*titla*) above Christ's head (3). The *bezpopovtsy* employ the monogram *IC XC* (*Isus Khristos*) while the people of Berezovka, along with the *popovtsy* and the Nikonites, adhere to *INCI*, which is the Slavonic version of Jesus of Nazareth, King of the Jews. My informants were not certain about the implications of the difference, which played a part in the fragmentation of the Old·Belief in the seventeenth and eighteenth centuries.

The cosmic significance of the crucifixion scene is alluded to by the depiction of the symbols for sun and moon above the hands of Christ (4). The sun face represents the east and is therefore placed above the right hand, and the moon face, above the left

Figure 5. *Raspiatie*: **(A) local** and **(B) doctrinal priestless.**

Traditional depiction of the crucifixion.
(Ikonenmuseum Recklinghausen)

hand, stands for the west. The crucified figure's arms are stretched out as far as possible, inviting, as my informants put it, the entire cosmos to follow suit. This universal gesture would be far less effective if Christ were hanging rather than standing. As local residents point out, Christ *stood* on the lowest slab of wood (5), designated as "foot rest" (*podnozhie*). Once Nikon removed this essential ingredient of the *krest*, the new *krizh* left Christ dangling, and the doctrine of His sacrifice had to be modified. The pictorial theology of the *raspiatie* ends with the skull of Adam (6), which complements the interpretation of the cross being not a "tree of death" but rather an extension of the "tree of life".

The local attention to iconographic details encompasses all sacred images: depictions of the Mother of God without a head cover are rejected for misrepresenting her marital status; wrong spellings of holy names, especially the aforementioned *Iisus*, make an otherwise orthodox icon heretical; and, above all, a saint performing the three-finger sign of the cross cannot be prayed to. All such images are said to be of dissimilar writing (*nepodobnovo pisma*) and are thus invalid.

The meticulous manner in which the Old Believers evaluate pictorial representations may be further illustrated with two examples drawn from the realm of secular imagery. Having been invited to attend a wedding in Berezovka, I was searching for an appropriate gift. By a stroke of luck, I happened to obtain a small reproduction of a famous nineteenth-century painting by Surikov, depicting the arrest of the boyarina Morozova, one of the early martyrs of the old faith. After I presented the newlyweds with this picture, there was considerable upheaval among the guests, and several elders began to scrutinize every detail of the depicted scene. Within a few moments, the elders declared triumphantly that the picture was not true to reality, because the sign of the cross made by the noblewoman had been painted incorrectly. The point here is not that in view of the tiny size of the sign it was impossible to analyze its composition. What appears more significant is the absolute unwillingness of the elders to concede that a non-"Christian" could correctly depict a religious topic. Needless to say, I have not seen my gift in the home of the young couple.

The second example is more difficult to understand. Towards the end of my field work, I wrote an article for a mass-circulation magazine which was intended to draw attention to the difficult educational situation of the Russian children. The piece contained some photographs of local residents, and I distributed several copies to my informants. Approximately a year later, I happened to talk to the *nastavnik* and his son, who accused me of having written "lies" about he community. When asked to supply evidence, the young man mentioned several statements whose content he had not understood because of his imperfect command of English. But then he pulled out the magazine and pointed at a photograph of adolescent boys taken some two years prior to our meeting. "Some of these boys have beards, you know," my accuser explained, "but in this picture, they are all beardless!" My arguments that this discrepancy between the past and the present was caused by the maturation process, something I had no control over, fell on deaf ears. The man continued to accuse me of having distorted the facts.

This anecdote invites a few remarks about the Old Believers' attitude to photographic reproductions of icons and the taking of photographs in general. Activities of the former type are strictly proscribed. Whether the icon is in church or at home, it may under no circumstances be photographed, a prohibition which extends to any other object found in the chapel. The only explanation for this provided by my informants emphasized the danger of the photograph's falling into hostile hands and being defaced. Hence there seems to be a postulated transference of identity between a painted original and its mechanical copy.

The taking of photographs of secular scenes is also officially prohibited, as is the mere possession of a camera. I do not have sufficient data to do justice to local explanations, but it seems that the opposition stems from the association of photographs with spying and with frivolous entertainment. Despite the prohibition, virtually every younger person owns and uses a camera, and every family has at least a few old photographs from China and many more from North America. I encountered few difficulties taking innocent pictures, but some elders refused to be photographed, or indeed to supply a reason for their refusal.

The people of Berezovka face something of a crisis because of a diminished supply of painted icons. The several thousand North and South American Old Believers are supplied by only two qualified icon painters, one in Bolivia and the other in Alaska. Both were trained by Russian-born specialists and "ordained" by means of a blessing (*rukopolozhenie*) accompanied by a certificate. Not unlike priests and *nastavniks*, these artists constitute a crucial link in the chain of orthodox tradition. Due to the growing population, however, more and more sacred images are manufactured from cast-iron by a commercial company located in the United States. Prior to their "activation", they are purified by the *nastavnik*.

All the icons in Berezovka are privately owned and inherited within the nuclear family. Parents usually present their children with sacred images upon the occasion of marriage, laying the foundation for a small collection in every home. The bride is most likely to receive an image of the Mother of God, while her husband is given an image of Christ. In order to set up house, the couple must possess these two icons and a *raspiatie*. Without them, other Old Believers would refuse to spend any time in their home, and the private performance of religious duties could not take place in the prescribed manner. The people of Berezovka do own other icons depicting several important saints, but the variety is limited. If a person has a painting of a saint whose deeds are about to be commemorated publicly, it is lent to the chapel for that occasion. When no such icon is owned locally, the congregation employs a "multiple icon", which is a panel containing tiny pictures of all the saints commemorated during an entire given month.

The primary function of sacred images is to promote communication between the congregation and God. The Old Believers consider the depicted saint as an intermediary or, as some of my informants put it, as God's secretary (*sekretar*), who takes on some of the responsibilities of his heavenly superior. Hence one prays not to the material image, but to the "prototype" it represents. The channel opened up by the icon seems, however, to be reciprocal, giving the saints a glimpse, so to speak, of human life. This belief underlies many of the purity precautions observed in the chapel and at home, such as the ban on animals, sinners, and pagans. When I inquired as to the reason for the requirement that I stand behind everybody else, including the women, I was told that the saints would be offended by my presence. I had to literally keep out of their sight!

The sight and the power of the holy figures can be somewhat regulated by the worshippers. The tools used to this end are pure beeswax candles, manufactured by the women and donated to the chapel. The candles are attached to the simplified iconostasis (*bozhnitsa*) in such a manner as to illuminate directly the eyes of the depicted saints. An old man shoulders the responsibility for adjusting the candles throughout the duration of the service, ensuring that the images can be seen by the congregation, and that the parishioners remain visible to the holy figures. As soon as the candles are snuffed out, the icons are "de-activated", and impure visitors may penetrate the sacred field along the eastern wall and examine the paintings at close range. Every public service begins and ends with the respective lighting and snuffing out of the candle which illuminates the *raspiatie* in the centre of the *bozhnitsa*.

Because of their elevated status, icons and crosses may not be disposed of in the same way as a secular object. They may not be sold or given to non-"Christians", and, in the case of serious damage, they must be committed to the waters of a river. The same treatment is prescribed for dilapidated liturgical books.

The final constituent of the *sviatost'* category is incense (*ladon*), known colloquially as *kadilo*. It is employed on a wide range of occasions associated with prayers and purification, and is seen as a complement to icons. While the substance itself is purchased in a store in Edmonton, it may only be used in a traditional version of the censer (*katsei*) which is not found in the reformed church. Unlike the censer employed there—a bowl suspended from chains—Berezovka's is attached to a long handle, which means that it is moved horizontally rather than swung. Any type of purification, be it applied to defiled icons, dishes, a newly constructed house, or the room in which a birth had taken place, may call for fumigation. Whenever possible, the *nastavnik* is asked to carry it out.

Sacraments

The people of Berezovka have access to a number of spiritual gifts which are explicitly or implicitly regarded as sacraments (*tainstvo*). Their status is made ambiguous by the absence of ordained clergy, but the extent to which the Old Believers themselves recognize and acknowledge this ambiguity varies from person to person and from sacrament to sacrament.

The equivocality is particularly marked in the case of what some people interpret as a substitute for the Eucharist, a substance referred to as *sviatynia*. This "sacred thing" consists of powerful water associated with Christ's baptism, which because of this association serves as the most potent external and internal cleansing agent. *Sviatynia* is prepared every year on the anniversary of Christ's baptism at Epiphany (*Bogoiavlenie*). It happens during a ceremony known as *kreshchenie*, a term related to the designation of human baptism and christening (*krestiny*). On two separate occasions, on the eve and in the morning of the holy day, a bucketful of water is fetched from the frozen river near the chapel and mixed with *sviatynia* preserved from the previous year. The water made in the evening becomes "small" (*malaya*), its counterpart mixed in the morning "great" (*velikaya*) *sviatynia*. The former is reserved for external purification of defiled objects and animals, such as household dishes, newly constructed homes, and cattle acquired from outsiders. Every household received a flask filled with the substance, which is then kept beside the icons at home. Great *sviatynia*, on the other hand, is used for internal cleansing.

The first cleansing occurs on the morning of Epiphany, immediately following the preparation of the powerful holy water. With the exception of excommunicated sinners, the congregation forms two long files segregated according to sex. Starting with the male side, pairs approach the "altar" and receive a white plastic cup filled with *sviatynia* by the *nastavnik* and his helpers. The men shake hands and kiss each other on the mouth three times, then drink three draughts of the water. While the pairs shuffle towards the eastern wall, a short tune commemorating Christ's baptism is repeated over and over again until all men and boys have partaken of the powerful substance. The entire sequence is then repeated for pairs of women and girls.

Sviatynia is drunk collectively on two further occasions: at the beginning and the end of Lent. On the first occasion, everybody is invited to participate in the manner just described, but on Easter Saturday, the consumption is restricted to those who have kept the fast conscientiously. Children, who are considered unable to sin wilfully, are never denied the holy water.

Further use of the great *sviatynia* is controlled by the confessors of individual parishioners. These elders receive a flask each at Epiphany to dispense the powerful substance every time after receiving the confession of their spiritual children. They or the *nastavnik* also administer the water to seriously ill patients.

I don't recall hearing anybody refer to *sviatynia* as communion (*prichastie*), but in its status and function the one does resemble the other. The affinity is particularly striking when one examines explanations of the power of the pseudo-sacrament. My informants admitted that, as is the case with the Eucharist, the transformation of ordinary river water into the powerful *sviatynia* cannot be accomplished without the intervention of a priest. Because they lack clergy, the local people can only add a fresh supply of river water to existing *sviatynia*, thus extending its lifetime but also reaffirming the continued dependence on an institution which is no longer believed to exist. The holy water thus constitutes an essential "iconic" link with the orthodox past.

From the perspective of the Old Believers, the only really indispensable sacrament is baptism (*krestiny*). Without it, one can never be considered a member of the community or hope to achieve salvation. Baptism is conferred on the eighth day after birth—unless the child is expected to die, in which case it takes place as quickly as possible. The parents choose a name, which should commemorate one of the saints celebrated in the period between birth and baptism. There are altogether around seven hundred potential male names and some two hundred female ones. Local residents have a definite preference for archaic-sounding names, except explicitly Jewish ones, such as Abraham, David, and Isaac. Common male names include Vasilii, Lavrentii, Leontii, Onufrii, Pamfil, Feodosii, and Stepan. Frequent female names are Anastasia, Agripina, Elena, Evdokia, and Feodosia. Although they are not found in the approved register, ordinary secular names such as Ivan and Uliana are popular too.

The ritual of baptism is preferably performed by the *nastavnik* in the chapel, but a ceremony carried out by any other Christian adult—except the child's parents—is also valid. Having recently given birth, the mother is considered impure and may not attend the baptism ritual. The father is present, but his participation is limited by the custom that whoever holds the child during the rite

John the Baptist immersing Christ in the Jordan.
(Ikonenmuseum Recklinghausen)

automatically becomes its godparent. Such status would provide
an unwanted kinship link between the child's father and mother,
making their marriage incestuous and forcing them to dissolve it.
In order to minimize the restrictive impact of this institution on

the marriage universe, the Old Believers tend to select godparents from close consanguines.

The godparent (*kriostnyi/kriostnaya*) brings the child to the chapel wrapped in a blanket, but otherwise naked. The father or some other relative fetches a high aluminum trash can stored in a closet for this express purpose, and fills it with water taken directly from the river. Local residents have no misgivings about using a font of this type and claim to have relied in the past on cauldrons and buckets taken straight from the kitchen. What counts above all is the purification of the water inside the container, which is accomplished with four lit candles attached to its upper border. The *nastavnik* fumigates the font with incense, asks the godparent to renounce the devil, and then immerses the naked child three times from head to toe.

The impurity discarded by the child during the immersion is seen as genuine material substance which has a defiling effect on the performer of the ritual. In order to minimize the "infection", the *nastavnik* washes his hands and arms with river water, and the content of the font is returned to its source. I was told that if a single drop fell onto the floor of the chapel, the entire building would have to be purified. The polluting effect of baptism extends to the four candles, which must be discarded along with the water.

Following the triple immersion, the child is dried off and given three objects of ritual value that define its Christian status. These are a small pectoral cross suspended from a string (*krestik*), a woven belt (*poyas*) fastened around the belly and conceived of as an umbilical cord connecting the child with God, and a white shirt (*riza*) to conceal nudity. Although these symbols of the Trinity may be exchanged for adult versions as the child grows up, they must be worn at all times. From now on, the child is protected by God, though still exposed to Satan's temptation. The struggle between the two entities is nicely expressed in the belief that every person possesses a personal angel and demon. The angel sits on the right shoulder and keeps track of one's good deeds. The demon hovers over the left shoulder and takes note of sinful conduct.

The people of Berezovka do not recognize the validity of any but their own baptism. This view is based on the premise that Christ himself was baptized by triple immersion (*pogruzhenie*), a custom that was to be followed by all Christians. The Latins, however, modified the ritual into a mere pouring or sprinkling (*polevanie*), setting an example for the Greeks and the Nikonites. The latter are also said to have started warming up the water, thereby denying the power of the Holy Spirit to keep the child comfortable even when immersed in ice-cold water. In addition, priests of the official Orthodox church are believed to hold the child with the left rather than the right hand and to employ an incorrect prayer formula. All these infractions of orthodoxy support the firmly held assumption that children outside the realm of "Christians" are baptized in the name of the antichrist. This is seen as a worse sin than lacking baptism altogether.

Local Old Believers do not have access to the holy oil required for chrismation, a ritual which normally takes place immediately after baptism. My informants confirmed that chrismation cannot be carried out without the assistance of a priest, but they nevertheless insisted on their baptisms possessing sacramental validity.

Similar incompleteness characterizes local marriage practices, defended in Berezovka as another true sacrament. This rite of passage consists of three separate ceremonies. The first one brings together the future bride and groom with their respective parents. Provided they agree with the proposed union, all four parents confer a blessing on the young couple (*svatat'*), followed by three collective prostrations before the icons at home. The young woman and man are then asked separately whether their decision is voluntary. This question (*ty volie idosh?*) is repeated three times; if the answers are affirmative, the couple is officially engaged.

The public announcement of the decision is made by means of a ceremony held at the bride's home at least a week prior to the wedding. Its name, *dievieshnik*, may be loosely translated as the "feast of the virgin". The bride invites her girlfriends to help prepare the clothing to be worn on the wedding day, and the groom and his friends visit in the evenings to join in the singing of traditional wedding songs and more or less explicit sexual teasing. The atmosphere is filled with joy and sadness as the girls discuss the advantages and disadvantages of married life.

The *dievieshnik* may be thought of as a transitional stage. Throughout its duration, the bride is freed entirely of her former domestic duties, and her membership in the parental household is symbolically minimized by the constant attention she receives from her girlfriends. The latter accompany the bride wherever she goes by day or by night, protecting her from the evil eye as well as from a premature loss of virginity. Adults may drop in during the evening performance of songs, but they may not interfere in anything that takes place. As a sign of her election and liminality, the bride wears a wreath (*krosata*) of flowers with long colourful ribbons hanging down her back. It symbolizes the transition from the uncovered hair of girlhood to the head cover associated with womanhood.

The wedding is almost invariably celebrated on a Sunday, immediately following the morning service. Prior to her arrival, the bride is washed in the *bania* by her assistants, who use a brush (*venik*) donated by the groom. She then enters the chapel in the company of several young people. The party consists, from left to right, of a close female relative of the groom (*svashka ot zhenikha*), the bridesmaid (*svashka nevestina*), the bride (*nevesta*), the groom (*zhenikh*), and the groom's best man (*druzhka [ot zhenikha]*). The members of the party are linked with white kerchiefs held in their hands. They remain standing in the centre of the chapel, awaiting the conclusion of the service.

The wedding ritual takes place with activated icons in the presence of a small group of adults. Because of its sexual overtones, children and single adolescents are required to leave. The first component consists of a benediction (*bogoslovenie*) conferred separately by all four parents. One by one, the parents enter the restricted space between the "altar" and the eastern wall to instruct the couple to live together in peace and in fear of God. The groom is then presented with a *raspiatie* whose *podnozhie* (foot-rest) he must kiss. The bride receives an icon of the Mother of God and kisses her right cheek, which is the one supporting Christ's head. The benediction ends with all participants exchanging three kisses on the mouth.

The second component leads to the "crowning" (*zavienchanie*) of the bride, carried out in the northwestern, that is, left corner of the chapel. The two female assistants remove the bride's kerchief, undo her single braid of hair, and arrange it into a double braid to represent married status. This is then topped with a triple cover of thin fabric, which must be worn by all married women. The cover is designated by several terms, such as *vienets* (wreath, crown), *obruchenie* (betrothal), *volosnik* (hair cover), *chin* (rank), *kitchka*, and *shoshmura*. Without yet delving too deeply into local hair symbolism, a topic discussed below, it is noteworthy that the head cover is made by the bride's mother-in-law and positioned by a relative of the groom, often his sister. Hence, as my informants clearly recognized, the "crown" becomes a symbol of the husband's authority over his wife. The groom is not crowned, because, I was told, a cover would interfere with his contact with God.

During the final component, the *nastavnik* hands out two wedding rings (*koltse*), which are worn on the right ring-finger by the bride and on the left by the groom. The rings are designated *obruchenie* (betrothal), a term deriving from the word *obruch* (hoop), implying a tangible connection between the husband and the wife. They may not be removed until death, at which time they are taken off before burial to allow the deceased to begin a new life.

Although the wedding ritual is presided over by the *nastavnik*, his participation is limited to giving a few words of advice and admonishing the bride to accept the guidance of her husband. The couple leave the chapel as *molodye* (newly-weds) and arrive at the husband's home to participate in the worldly celebration (*svadba*) of their new status, which spans several days and includes the adults of the entire community.

Compared with a marriage performed by an Orthodox priest, the ritual conducted in Berezovka appears incomplete. Virtually all of the enumerated components are part of the preliminary office of betrothal (*obruchenie*), which does not constitute a sacrament. Sacramental validity is bestowed by the office of crowning (*vienchanie*, *brak*), which must involve the bride as well as the groom. These deviations do not concern local residents, who appear to be unfamiliar with the conduct of a proper Orthodox wedding ceremony. They refer to their version as *vienchanie* and *brak* and treat it as a full sacrament.

The situation is similar with respect to confession. Although the spiritual father or mother provides advice and imposes penance (*epitimia*), the prayer of sacramental absolution is not pronounced. My informants agreed that the latter may be given

Berezovka's cemetery. (Detmar Schmoll)

only by a priest, but they seemed confident of receiving absolution directly from God.

The anointing of the sick, which under normal circumstances consists of confession and absolution, is limited to a simple confession followed by the administration of *sviatynia*. However, many Old Believers die from injuries incurred in the bush or on the road, so that far more importance is attached to funerary and post-mortuary rituals than to practices conducted prior to death.

A dead person is supposed to be buried three days after passing away, ostensibly to minimize the danger of mistaking apparent for genuine death. The waiting period can be eliminated in cases that are beyond doubt. The body is wrapped in a special outfit whose white colour underlines the parallel with birth. It makes no distinction between men and women, poor or rich, expressing simplicity, resignation, and the expectation of resurrection.

The responsibility for making the outfit rests with an old widow, who is selected and blessed by the *nastavnik*. She is required to use cloth made from locally grown flax and stitched together by hand. The shroud (*savan*) consists of an over-size, long shirt (*riza*)—an adult version of the baptismal shirt—wide, knee-high socks (*noski*), the actual *savan*, which resembles a sleeping bag covering the entire body except the face, and two long sheets (*postilki*) attached to the front and the back of the body. The shrouded corpse is tied with white strings woven from flax (*piliny*), which are believed to keep it from falling apart during the stormy journey to heaven. The feet are left unobstructed in order to facilitate resurrection.

The body is buried in the praying posture, with arms crossed and a rosary and prayer-pillow placed in the hands. The right hand clutches also a Slavonic certificate (*rukopisanie*), likened to a passport, signed by the person's confessor and attesting to his or her Christian status. A crown (*vienets*) made of cardboard and inscribed with prayers and religious symbols is placed upon the head, and the old pectoral cross (*krestik*) is exchanged for a new one, hanging on a white string. A person in good standing is interred in the central part of the cemetery (*kladbishche*); an excommunicated member is banned to a small fringe, clearly separated from the rest. In either case, the body must face east, from which direction the signal for resurrection is believed to come. The grave is marked with a large white cross (*krest*) made of wood.

On the third day after death—hence usually immediately following the funeral—the deceased person's relatives invite the rest of the community to a commemorative meal combined with a short vigil (*pominki*). A ceremonial dish, consisting of boiled wheat with honey (*kutia*) is served prior to the singing of funerary songs known as *ponekhidy*. These gatherings are repeated on the ninth, the twentieth, and the fortieth day.

The purpose of the *pominki* is to support the soul of the deceased on its journey through the heavenly spheres (*mutarstvo*) in search of a niche where it awaits resurrection. The body remains for the time being on earth, undergoing natural decay, which supposedly will be reversed when the body is called upon by Christ to rejoin the soul. The corpses of saints and martyrs alone are held to be immune to decay, awaiting resurrection in their original state.

My informants could not agree on the composition of the heavenly realm. They all subscribed to the notion of its being divided into a number of separate fields (*mutarstvo*), but some insisted on two and others on four such divisions. The two-fold version holds that the sinners are housed in a dark sphere and the pious people in a light one. The four-fold version has one layer resembling hell (*ad*), a second one just like earth, a third of elevated beauty (*israelskoe miesto*), and a fourth location akin to paradise (*rai*).

The soul of the deceased undergoes a rigorous examination which determines its place of waiting. The examination is carried out by angels and demons who compete for the soul on the basis of written evidence assembled by the deceased person's angel and demon. The *pominki* are held to influence the decision by persuading the judges of the person's Christian background. Since the verdict is believed to be announced on the fortieth day after death, the last commemorative session is of special importance.

Asked about the sources of their funerary practices, my informants pointed out iconographic depictions of scenes such as the raising of Lazarus, the falling asleep of the Mother of God, and the resurrection of Christ, all of which reveal a mortuary appearance structure akin to Berezovka's. At the same time, although the local practice is considered the only way to continue such divine prototypes, I found surprisingly little evidence of explicit attempts to discredit "pagan" death-related rites. With the exception of cremation, which is held to deprive the soul of its body, the Old Believers seem unaware of and uninterested in mortuary practices observed in other Christian denominations.

Whether we discussed Roman Catholic ordination, Protestant communion, or Greek Orthodox confession, local residents always returned to two fundamental reasons underlying their alleged invalidity. Firstly, the "pagan" so-called sacraments are prepared and administered in conjunction with false sacramentals, ranging from the sign of the cross to icons and prayers, which discredit the entire ritual occasion. Secondly, even if the employed sacramentals were orthodox, they become ineffective when used by people lacking proper baptism. Hence the sacramentals and baptism should be considered the dominant symbols of local ritual orthodoxy. In both instances, there is tremendous interest in showing off the continuity of the "iconic principle" and its absence in "pagan" versions.

The selectivity in the choice of self-identifying symbols is surely related to the role of priesthood in their "construction". By insisting on the dominance of symbols which do not require priestly intervention, the people of Berezovka have been able to reconcile their definition of orthodoxy with its pre-Nikonian prototype.

Symbols of Orthodoxy: The Home

This chapter continues the description of Berezovka's symbols of orthodoxy, but focuses now on the context of the home. It has been shown that proper baptism establishes a person's Christian status, which is then upheld by continued adherence to ritual orthodoxy. However, there are several other criteria that must be fulfilled in order to maintain orthodox status. Foremostly, an Old Believer is required to observe numerous standards of correct diet, appearance, and sexual expression, which could be said to certify his or her bridging of the abyss between nature and culture.

Because these norms are designed to regulate the contact between the ritual and the natural domain, I employ from time to time the term "natural purity" to express the contrast to the "ritual purity" dealt with in chapter 6. This semantic distinction is not meant to obscure the interdependence and similarity between the symbols associated with ritual and natural purity respectively. Proper prayers or baptism alone are as insufficient guarantees of orthodoxy, as are proper diet or appearance on their own. It is the combination of the two classes of symbols which denotes Christian status in the manner understood by the Old Believers. The affinity between these symbols can be further detected in the continued, albeit somewhat modified, importance of the "iconic principle".

The reason why I nevertheless discuss natural purity separately from ritual purity lies primarily in the association of the former with the Christian home. The home might quite usefully be conceived of as a filter between the raw and chaotic forces of nature and the ordered world of Christian culture, for it is here that wild elements are classified and held back for fear that they should threaten the maintenance of ritual purity. The home constitutes a buffer zone between the heterogeneity of the "outside" and the carefully guarded homogeneity of Berezovka's "inside", the chapel. What I am primarily concerned with in this chapter is the logic behind the filtering process which determines what of nature may proceed into the home and how much of it is elevated to a symbolic status.

Nature and the Christian Home

The dwellings of Berezovka differ little from ordinary Canadian homes. They are either trailers set up by newly-wed couples prior to the construction of a permanent house, or they are spacious bungalows of the design that can be encountered anywhere in North America. These standardized structures have nothing Russian about them: no carvings, bright colours, or peasant stoves. Even the large gardens surrounding them appear quite unexceptional, and were it not for the long, single road connecting all the houses, the community would hardly stand out in the Alberta landscape.

The interiors look perfectly ordinary as well. There are the usual kitchen appliances, and the rooms are furnished somewhat sparsely but in the style and material encountered everywhere in rural Alberta. The walls are covered with huge canvasses displaying some mass artist's rendition of a bull moose wading through a pond against the backdrop of the Rockies, or a grizzly baring its jaws at an invisible intruder. Only the conspicuous absence of a television set creates a slight impression of unconventionality.

Despite its ordinary appearance, the home is considered a place of elevated ritual status. If one sees a genuine church as a reflection of heaven, and the local chapel as the reflection of a church, then the home may very well be understood as a reflection of the chapel. It is the lowest link in the chain connecting both God with His followers and the past with the present.

The ritual status of the home derives from a miniature temple referred to as the beautiful corner (*krasnyi ugol*), which is located in every commonly used room. It consists of a small iconostasis with several holy images, a flask with *sviatynia*, a few dyed eggs blessed at Easter, and, occasionally, a censer. An embroidered curtain adds a touch of beauty and decorum. When sexual intercourse takes place, the curtain is drawn over the *bozhnitsa*, concealing the act from the sight of the saints.

The "beautiful corner" in the main room is located above the dining table in full view of visitors entering the house. Here, the family gathers for the performance of collective prayers before and after formal meals and during minor feasts, when a visit to the chapel is not deemed essential. When visitors arrive, they perform three prostrations accompanied by signs of the cross and a short prayer. Only then do they greet the occupants of the house. The expectation of being in a Christian home is conveyed by the question asked by a person unable to locate the icons; he or she asks, "Where is your God?" (*gde vash Bog*).

The house provides an environment where sacred and profane forces meet, and, depending on their status, these forces are either allowed to mix or not. It is almost as if the dwelling were equipped with two doors, one leading to the chapel, the other to the world outside, including the "pagan" society. The occupants open and close the doors in such a manner as to maintain an appropriate mixture of the two currents. Too much ritual purity makes human life difficult, if not impossible. Hence when sexual intercourse is contemplated, the eastern window is shut with a curtain over the icons. Conversely, a powerful pollutant, such as a dog or a smoker, must remain outside for fear of defiling the atmosphere. Should one gain entry, the eastern door must be flung open to admit potent purifiers from the chapel. This is the essence of the simile comparing the home to a filter.

It would be a considerable and somewhat redundant undertaking to attempt to chart the workings of this filter in all its complexity. Instead, in the following pages, I make a sketchy attempt at designing a basic model which contains only elements that possess great symbolic value. Particular attention is paid to those associated with natural as well as ritual purity. I begin with the symbolic connotations of natural liquids, depicted in Table 5.

Starting at the top, *sviatynia*, the least natural element, occupies the highest position as a most potent purifier that cannot defile anything or anybody. Without further precautions, it may be employed in the chapel as well as at home.

Ordinary water is a more complex substance whose status depends on its source. The rapid flow of rivers and creeks is believed to act as a mechanical cleansing agent, and this is one reason why the Old Believers locate their settlements along rivers. A second explanation advanced for the preference contains a supernatural component. It is believed that every morning, God dispatches two angels who hover above a river used by Christians, with the task of eliminating any further impurity. For this reason, the water is pumped into homes with no doubts about its quality. It is drunk and used for cooking, washing, and bathing. Although weaker than *sviatynia*, river water can become a source of ritual purification when complemented with other purifiers, such as incense and candles. The best example was supplied in the discussion of baptism. Because of these properties, river water may be brought to home and church without any precautions.

Sources of water that occupy an intermediate position are wells and springs. Held to be fed by an underground river, wells are not entirely stagnant, but their quality must be improved through a short prayer and fumigation with incense. The water then becomes fit for human consumption, but it may not be used in any ritual context. The residents of Berezovka rely on wells

TABLE 5
Natural Liquids and Their Secular and Ritual Status

ELEMENT	SOURCE	ASSOCIATION	SECULAR USE	RITUAL USE
Holy Water	Jordan	Christ	none	purifier
	rivers/creeks	angels	human consumption	purifier
Water	wells	Christians	after purification	none
	ponds/lakes	demons	animals	pollutant
Blood	edible animals	pagans	medicinal	pollutant
	inedible animals		pollutant	pollutant

only where access to a river cannot be gained. Without such access, ritual life would come to a standstill.

The opposite of flowing water is stagnant water, found in lakes, ponds, and puddles. It is considered impure and polluting on the basis of two explanations. Firstly, the accumulation of a body of water that doesn't move is believed to prevent the discharge of harmful organisms. Secondly, stagnant water is held to be a favourite habitat of demons (*biesy*) whose presence can be detected from the foul smell emanating from such reservoirs of pollution. The demons, who are Satan's helpers, are invisible, and their primary task consists of trying to penetrate the human organism. The symptoms of demonic infiltration are said to resemble those resulting from poisoning and mental illness. In some cases, the victim can free him or herself through a combination of prayers and proper diet; in other cases, the damage may be permanent.

While cattle are allowed to consume stagnant water, the Old Believers themselves do not use it at all. I was told that although it would not cause any harm if it were employed in the washing of a truck or animal, its mere presence in the chapel would require purification of the icons.

The least acceptable natural liquid is animal blood, which evokes the strongest possible fears. The status of blood depends on its source. If it derives from an edible animal, it may be drunk sparingly as a remedy against anaemia, but only if drained from the right side of the animal. Consumption of any other type of blood, on the other hand, is considered strongly polluting. It is for this reason that carnivorous animals are not tolerated within the chapel or, with the exception of the cat, the home.

This tripartite classification of liquids demonstrates in a nutshell the buffer-zone function fulfilled by the home in maintaining the separation between the sacred culture of the church and the profane character of the natural environment. It is noteworthy that the consumption of blood is one of the serious sins attributed to "pagans" of whatever persuasion. Although my informants could not supply concrete examples of the consequences of ingesting blood and blood products, they all agreed that the substance constitutes the "soul of animals". Their testimonies implied that the incorporation of this essence of animality would lower humans from the realm of culture, that is, "Christianity", to that of nature, a status which is synonymous with "paganism".

River water, on the other hand, elevates humanity from the domain of nature to that of culture. It does so primarily because of its association with the sacred *sviatynia*, which may be regarded as the divine prototype of pure water. The iconic principle is unmistakable here. The sanctity of the Jordan River is reflected in other rivers, just as Christ's baptism lends validity to ordinary human baptism. The link between a natural element and a ritual occasion makes water a powerful symbol of natural as well as ritual purity.

Unlike blood, which derives from an altogether different source and belongs to a different domain, stagnant water should be considered a caricature of river water. It looks the same, it tastes the same, but while the one is protected by angels, the other is inhabited by demons. This crucial distinction derives from the much weaker connection between the divine prototype—Jordan River—and a lake or pond. Hence just like heterodox baptism, stagnant water becomes the symbol of pseudo-Christians. This association can be seen in the Old Believers' refusal to modify in any way the water employed in baptism. Should they heat it or use even a lake as its source, the reflection of the prototype would be unacceptably diminished.

The next realm of nature which evokes considerable symbolic connotations consists of plants and plant products. The overwhelming majority of plant species, including poisonous ones, are considered pure and ritually harmless. The exceptions are the hop, the vine, and the tea-, coffee-, and tobacco-plants. The Old Believers are divided over whether these plants are inherently impure or whether their polluting effect is limited to their consumption. Those who subscribe to the former opinion attribute their origin to Satan; the other interpretation regards Satan's role as confined to prompting humans to partake of products that should remain untouched.

The impure plants share two crucial qualities. They are considered "alcoholic", in the sense of modifying one's behaviour, and their origin is sought outside Russia. With the exception of tea, which is known to have been imported from China, these alcoholic substances are believed to have spread form the Near East immediately following Christ's crucifixion. Satan, jealous of God's successes, is blamed for having introduced the local population to smoking and drinking in order to cloud the minds and weaken the bodies of potential followers of Christ. The first victims are said to have been the Arabs and the Turks, who in turn seduced the Latins and the Greeks.

Of all these intoxicants, the greatest polluting potential is ascribed to tobacco: its consumption in any form evokes the strongest fears of natural and ritual defilement. The substance is held to defile one's body and soul on account of being alcoholic, and to destroy the beneficial power of sacred objects on account of being a "pagan" version of incense. The latter association was not made explicit by my informants, but I deduce it from several examples in which a clear connection was established between any type of smoking (*kurenie*) and what the Old Believers consider to be pagan rites. North American Indians, Manchuria's aboriginal peoples, or even witches and sorcerers—all of their ritual performances are believed to revolve around the consumption of tobacco. As has been shown already, the same link is seen between Nikonites' snuffing and their making the wrong sign of the cross.

Although strangers who happen to smoke are not barred altogether from visiting local homes, they are denied access to liturgical books and icons, objects whose effectiveness is believed to suffer from even indirect contact with tobacco. Outright smoking, an act unheard of within the home, is held to completely destroy the power emanating from the icons, which would then have to be purified with *sviatynia* and incense. Still, despite the extremely negative connotation of tobacco, a few adolescents and young men indulge in smoking outside Berezovka's confines.

Aside from the small class of intoxicants, plants are highly regarded as nutritious food and effective medicine. I was told of skilled herbalists whose superb knowledge of a wide range of vegetation made them capable of curing any type of illness with perfectly natural methods. Although no such specialist lives in Berezovka, every older resident has some of these skills and applies them in the treatment of the minor ailments experienced by humans and animals alike. Because northern Alberta is said to be poor in medicinal herbs, local healing efforts depend to some extent on supplies of tropical plants received from South American relatives.

The classification of animals is based primarily on the criterion of edibility. Those that may be consumed are considered pure (*chistye*), the remaining ones are held to be impure (*nechistye*). This dichotomy resembles the classification of plants, as it pertains in the first instance to the purity of the human body. Strong fears

TABLE 6
Animal Classification According to Edibility

HABITAT	FEET	FOOD	OTHER CRITERIA	STATUS
AIR				
	red feet			edible
	toes with membrane			edible
	thin hairs below knees			edible
	naked below knees			edible
	naked above knees			inedible
			live in couples	inedible
LAND				
	hooves			edible
	cloven hooves			edible
		chew cud		edible
		don't chew cud		inedible
		predators		inedible
	uncloven hooves			inedible
	hoofless			inedible
	dog's paw			inedible
WATER				
		predators		inedible
			scales and eight fins	edible

of ritual defilement are expressed only about a subclass of *nechistye* animals, namely those designated as "pagan". The latter can be compared to tobacco insofar as they too pollute human bodies and ritual objects alike. The criteria employed in the differentiation of pure from impure animals are summarized in table 6.

The criteria listed in table 6 were all mentioned by informants asked to enumerate characteristics associated with animal purity and impurity respectively. I wish to make it clear that individual persons displayed preferences for just a few criteria, which did not necessarily overlap with those mentioned by other informants. For example, one resident might use "red feet" as *the* sign of purity in birds while another would insist on "naked feet". Similarly, land animals could be classified according to their feeding habits or the constellation of hooves. This lack of agreement does not derived from uncertainty about the status of a given animal, but rather from the peculiar manner in which most Old Believers go about creating order in this domain. Instead of evaluating animal status on the basis of unchangeable criteria, they move in the opposite direction by designing their criteria to justify the traditional status of a given animal. Thus while the signs of purity or impurity differ from informant to informant, everybody agrees on which animals are edible and which are not.

The status of birds is most commonly associated with the appearance of their feet. Those with red feet (*krasnolapye*), with a membrane between the toes, or naked (*nagatye*) below the knees are considered pure and edible, but these criteria are applied so broadly that virtually any bird that does not feed on carrion or other animals falls into this category. Indeed, it appears that the dividing line between edibility and inedibility coincides with the distinction between herbivores and carnivores, and that the preoccupation with feet may be an attempt at concealing the carnivorous tendencies of the chicken. The latter is considered a pure bird and is a major source of festive food.

One interesting class exempted from the equation between edibility and purity consists of birds living in couples (*parenni*). They are considered pure but may not be killed because of their resemblance to humans. Like a husband and wife, if one member of the pair dies, the other suffers and may perish from sadness. This parallel was drawn to explain the status of swans, but I strongly suspect that it extends to other birds of pure feeding habits, such as doves. The dove is of course a well-known symbol of the Holy Spirit, and to the best of my knowledge it is not eaten in Berezovka. But I failed to inquire about its status during the field work.

Animals living on land are classified on the basis of their feet and/or feeding habits. Some of my informants associated edibility with the mere possession of hooves (*kopyta*) combined with the chewing of cud (*zhevat'*), while others insisted on the hoof's being cloven (*razdielennye kopyta*) as the sole sufficient characteristic. Thus the swine, which is of great local importance, is held to be edible on account of having cloven hooves while the hare, in spite of its feeding habits, is considered impure because of its feet. The horse and similar chewing but improperly "footed" beasts are also inedible.

Despite their inferior status, animals which have uncloven hooves and vegetarian feeding habits do not evoke sentiments associated with ritual purity. The situation is entirely different with respect to hoofless creatures, especially when they feed on other animals. All predators (*grabitel'skii zvier*) are unfit for human consumption and are *pogany* in the sense that they defile ritual settings. Their classification resembles a pyramid whose top is occupied by the dog, an animal considered most profoundly polluted and polluting. Although dogs are kept and cared for locally, they are rarely touched and never let into the home. Should a dog succeed in sneaking inside, the occupants would be required to have their icons purified. Like tobacco, the dog is believed to defile all ritual objects.

The justifications supplied for the local aversion to dogs consist for the most part of references to impure feeding habits. In addition to subsisting on the blood of other animals, the dog is held in contempt for lapping up vomit and for being preoccupied with feces. In view of its excessive salivation, the dog is seen as a most likely transmitter of disease and dirt (*griaz*) and as the prototype of a "pagan" animal.

The iconic relationship between the dog and other naturally and ritually impure animals is expressed in the term "dog's paw" (*lapa sobachi*). When asked about the status of such diverse animals as the bear, the tiger, the cat, or the mouse, informants classed them all as pagan on account of their sharing the dog's paw. Although this attribute is defined rather widely in order to allow the inclusion of not necessarily carnivorous but otherwise distasteful creatures, the primary criterion remains the killing and eating of other animals. Consequently, paganism in animals is synonymous with rapacity.

The Old Believers do, however, distinguish between more and less pagan creatures. This can be seen in the treatment of the cat, which occupies the bottom of the pyramid presided over by the dog. Unlike the latter, the cat is admitted into the house, and kittens are given to small children as presents. The differential treatment is explained by pointing out the cat's hygienic habits, which make it a suitable domestic companion. Another, perhaps even more important reason, derives from the contribution of the cat to keeping the home free of mice. Still, the cat is a carnivore and may therefore not be allowed direct contact with icons or liturgical books.

One class of animals considered pagan but lacking the dog's paw consists of snakes and other reptiles, known collectively as *gadina*. These creatures are subsumed in the category of predators, and the derivative verb *gadit'* is applied to a wide range of distasteful behaviour.

Finally, aquatic organisms fall into either of two classes. Fish (*ryby*) are always pure and edible, regardless of their habitat, if they possess scales and eight fins. Unlike any other animal, a fish may be eaten with its blood. Shellfish, sharks, seals, and all other creatures living in water and not belonging to *ryby* are known as sea animals (*morskii zvier*) and may not be consumed. As the core of this class consists of predators, it would appear that *morskii zvier* is the aquatic equivalent of the more inclusive category of *grabitel'skii zvier*.

This is, in summary, a picture of the most significant features of the "Christian" environment outside the chapel. The details of the sketch are provided in subsequent sections, where the implications of local views on natural purity are discussed as they concern daily life. At this stage, I will offer a few concluding remarks on the commercial use of impure plants and animals, a point which should further clarify their status.

There is no indication that the idea of natural impurity would prevent the Old Believers from handling substances considered defiling when such use can be converted into a profitable occupation. This is made abundantly clear by the long history of commercial activities involving impure plants and animals. During their sojourn in China, several local residents participated in the growing and smuggling of opium, a highly "alcoholic" plant indeed. The economy of the *Kharbintsy* depended to a great extent on tigers, bears, and other impure beasts of the forest sold to Chinese merchants. My informants extolled the medicinal properties of bear fat and ground tiger teeth, and expressed regret at having been deprived of these and other folk remedies due to their "pagan" origin.

Today, many of the Oregon-based Old Believers derive a good income from harvesting hops, and the breeding of foxes was a fairly popular enterprise until very recently. Most of the settlers in Alaska subsist on fishing, and they catch and sell shellfish with little regard for its impure status.

Food and Drink

The people of Berezovka are extremely attached to good food and drink. Every major social occasion calls for the preparation of elaborate meals, and the status of individual households is determined to a considerable extent by the hospitality of its members. A good wife is expected to know how to prepare vast quantities of various traditional dishes, and her skill in the kitchen is measured to a great degree by her girth, and by that of her family. Although the standard is shifting somewhat under the influence of North American popular culture, older residents regard a well-rounded figure and glowing cheeks as primary indicators of feminine beauty. A corpulent woman is believed to work hard, experience little difficulty in childbirth, and take good care of her husband. A portly man is said to demonstrate a happy home environment.

The local diet consists for the most part of traditional Russian peasant fare with a sprinkling of recently introduced dishes, such as pizza and spaghetti. The meals lack variety, and their nutritional value is diminished on account of too much starch and little protein. The basic staple is heavy bread baked from white flour and served in abundance with every meal. It is supplemented with raw vegetables and a vast number of dumplings and pies stuffed with mushrooms, cooked peas or beans, and, more sparingly, minced meat. Meat is reserved for festive occasions and is usually served well cooked and mixed with a greasy soup. Fish is eaten occasionally, most often dried or smoked. The separate dishes are all served at once, and the sequence of consumption is up to one's own taste.

The Old Believer diet is influenced by the distinction between pure (edible) and impure (inedible) natural substances as outlined above, and an elaborate feast-and-fast cycle which is part of the ritual calendar. The latter consists of the already mentioned dichotomy of *post* (fast) and *miasoyed* (meat-eating), which in theory constitutes eight long blocks of time coinciding with the restricted and unrestricted diets respectively. In reality, there are several mechanisms built into the ritual cycle to bridge the gap between *post* and *miasoyed*. For example, when a holy day falls on a Wednesday or Friday, the requirement to fast is set aside. On the other hand, the theoretical dietary freedom of *miasoyed* is overridden by the demand for fasting on an ordinary Wednesday and Friday, and many of the numerous holidays celebrated in Berezovka call for some dietary restraint during fast-free periods. Hence the type and quantity of food consumed on a restricted day during *miasoyed* can be identical with that allowed on a lenient day during *post*.

The Old Believers view fasts as a time of introspection and intensified demonstration of the spirit's mastery over the body by means of sexual and dietary abstinence (*vozderzhanie*). The demand for fasting is justified on the basis of the prophecy of Isaiah (Is. 65); it is associated with the setting aside of a tithe of land (*desetina*) left fallow in the expectation of future harvest, which will benefit only the obedient farmer. Although sexual activity must cease entirely, the intake of food and drink is merely curtailed in terms of quantity and quality. In order of severity, then, one's diet changes from including meat to consisting of nothing but water. The highest degree of *vozderzhanie* applies to the last week of Lent.

The gradual descent from unrestricted to severely limited meals is conceived of in terms of three pairs of opposites which express the composition and mode of preparation of a given meal. These pairs are hot:cold (*gorkoe:studenoe*), oily:dry (*maslianoe:sukhoe*), and cooked:raw (*varenoye:syroye*). The *ustav* uses these terms in stipulating proper diet for individual days, and they are translated into meals by the cook. Thus, the least restrictive fast contains cooked, hot, vegetarian—and, from time to time, dairy—food, while the strictest regimen, except for the last week of Lent, requires cold, dry, and raw food. The six attributes make it possible to combine different elements, thereby preserving some variety and accommodating fluctuations within a given fast.

It is apparent that the views underlying the distinction between fast and fast-free meals are related to the principles separating pure from impure natural substances. In both instances, we see a very marked gap between blood and water on the one hand, and between meat and vegetables on the other. This can be represented as a double dichotomy of "blood...meat:vegetables...water". It can then be expanded into a basic model of the distinction between carnal and spiritual life, which coincides to a considerable extent with the differentiation of pagans, and Christians: "blood...meat...hot...sex: sexless...cold...plants...water".

The ideals of vegetarianism, chastity, and spirituality are felt very strongly during protracted fasts, particularly Lent. One could say that the Old Believers are filled at such times with the desire to emulate the desert fathers and other famous ascetics. But this desire is rarely translated into reality, as one's sustenance derives from the vision of the end of the fast rather than from the spiritual rewards stemming from *vozderzhanie*. People complain about the rigours to be endured, and little secret is made of their inability and unwillingness to permanently suppress carnal urges. But they also pride themselves on fasting more rigorously and conscientiously than any other Christians.

Ideally, some form of dietary abstinence (*vozderzhanie*) should be observed during fast-free periods as well. Because most people are unwilling to practise voluntary restraint from food, they compensate for it by limiting the intake of strong drink. Here we come back to the status of "alcoholic" beverages derived from impure plants, an issue that is both complex and murky.

Berezovka's residents expend much energy in the manufacture of two kinds of fermented beverage, which are consumed in every household. There is, first of all, the only very mildly alcoholic *kvas*, derived from a mixture of water, bread crumbs, and berries. Local people do not consider it alcoholic, and *kvas* is drunk by young and old alike: in this respect, it can be seen as a traditional version of the North American soft drink. *Braga*, a fruit wine of considerable potency, is another story. It is prepared from berries or other types of fruit mixed with water, sugar, and yeast, and fermented under carefully controlled conditions. The effect of *braga* is comparable to that of strong wine, a parallel drawn by the Old Believers themselves when they often refer to *braga* as *vino* (wine). Like wine, it comes in both white and red varieties, and its quality depends on age.

The consumption of this beverage approaches the status of a local cult. Life without *braga*—or rather *brashka*, as it is tenderly known—would be unthinkable. Every self-respecting household head cultivates a large collection of huge plastic barrels filled with gallons and gallons of *braga*, arranged according to age, fruit base, and taste, and awaits an appropriate social occasion. Although one may empty a few cups after the main meal at home, *braga* is a social beverage whose enjoyment—and, it seems, potency—increases with the number of people who partake of it together. This can be seen at any wedding celebration, where specially appointed "waiters" do not much else but watch for empty cups, which they constantly refill. Within a few hours, most guests are fairly inebriated. At the end of the three-day celebration, the home and yard are strewn with motionless figures that must be loaded up on a truck and driven to their respective houses.

Despite the nearly universal weakness for *brashka*, many Old Believers deny its alcoholic properties. Alcohol is associated with the prohibited plants and with hard liquor, such as vodka, which is believed to derive its potency from raw alcohol added to it during the manufacturing process. Hence *vozderzhanie* is understood primarily as an abstention from strong beverages, including tea and coffee, imported from outside of Berezovka rather than as an abstention from locally produced liquor. There is, however, one apparent exception within the dichotomy of self-made and imported alcohol. Beer (*pivo*) was a popular beverage of the Old Believers in Turkey, and the *Turchane* of Oregon managed to have it exempted from the category of forbidden liquor. Still, the Turkish minority is expected to adhere to the same rules as the remaining residents of Berezovka, and public consumption of beer is not tolerated locally.

Hard, that is, imported, liquor is compared to an axe (*sekyra*) in the sense of a threat to human life. The consumption of alcohol is said to lead to the state of being hot and wild (*goriachi*), which is the opposite of the ideal of "cold" sobriety aspired to by the local residents. One could argue that the distinction between *braga* and foreign alcohol fits into the tension between water (Christianity) and blood (paganism). Unlike *braga*, an essentially "cold" drink made from river water and edible vegetables, imported liquor is a "hot" beverage whose consumption transforms the drinker into a senseless animal. Hence the effect is not at all dissimilar to the dangers associated with the eating of blood.

The differentiation between local and foreign liquor is but part of a much wider range of food and drink classified according to its origin. Just as ritual elements formulated and/or acted out by outsiders are feared as pollutants of the ritual domain, so too local natural purity is believed to depend on the isolation of food and drink from the external, "pagan" world. Where such distance is not maintained, the threat of pollution intensifies.

The belief in the defilement of food and drink as a consequence of insufficient boundaries between the inside and the outside worlds can best be demonstrated with the help of the already mentioned fear of demonic infiltration. Owing to their preference for standing water, demons are held to penetrate not only lakes and pons but any type of liquid stored over a period of time. This fear prompts the covering of all containers filled with milk, water, *braga*, or *kvas* with a lid, which is removed only to allow the liquid to be poured out. Generally speaking, the thinner the liquid, the more elaborate are the precautions that accompany its storage and consumption. Anything that is drunk must be exorcised with the sign of the cross and a short prayer, a ritual rarely omitted even by *braga*-drinkers at the height of inebriation.

Liquids must be guarded not only against contact with demons but also against the saliva of impure animals and people. The fear of contamination underlies the Old Believers' refusal to drink from a vessel employed by an outsider or to serve the latter from their own dishes. Visitors receive their share from a special set of dishes, usually made from plastic, which is known as *mirskaya posuda* or *chasha* (worldly crockery or cup). This precaution is required in view of the table manners adhered to locally, whereby soups, salads, and broths are shared by several persons, each equipped only with a separate spoon. The visitor is seated either at a different table or at a place segregated from the rest by means of a small tablecloth. The strict polarization between "Christians" and "pagans" is reminiscent of the exclusion of visitors from any ritual action, including the partaking of *sviatynia*.

The ban on eating with "pagans" is related to the latter's alleged consumption of unbled meat, impure animals, tobacco, and other defiling substances. It is observed very conscientiously, and an ignorant visitor can cause a great deal of misery by not following the rules imposed by his hosts. But even a sympathetic and fairly knowledgeable outsider can run into trouble, as I did on several occasions. Once I caused great consternation when I attempted to wash my hands in the kitchen sink, something done frequently by the Old Believers but not permitted to an impure "pagan", who would defile the dishes washed there *in the future*. Equally inappropriate was one of my less successful responses to the pressure put on me at a wedding to drink as much *braga* as other "real men". I sneaked with my full cup to the sink and emptied it with a quick gesture. One of the bystanders raised havoc, and the entire company joined in and lamented my unwise move. I was given to understand that despite my assurances of not having touched the cup with my lips, it was a "worldly" container whose contents should not be deposited in the "Christian" sink. The family would have to stop using the sink and await its purification by the *nastavnik*.

The fear of contamination is also responsible for several rules prohibiting the purchase of commercially prepared juices, ice cream, canned soups, or any other type of liquid food. Solid staples, on the other hand, such as flour, sugar, salt, and rice, may be acquired outside Berezovka. The distinction between liquids and solids makes the consumption of solid food a far less dangerous activity, and I was always encouraged to help myself to bread, pancakes, and raw vegetables from the dishes used by my hosts. What is at issue here is the role of saliva in the transmission of contamination.

Food and drink can be defiled not only by direct contact with the human or animal agent of pollution but also by being prepared with impure household utensils. The Old Believers are supposed to refrain from acquiring used equipment of this kind and to purify new, never-before used, dishes prior to their incorporation into the kitchen. Existing crockery defiled accidentally within the home environment must also be purified before being used again.

The elements involved in the cleansing of defiled dishes include prayers, water, fire, incense, and icons. Brand new objects are merely washed in the river and prayed over. Second-hand equipment, acquired from outsiders, undergoes identical treatment but only at Epiphany, when the river is held to be imbued with additional power. Dishes polluted by contact with "pagan" animals and humans must be taken to the chapel, where they are exposed to the purifying effect of icons, incense, and prayers before being cleaned with small *sviatynia*. Some informants insisted that the first step in this process requires the object to be placed in a fire, but this custom seems to be declining with the growing popularity of plastic.

There are, however, two irremediable types of defilement: the first involves any direct contact between a household dish and a dog. The second instance applies to utensils tainted by the urine of a girl. Such objects must be discarded. My informants did not explain what makes the urine of a girl that much more dangerous than that of a boy, but the distinction seems to derive from the belief that women pose inherently more of a threat to purity than men. This point is discussed further below.

The fear of being polluted as a result of physical contact with certain impure substances affects the healing methods resorted to in Berezovka. Although professional physicians are consulted for serious ailments, indigenous techniques are always tried first. Minor disorders, such as fever or muscle ache, are expected to vanish after the patient's exposure to the hot steam of the *bania*. Graver internal disorders are cured with herbs and other plants, which are administered either in the form of a strong tea, or dried, ground up, and mixed with ashes and other organic matter. Because there is no local herbalist, many patients rely on catalogues of various "herbologists" in and outside Alberta and order appropriate medicine via this route. When a professional physician must be consulted, the Old Believers strongly prefer a person with a holistic background, and they are ready to travel to Saskatchewan or British Columbia to obtain the appropriate type of treatment. One such specialist, a Korean practitioner of acupuncture from British Columbia, pays annual visits to Berezovka, and the demand for his service is considerable.

The preference for natural and holistic healing methods is understandable in view of the Old Believers' social and geographical isolation. But their fear of defilement plays some part as well. Pills and injections filled with strange-looking and -smelling matter are regarded with great suspicion, and although blood transfusion is allowed to occur when really necessary, this procedure causes considerable trepidation.

To conclude this exposition of local rules governing dietary purity, I wish to emphasize once again the inability of my informants to identify exactly the sources of these precepts. The justifications ranged from theological arguments to appeals to common sense based on hygienic considerations. For example, the distinction between pure and impure animals and plants was claimed to be derived from the Bible and orthodox "old books", but the prohibition of pork in Levithicus was discounted as a Jewish tradition which does not apply to Christians. On the other hand, Moses' alleged refusal to eat with "pagans" in Egyptian exile was acknowledged as the source of an orthodox tradition that should be adhered to by Christians as well.

The overlap between theology and hygiene can be seen in statements which I received concerning the apparent purity of wine as demonstrated in biblical writings. Those informants who were less inclined to associate the vine with Satan explained that wine used to be pure in the past, when it was manufactured at home, just as *braga* is today. Later, however, it began to be made in "factories" where hired workers crushed the fruit no longer with clean hands but with dirty feet. Who would want to drink that?

The reference to dirty feet surfaced once again when I tried to elicit information concerning the extent to which the purity precautions have changed over time. It appears that prior to the emigration from Russia, the Old Believers were allowed to purchase butter from outsiders. Upon their arrival in Manchuria, however, they were shocked to learn that local butter was apparently made by hired peasants with their feet, and it was decided not to consume such an unhygienic product. Today, living in a society preoccupied with germs and pollution, some Old Believers feel safe in relaxing some of the precautions guarding the purity of edible food and drink. This applies primarily to the class of commercially produced soft drinks, which, while still officially banned, are enjoyed occasionally. I was told that this was only a minor infraction in view of the hygienic purity surrounding the manufacturing process of these beverages.

Despite the gradual relaxation of some of the precautions regulating the flow of food and drink from the "pagan" to the "Christian" society, it would be erroneous to equate the Old Believers' understanding of hygiene with the scientific concept. Some older residents insist on washing unpeeled oranges and bananas, and I was told of several cases of the Russian children refusing oranges distributed by their teachers at school. Fruit and vegetables grown in Berezovka are, on the other hand, eaten unceremoniously, often without any type of cleaning. Hence, even in those instances where local dietary taboos seem to derive from scientific principles, religious factors are still far from irrelevant.

Appearance and Sexuality

The analysis of dietary rules is of some importance in the context of sexual behaviour. Indeed, in several respects, proper sexual conduct parallels orthodox dietary practices. Just as vegetarianism is considered more admirable than the consumption of meat, so too a life of restricted sexuality is valued more highly than an existence dominated by carnal desire: The example of the pious, chaste, and solitary *inok* (hermit, monk) is used rather often to describe ideal Christian attributes. The Old Believers do not credit many people, however, with the strength required for attaining this ideal stage. As with their diet, the people of Berezovka exhibit sexual attitudes which are designed to curb excesses without resulting in a complete suppression of sensuality.

In agreement with this strategy is the insistence on regulated sexuality, a condition defined as the conjugal relationship between two members of the opposite sex. Unregulated sexuality, such as masturbation, sodomy, pre-marital and extra-marital intercourse, is considered aberrant and sinful. Although the material collected on this topic is sketchy, it is apparent that pre-marital relations do occur sporadically, in spite of, in particular, the desirability of female virginity. Early marriage functions as one of the precautions against pregnancy and social disgrace. At the same time, it expresses local unwillingness and inability to postpone sexual gratification.

Regulated, that is, marital sexuality, is regarded with a mixture of pleasure and fear, resembling the attitude towards the consumption of tasty food. As long as obsession and gluttony are avoided, copulation and eating are accepted as normal processes of life. Both realms are controlled by rules of abstinence and moderation (*vozderzhanie*), which ensure that behaviour which is on the borderline between purity and defilement does not become excessively dangerous. This applies primarily to periods of increased ritual significance, such as fasts, as well as to the night preceding a church service, when sexual activity must not take place.

Despite the clear parallel between food and sex, the latter domain is subjected to several further precautions, which demonstrate its riskier nature. As I have already indicated, the *iconostasis* at home is equipped with curtains that can be closed when sexual intercourse takes place. Given the delicate subject matter, I refrained from a systematic inquiry into the extent of and justification for this custom. But even the incomplete evidence at my disposal demonstrates quite conclusively that what makes intercourse distasteful to the eyes of the holy figures is the animal-like passion which often accompanies it. Like excessive drunkenness, sex can be "hot" and "wild", the opposite of the ideal of restraint. But unlike alcoholism—or, for that matter, the drinking of blood—marital sexuality is not an infraction against the "law" but rather an institutionalized "breach of decorum". Hence it seems that the drawn curtain should be seen as an admission of guilt in a permitted but improper situation.

The guilt is alleviated somewhat by shifting the responsibility for sexual desire onto the woman and her primeval ancestress, Eve. The Old Believers, especially the men among them, are very fond of narrating the story of Adam's fall, and they never fail to draw the conclusion of the female gender being naturally inferior. Although Eve too is held to have been created in God's image, her status is claimed to have been intended to remain below that of Adam. This postulate is proven allegedly by the creation of the woman from the body of the man, and, as if this were not enough, from his *left* rib. Whenever the creation story was narrated, I would be encouraged to verify it by counting my ribs to see that one on the left side is missing. The fall of Adam is attributed to his foolish willingness to allow a creature that was in more than one sense his property to act autonomously. Since Eve allegedly lacked the moral will and ability to follow God's commands, she snared Adam by attracting him to her beautiful body. Ever since, the woman has been used as a bait by Satan, and her lasciviousness must be subjected to strict controls imposed by the inherently more spiritual man.

The most important visible symptom of the greater animality of women is their periodic discharge of blood in menstruation (*miesichnaya*) and childbirth. A menstruating woman is regarded as a source of defilement of the ritual domain, on account of which she is barred from the chapel. This condition does not seem to affect her natural purity, as she is allowed to engage in the usual duties, including the preparation of food. Childbirth, on the other hand, requires that the mother be segregated from the family and use her own set of dishes. The period of impurity lasts for eight days if the child is a boy and forty days if a girl. A prayer read over the mother by the *nastavnik* at the end of the purification period restores her previous status.

The onset of menopause signals the loss of the woman's natural attractiveness and, especially when combined with widowhood, some elevation of her ritual status. Currently, the responsibilities she may be entrusted with are menial compared with those of men, such as the manufacture of candles for the chapel or the sewing of the mortuary shroud. In the past, an old woman could occupy the prestigious position of *zhakharka*, the healer who cured with the help of powerful prayers. With the disappearance of this occupation after the exodus from China, female elders have lost a prestigious niche. But despite the lack of formal recognition, old women tend to be respected and even feared for their sharp tongue by Berezovka's official elders, all of whom are male.

Many of the local attitudes towards sexuality and gender distinctions are entrenched in the physical appearance of Berezovka's residents. The Old Believers stand out not only because of their robust physique, but equally because of their colourful apparel, which makes them an object of curiosity wherever they go. The rules governing the human exterior are intended to accentuate the Old Believers' orthodox status by preserving a measure of visual continuity between Christ and his early followers, and their present-day successors. The iconic principle is unmistakable in this realm, and my informants agreed that they strive to the best of their ability to emulate the appearance of saints as they are depicted in sacred images. This copying activity should, however, not be interpreted too literally. What matters is not the preservation of every detail associated with a particular famous figure, but rather the continuity of the *structure* of appearance exhibited by the early Christians. After all, the Old Believers do not see themselves as being part of a reincarnation process, but merely as guardians of those traits which should be shared by all Christians. Consequently, an adult man's beard is not expected to be identical with that of Christ, St. Paul, or St. Nicholas, but rather to preserve the attributes of the wider *Christian* prototype. The characteristics of the appearance structure can best be supplied by following the life-cycle of a male and a female resident.

The ritual reception of a new child into the Christian society has already been described, and I merely wish to point out again that the baptismal outfit is identical for boys and girls. The lack of attention to the child's sex continues to shape its appearance during the first two years or so. Both boys and girls are dressed in a simple long-sleeved shirt which reaches half-way down the thighs, and, depending on their activity, swaddling clothes.

After mastering the art of walking, children are slowly prepared for participation in ritual activities, which requires segregation between males and females. A girl receives a miniature version of the outfit worn by women, consisting of a long shirt (*rubakha*), an almost ankle-long dress (*sarafan*), and a somewhat shorter apron (*zapon*). A large kerchief (*platok*) is placed over her head on ritual and other formal occasions. A boy is equipped with long pants (*shtany*) and a long-sleeved shirt (*rubakha*), and his head remains uncovered. The far more elaborate clothing worn by girls signals an important gender-specific distinction in the tolerance of nakedness. Unlike boys, who may wander around with exposed buttocks and genitals, girls are severely

Characteristic appearance of girls. (Detmar Schmoll)

reprimanded for baring their private parts in public. A girl is taught to keep her legs together, and, during activities which make it impossible, she is furnished with long pants that are worn underneath her dress.

The unequal tolerance of male and female nakedness continues into adolescence and adulthood. Girls have understood by this time that any unnecessary exposure of flesh may be interpreted as a sign of lewdness, which could jeopardize their marital prospects. Their shirts always remain buttoned up all the way to the neck, and their arms are covered by long sleeves at all times. Boys and men, on the other hand, are permitted to expose the upper part of the chest during informal occasions, and they are increasingly becoming accustomed to wearing short-sleeved shirts when they engage in hard work in hot weather. Young women are allowed to *add* some new elements to their basic outfit, such as fashionable shoes and even earrings. But no such innovation is allowed to *replace* a traditional item.

One symbol of Christian appearance which receives extraordinary attention is the gender-specific hair style. Female hair is charged with sexual connotation and is regarded as an important component of attractiveness. Simultaneously, since its style changes with marriage, it expresses the woman's subordinate status and need for guidance. Male hair symbolizes sexual prowess and dominance over the woman. In both instances, hair is arranged in accordance with divine examples furnished by Christ and male saints on the one hand, and the Mother of God and female saints on the other.

Female hair is never cut. This prohibition was explained to me as a strategy aimed at emphasizing its beauty and at the same time maintaining the contrast with men, whose hair must be kept short. Prior to adolescence, a girl wears her hair loose or tied in a single braid. The latter arrangement prevails during the courting period, when the braid signals virginity and availability. The braid (*kosa*) is sold symbolically to the groom by the bride's brother on the eve of the wedding, expressing the girl's transfer from one household to another. Then, during the already described crowning ceremony (*zavienchanie*), the bride's hair is modified into a double braid, which signifies marriage.

From this point on, the woman's hair must remain covered at all times. The triple layer (*chin*)—consisting of a thin cap worn directly on top of the hair (*shoshmura*), a larger cap or small kerchief (*sorochka*), and a large kerchief falling over the shoulders and concealing the neck (*platok*)—is interpreted as a sign of submission to the husband, who, symbolically, is placed above his wife's head. In future, the only man allowed to see the hair exposed will be the husband, the sole legitimate sexual partner.

The hair of boys and men is kept short, so as, I was told, to facilitate communication with God, who is considered the "head" of men. This departure from iconographic examples—which depict Christ and male saints with long hair—is justified with reference to the congregation's priestless status. Only an ordained priest, bishop, or some other ecclesiastic is worthy of imitating Christ's long hair—or correspondingly, of covering his head in church. Ordinary laymen must keep their hair short and bare their heads in church. I suspect, however, that short male hair has an additional sexual connotation, expressed in the local injunction

Young boys with traditional hair style. (Detmar Schmoll)

against women cutting the hair of men or boys or even witnessing the event.

A more explicit symbol of male sexual ritual maturity is the beard. Like the hair of women and girls, the beard may not in any way be tampered with. However, Berezovka's girls express a strong preference for suitors with smooth skin, and the plucking of unwanted facial hair is known to be practiced secretly. Once married, a young man is unlikely to obstruct the growth of his beard, as it gives him access to full social and ritual participation. Beardless visitors are ridiculed and likened to women. Particular contempt is shown for men with moustaches, who are said to resemble cats.

There is a strong motif underlying the local appearance structure, which consists of a reluctance to "falsify" one's natural appearance. The argument goes that since humans are created in the image of God, any artificial intervention in the creation process would distance the creator from His "product" and perhaps wipe out the divine imprint altogether. Consequently, the Old Believers fear that a person who has modified his or her "true" appearance with plastic surgery, cosmetic aids, a wig, or dyed hair will not be recognized by God and will be treated as any other violator of the iconic principle. This fear underlies the local rejection of cosmetics (lips covered with lipstick may not kiss an icon), shaving, or any other significant modification of the "original" body.

Worst of all is the fate of deceased pious persons who, through no fault of their own, are subjected to an autopsy. It is expected that because they are missing certain parts of the body, victims of autopsies will experience difficulty in resurrecting. The "passport" certifying the bearer's Christian status is hoped to alleviate his or her suffering, but many people are genuinely afraid that their mutilated bodies will be unrecognized by God.

The strong desire to pass through life without a major distortion of the image received at birth is perhaps best reflected in the parallel between a baby and a corpse. As has already been pointed out, it is only at birth and at death that all social and sexual distinctions are disregarded. One enters the world as a *Christian*, and one hopes to leave it in the same way. The similarity between the baptismal and the death shroud underlines the desire to minimize the impact of the years separating birth and death. After all, the longer ones lives, the more removed one becomes from the sinless existence of early childhood, or, in other words, the fainter the imprint of God's image. By structuring death as a second birth, one's original image is renewed.

Old Belief in Context

What are we to make of all the ethnographic details amassed in the preceding chapters? What, if any, relevance do the people of Berezovka have for the study of society and culture? I attempt to provide several answers to such questions in this concluding chapter. My concern here is still to grasp the essence of the beliefs and values embraced by "my people", but instead of looking at them from within, I now modify my perspective to observe them from afar.

The widened angle of my analysis invites comparison with other societies that share some of the Old Believers' principal traits, and it encourages a multidisciplinary search for models which can bring us a little further towards grasping the context in which Old Orthodoxy has evolved. The main thrust of my argument is that the examination of Berezovka's culture provides a vivid illustration of some rather important but largely neglected differences between eastern and western Christianity. Theologians, church historians, and religious scientists are not generally inclined to pay much attention to dietary prohibitions, the configuration of fingers in the sign of the cross, the composition of holy water, the depiction of Christ the crucified, and a myriad of other details which the people of Berezovka employ in their definition of orthodoxy. Such indicators of faith are usually glossed over or treated as an example of "folk religion", which, as an aberration of true religion, is delegated to anthropologists, folklorists, and similar specialists in cultural idiosyncrasies. Yet as I try to show in this chapter, the ideas of the Old Believers about orthodoxy are not idiosyncratic bits and pieces which possess no relevance beyond an obscure community in northern Alberta. They are the manifestation of divergent developments in eastern and western Christian attitudes to the relationship between ritual and dogma, between the home and the church, and between the present and the past. Far from confining us to an isolated community, the study of Berezovka's culture helps us grasp some unrecognized differences between Russia and the West, and, at an even higher level, between tradition and modernity.

In a nutshell, then, I try to demonstrate here the feasibility of extending the anthropological analysis of a small community—which has been the traditional focus of the discipline—to encompass national and even supranational cultures. Such an increase in scope, especially in as underdeveloped a field as Russian studies, must by necessity involve the construction of new models by trial and error. What follows here is not a watertight theory but rather a wide-ranging exploration in search of such models.

Puritanism

Perhaps the most striking feature of Berezovka's Old Believers is their fastidious separation of things considered pure from those held to be impure. As we have seen, this polarization pervades the entire physical and social universe, extending all the way from the contrast between Christians and pagans to the dichotomies of water:blood, incense:tobacco, *krest:krizh*, and Christ:antichrist. It is anchored in the injunction against "mixing up" (*pomeshanie*), which is so important in shaping Berezovka's culture that one cannot imagine the Old Believers surviving as a distinct society without that polarizing tendency.

In her seminal *Purity and Danger*, Mary Douglas identifies the separation of purity and pollution as a universal social preoccupation stemming from the ever-present fear of chaos and disorder (1966:2-4). Following in the footsteps of Emile Durkheim and Marcel Mauss, Douglas reiterates the main conclusion of their *Primitive Classification* (1903) by suggesting that, far from reflecting some scientific or proto-scientific concerns with hygiene, categories of purity and pollution express ideas about *social* relations (1966:128). This means, for example, that minority groups which feel threatened are more likely to erect boundaries based on the pure:impure dichotomy than are groups whose members feel secure in their position. In this manner, pollution beliefs can and often do crystallize into full-fledged ideologies which justify various forms of *apartheid*.

Douglas' sociological model of "puritanism" can be easily applied to the Old Believers with their long history of marginality and persecution. Indeed, as I argue further on, ample evidence suggests that the borderline existence thrust upon the Old Believers following the *raskol* contributed significantly to the elaboration of their views on purity and pollution. But it would be unwise to attribute the origins of such views to the schism itself. The purity system encountered in Berezovka is of much greater antiquity than the *raskol*, and we must immerse ourselves in the early Christian era in order to grasp its roots.

During the first five centuries of its existence, the Christian church underwent numerous internal conflicts as it sought to define the basic tenets of the new faith. Perhaps the gravest dispute pitched theologians who subscribed to *monism*—a doctrine which holds God responsible for the entire creation, including evil forces—against those who attributed evil to a second creator, an "anti-god" independent of God. The latter theology of *dualism*—represented particularly well by the Gnostics—was eventually repudiated by the church as heresy, but it left an indelible imprint on Christian diabology (Russell 1981). For centuries to come, while the western as well as the eastern church emphasized the monist view of God as the sole source of good *and* evil (Pelikan 1974:221), manifold dualistic currents continued to spread the view of the devil as a competitor rather than a servant of God.

These dualistic tendencies made themselves felt more in the East than in the West (Pelikan 1974:216-220; Russell 1984:28-51), and they were eminently suitable as a theological justification for the polarization of purity and pollution. Building upon the ancient Jewish purity system, early Christian theologians, such as Tertullian and Origen, developed a systematic diabology in which the devil, or antichrist, came to play the part of the master over physical and corruptible elements, while God, or Christ, exercised control over spiritual and eternal elements. This dualistic arrangement lent itself to the conceptualization of existence as an ongoing cosmic battle between God and Satan, which involved humanity in the form of a struggle between Christians and pagans, orthodoxy and heresy, spirituality and sensuality, all of which manifested itself in the constant requirement to distinguish purity from defilement. Mindful of Tertullian's warning that "God plants a field with wheat, and the Devil strews it with weeds" (in Russell 1981:95), the early Christians were expected to internalize the distinction between purity and pollution as a weapon against Satan's desire "to destroy the truth, corrupt virtue, and pollute beauty" (Tertullian quoted in Russell 1981:95).

The essential properties of the early Christian purity system resemble very closely that adhered to by the Old Believers of Berezovka. The affinity, and the dualism of both, is nicely summarized in Origen's view of demons as the principal messengers of Satan and transmitters of pollution. Each person, he argued, possesses a guardian angel and a demon, with the latter trying to invade the body through ingested impure food, such as pagan meals and blood (Boeckenhoff 1903:55-59; Russell 1981:135). Later assertions that demons and other forces of evil were repelled by rivers and fresh water in general (Russell 1981:191) contributed to the entrenchment of the association between blood and illness, and water and health.

The specific features of Berezovka's model of food purity derive from the Old Testament, but they found their way into Christian culture via Greek Orthodoxy. At the beginning of this process was the Synod of Jerusalem, held in the year 48 in order to reconcile Jewish and Christian views on purity. It demanded abstention from "things sacrificed to idols" and from "blood and what is strangled" (Acts 14:29). In view of the rejection elsewhere in the New Testament (Mk 7:15; Matt 15:11; I Tim 4:4) of the Mosaic idea that any part of nature could have a defiling effect on humans, the synodal injunction against blood and carrion has been interpreted as a metaphorical admonition against violence (Boeckenhoff 1903; Cochrane 1974; Dix 1953; Hennisch 1976). However, possibly as a result of the elaboration of demonology in subsequent centuries, with its emphasis on pollution as a physical rather than merely spiritual condition, some local councils began to tolerate the distinction between *clean* and *unclean* food, albeit with the qualification that it derived from human rather than divine taste (Boeckenhoff 1903:129). Eventually, this concession to human weakness changed into a *prohibition* of unclean food and found its way into some Greek penitentials. With the exception of the swine—defined as pure and edible in direct contradiction to the Jewish law—the Orthodox model of dietary purity derived in most details from Levithicus (Boeckenhoff 1903:130-135).

Events took a different turn in the West, where the Latin church fell short even of the minimal injunction against blood (Boeckenhoff 1903:69; Haberland 1887,17:364; Hein 1973:84). At first, this unwillingness to enforce an apparently authoritative dictum led to mild rebukes from the East—such as the disapproving reference to the eating of sausages made by the Sixth Ecumenical Council (*Kormchaia kniga* 1650:199)—which grew sterner as they were repeated over and over again by the Patriarch of Constantinople and other dignitaries of the Greek church (Popov 1875:9-13, 33-36. 46).

While the hierarchs took the Latins to task for violating an indisputably traditional principle, members of the lower clergy and private citizens expressed indignation over departures from uncanonical and specifically eastern views on dietary purity. Thus the western "Franks" were rebuked by their Byzantine brethren for allegedly drinking from glasses that had contained blood (Geanakoplos 1976:166), for feeding dogs from plates used by humans (*ibid.*), and for eating hedgehogs, bears, otters, turtles, crows and "even filthier animals" (Geanakoplos 1976:167; Popov 1875:62). These accusations increased in intensity as the two churches drifted apart in the course of the Middle Ages.

It was the Greek *folk* system of dietary purity which penetrated Kievan and later Muscovite Rus'. As in Byzantium, the Muscovite distinction between pure and impure food reflected the Mosaic laws (Kostomarov 1905:70; Kozhanchikov 1863:260; Smirnov 1914:121-136; Zelenin 1927: 116-117), and the Latins were held in contempt for their postulated proclivity for sharing meals with dogs, drinking blood, and eating the meat of defiled animals (Akademiya nauk SSSR, 1941:351; Arkheograficheskaya kommissiya 1897:60; *Kormchaia kniga* 1650:16). Unlike in Greece, where the church saw no harm in its members' sharing meals with the Franks, Muscovite clerics warned of the consequences of any intimate contact with westerners, including the sharing of food and drink (Pavlov 1908:54, 62, 102; Popov 1875:318; Smirnov 1914:73-75, 121-126, 144-146).

Moving into the realm of ritual purity, there is a clear continuity between the Byzantine and the Russian definition of proper baptism. The insistence on performing the sacrament with a triple *immersion* goes back to the formative era of Christianity (Bullough 1963; Hein 1973), and it was reinforced as a result of the Latin tendency to substitute *effusion* for immersion. That prompted some Greek clerics to deny the validity of western baptism (Dvornik 1961:54; Geanakoplos 1984:208-210), foreshadowing objections raised by the Old Believers. The same can be said about the sign of the cross, which developed in early Christianity as a shield against the devil (Russell 1981:100). Following centuries of indiscriminate usage, the heretical Monophysites—who denied Christ's divinity and dwelled on his humanity—adopted the habit of erecting a single finger, to which the Orthodox responded with two fingers (Koch 1962:95). At some point during the Middle Ages, the Latins came to sign themselves with all five fingers joined, and by touching the left shoulder before the right one (Cabrol & Leclercq 1914:3144; Popov 1875:64). This departure from the common tradition triggered protests in the Greek church (Geanakoplos 1976:166; Popov 1875:64).

Sacred words constitute another significant ingredient of the Orthodox purity system which connects the Old Believers with Byzantine models. The link made in Berezovka between incorrectly copied or pronounced words and the antichrist as the source of heresy has roots in early Christianity (Hefele 1896:232; Russell 1981:95) and especially in Eastern Orthodoxy, where it seems to have been taken far more seriously than in the West. The postulated association between wrong prayers and the devil led to the exclusion of pagans and heretics from all Christian rituals (Hein 1973:315; *Kormchaia kniga* 1650:3,21,50,73,79)—a practice still prominently observed in Berezovka.

In their appearance too, the people of Berezovka adhere to principles sanctified by the Greek church. This applies particularly to the Byzantine injunction against any significant distortion of one's natural image. Indebted to the iconic relationship postulated between God and humanity in the Old Testament (Gen 1:27), the prohibition of wigs, make-up, hair-dye, and similar beauty aids (I

Tim 2:9; Cooper 1971:101-102; Haussig 1971:126; Mango 1980:225-228) which we encounter in the early Christian and Byzantine literature was explicitly directed against Satan's desire to falsify the truth of creation (Russell 1981:95, 99). This fight culminated in the demand of the church that clergy refrain from shaving out of respect for Christ—a call that was heeded in the East as well as the West (Cross 1958:144; Reynolds 1950:99-101). In the course of the second half of the first millennium, however, Roman Catholic ecclesiastics aborted the custom, leading to protracted conflict with the East (Popov 1875:9-13; Reynolds 1950:106) and eventually culminating in the first schism in 867 (Geanakoplos 1984:208-212).

This short overview of the parallels between the key symbols of purity and pollution in Berezovka and Byzantium could be continued, but for now it suffices to have demonstrated a clear continuity between the two systems. Whether we examine food, baptism, iconography, religious formulas, or appearance, we discover that most of the markers employed in Berezovka to distinguish "Christians" from "pagans" served the same function in early Greek Orthodoxy. In both settings the sign of the cross, the triple immersion, the beard, and the abstention from blood and other unclean food serve as an important badge of orthodoxy and as a weapon against the devil.

The continuity between Byzantium and Berezovka must not obscure an important transformation of the Greek purity system in Muscovy. I alluded to it in the description of the evolution of dietary practices when I indicated that while Greek clerics saw little harm in the sharing of meals with western Christians, their Russian colleagues preached against it. What we see here is the nucleus of the Kievan and Muscovite proclivity to apply purity rules employed in Byzantium only in the *ritual* realm to a much wider gamut of settings. The warning against the sharing of *ordinary* meals with western "pagans" is a case in point, because it grew out of occasional refusals of Greek clergy to admit Latin visitors to partake of the Eucharist (Popov 1875:9-13; Reynolds 1950:106). Another instance of the tendency to extend ritual prohibitions to the secular domain is afforded by the treatment of beards. As numerous paintings demonstrate, the demand for beards applied in Byzantium only to the clergy, and secular dignitaries, including some emperors, continued to prefer a clean shaven face (Haussig 1971). Such a state of affairs was unthinkable in Muscovy, where the church insisted, successfully, that all men imitate Christ by letting their beards grow (Buslaev 1861,2:228; Kozhanchikov 1863:124; Pavlov 1908:880).

The Russian extension of "ritual value" (Radcliffe-Brown 1952) to a domain which in Byzantium remained unmarked was combined with an elaboration of the imported purity system. Whether we consider food, appearance, sacraments, or rituals, where the Greeks insisted on one or two criteria to certify their orthodox status, the Russians stipulated a few more. For example, the bread used in the Eucharist could no longer be baked with *any* water; its preparation now required river water *warmed up* to the temperature of the Holy Spirit (*Kniga o vere* 1648:48-49; Kozhanchikov 1863:68).

How can we explain the explosion in the number of rules guarding the domain of purity? I think that it is useful to try and distinguish at this point two types of concern with purity maintenance. The first kind is a more or less permanent form of purism which is absorbed, often in conjunction with religious dualism or some other expression of binary oppositions, as a relatively stable cultural routine, which may persist in the same form for centuries. The second kind, on the other hand, is a dynamic and unfolding purism that comes into being as part of a social movement, which escalates the search for perfection and hence accentuates the gulf between good and evil, lie and truth, defilement and purity. Because of its association with a specific historical phenomenon, the accelerated quest for purity may be designated as *puritanism*. The distinction has blurred edges, but I think it is useful to consider the transformation undergone by the Byzantine purity system in Russia as an example of the change of ordinary, stable *purism* into *puritanism* triggered by a social movement.

The phenomenon of puritan movements has recently received attention from a group of Dutch anthropologists and religious scientists. The analysis, which ranges from the English Puritans to Islamic fundamentalists and Soviet communists, postulates that all puritans are driven "by an inexorable desire to cleanse the world and themselves of evil" (Velzen & Beek 1988:3). The mind set that gives rise to such a desire is apparently susceptible to a degree of polarization by which everything is assigned on the basis of the *either/or* principle: "The world is divided between good and evil with no ground in between, and a person who tries to create a neutral territory where parties can negotiate their differences stands condemned" (*ibid.*:24). Evil is apparently associated with physical comfort, sexual pleasure, free will, and disrespect for tradition (*ibid.*7-9), which explains why art is frowned upon as frivolity and science distrusted as a potential source of conflict with religious dogma. The past is glorified as the revelation of Truth, and the future is awaited only to the extent that it promises to bring about a return of the culture hero who is venerated as the source of perfection (*ibid.*:14-15).

It requires little imagination to fit late-sixteenth- and early seventeenth-century Muscovy into this model. Threatened by the influx of western ideas, the traditionalists who joined the Zealots of Piety and similar revivalist circles shared the same concerns as the followers of Calvin in Geneva, the Puritans of New England, or the clerics of the Iranian Islamic Republic: they wanted to expel evil from their midst. And they went about doing it by adhering to a pattern which, in view of the puritan unwillingness to tolerate a secular, neutral domain in between good and evil, was predictable: they burned musical instruments, smashed pictures that smacked of "profanity", banned the use of alcohol, and converted tobacco into Satan's weed. As is customary in societies in the grip of puritanism (Velzen & Beek 1988:11), the Muscovite movement against evil dissolved the distinction between civil and religious authority, and placed the *Book* above all mundane concerns.

According to Velzen and Beek, puritanism is a "greedy ideology" which is rarely sustained over a long period of time (1988:16). Eventually, the quest for purity leads to the realization that it makes ordinary human life exceedingly difficult, and the massive support characteristic of the early stages dwindles. At this point, when the larger society has resumed its indifference to puritanical fervour, the latter can be preserved through the colonization of new lands where isolation and hard work counteract doubt (*ibid.*:22-23). Once they secede, the puritans withdraw from the "City on the Hill"—the New Jerusalem—and disperse into small "island communities" where "there is little to gain from interaction with the enemy, nothing to learn, nothing useful to expect" (*ibid.*:10).

The *raskol* and, subsequent to it, the reforms enacted by Peter the Great, forced the Muscovite puritans to abandon the Third Rome and to seek refuge in rural communities resembling Berezovka. Here, far from forsaking the puritanical zeal of their ancestors, the Old Believers added a further layer to the Byzantine foundation. The contribution they made to the ancient purity system was twofold. For one, they further restricted the unmarked ground between clean and unclean phenomena, intensifying the polarity of their brand of Orthodoxy. Second, the Old Believers brought about a more complete overlap between the theory and the practice of the Muscovite purity maintenance than had been the case prior to the schism.

This trend can best be demonstrated with examples drawn from the realm of food and drink. Unlike the Greeks, whose purity precautions did not extend beyond food derived from animals, the Muscovites displayed a preoccupation with products made from "alcoholic" plants, such as hops, vine, and tobacco. Arguing that these plants were used by the devil to confuse Christian minds, Russian moralists preached against the consumption of beer, wine, and tobacco in most every religious tractate (Akademiya nauk SSSR 1947:90, 1948:288,334; *Kniga o vere* 1648:124-132; Kostomarov 1860, 1:137-138, 2:427-435, 447-449; Kozhanchikov 1863:166,299). In the case of tobacco, the rapidly spreading view that it constituted a ritual pollutant which defiled icons (Baron 1967:146; Rushchinskii 1871:99) prepared the ground for an outright ban imposed in 1634 (Rushchinskii 1871:99). This opinion was clearly at odds with Greek practice, and the discrepancy contributed to Muscovite criticism of the mother church (Aleppo 1873:64; Bolshakov 1903:22-23).

But when we examine the degree to which the clerical campaign against alcohol and tobacco found a response among ordinary people, we detect widespread indifference and resistance. Far from evoking fear, hops continued to be used as a fertility symbol (Olearius 1656:215), and the brewing of beer retained its ancient image of health and sociability (Staden 1964:215). Wine, beer, hopped *braga*, and strong spirits introduced from the West are reported to have been consumed on a scale unknown in other

European countries (Olearius 1656:30; Smith & Christian 1984). In spite of the harsh penalties meted out to Muscovites caught snuffing and smoking—reportedly their noses were cut off (Ruschinskii 1871:99)—the use of tobacco spread like a wild fire (Laufer 1924).

Overwhelming evidence indicates that the considerable discrepancy that prevailed in Muscovy between the theological and the popular view of intoxicants was not tolerated in Old Believer communities. This applies particularly to tobacco, which, because of its postulated defiling effect on icons, was universally shunned (Akademiya nauk SSSR 1947:89, 92; Begunov 1969:511; Goehlert 1863:485; Kaindl 1897:360; Kelsiev 1866:435; Popova 1928:23; Rochow 1799:412; Tetzner 1908:351).

Unlike ordinary Russians (Olearius 1656:597-600), the Old Believers perceived tea and coffee as intoxicants and refrained from their use almost as conscientiously as from tobacco (Andreev 1870:135; Blomkvist and Grinkova 1930:33; Goehlert 1863:485; Kaindl 1897:360; Kelsiev 1866:427, 434; Popova 1928:14; Tetzner 1908:352; Zelenin 1927:117). Both beverages were associated with the antichrist and his allies, the fallen Latins and Greeks (Akademiya nauk SSSR 1947:90-91, 1948:335; Andreev 1870:135; Blomkvist & Grinkova 1930:33).

This unqualified opposition of the Old Believers to coffee, tea, and tobacco appears as somewhat of an anomaly. Ethnographic evidence indicates that plant products are rarely defined as pollutants (Schurtz 1893:14-16), and when they are, the restrictions to which they are subjected usually fail to find widespread support. This is demonstrated in the case of tobacco, which, following its introduction to Europe and Asia in the late sixteenth and early seventeenth century, encountered occasional clerical and civil resistance similar to that reported from Muscovy (Cudell 1927; Fisher 1939; Laufer 1924; Mackenzie 1957). But wherever the initial bans endured, they were clearly defined as *ritual* prohibitions, which had no bearing on behaviour outside the ritual setting. The papal bulls issued in the West against snuffing and smoking are a good case in point. They proscribed the use of tobacco in church, but once outside, clergy and laity alike were free to indulge in the new vice (Cudell 1927:70-71; Fisher 1939:61). A similar situation is reported from seventeenth-century

New England, where the Puritans could smoke as much as they pleased except within two miles of the church (Mackenzie 1957:150).

Tea and coffee have never encountered ritually-motivated sanctions in the West, but some Islamic societies have occasionally tried to regulate the use of coffee on religious grounds. Using the argument that coffee was an intoxicant which, akin to alcohol, exposes the "drunk" to the machinations of the devil, several influential clerics in sixteenth-century Arabia, Egypt, and Turkey tried to make its consumption illegal (Hattox 1985). Their opposition was effectively silenced by experiments which established that far from dulling the mind, coffee made it more alert and thus receptive to God (Hattox 1985:58-60).

The ability of the Old Believers, then, to effectively ban the use of tobacco, tea, and coffee for more than three centuries is quite exceptional. Although the classification of these three substances as intoxicants facilitated their incorporation into the Orthodox model of purity and pollution, it is probable that at least tea and coffee were classified in this manner not because of empirically established conclusions, but rather in consequence of their foreign origin. Beginning with hops and vine, the trend to associate products introduced from abroad with defilement and the devil gathers momentum with tobacco, to be extended to tea and coffee, and later even to potatoes (Akademiya nauk SSSR 1947:89, 91; Andreev 1870:135; Dal 1862:909; Zelenin 1927:117), pepper (Tetzner 1908:352), and several exotic spices. This trend demonstrates that while the Muscovites were unwilling to censor *plant* products without real evidence of their harmful consequences, the Old Believers inferred the latter simply on account of the plant's foreign origin. At times the use of such exotic products evoked so much resistance that anything defined as "vegetables from beyond the sea" (*zamorskiya ovoshchi*) was classified as a pollutant (Unkrieg 1933:81).

Unmistakable traces of a growing proclivity to attribute defilement to sources outside one's own society can be seen in the virtually universal exclusion of non-"Christians" from Old Orthodox prayers and meals. The ban on the participation of "pagans" in religious services (Ammann 1937:190; Arsenii 1885:169-170; Goehlert 1863:484; Kaindl 1897:360; Marchadier

1977:443; Rochow 1799:420; Subbotin 1881:279; Vasilev 1694) can be seen as a mere continuation of a well-established Muscovite tradition. The reluctance to share meals with outsiders, on the other hand, realized its full potential only among the Old Believers. Despite the already noted clerical exhortations to this effect, there is no evidence proving that foreigners were indeed excluded from Muscovite meals. On the contrary, we know from eyewitnesses that some western visitors received treatment that was normally reserved for the most esteemed guests (Olearius 1656:206). The literature is unequivocal with respect to the Old Believers' unwillingness to admit outsiders to their tables (Andreev 1870:129; Crummey 1970:120; Gerss 1909:57, 1910:416; Goehlert 1863:484; Iwaniec 1977:282; Katunskii 1972:89; Kolarz 1961:146; Peskov 1982; Vasilev 1694:41-45; Zhuravlev 1831:135). It became famous throughout the country and even entered the repertoire of Russian proverbs (Dal 1862:908).

This review of the history of Orthodox puritanism could be continued for many more pages with examples from several other domains, all of them demonstrating the same pattern. Whether we look at rules governing proper diet, appearance, sexual conduct, iconography, or ritual behaviour, we see the Old Believers as exemplifying an approach to matters of purity and pollution that could be termed "Pharisaic". Grounded in Eastern dualism, Greek susceptibility to folk models based on the Mosaic law, and Muscovite elaboration of this heritage as part of the ideological war with the West, the Old Orthodox Pharisaism must be regarded as the culmination of a centuries-long development during which evil and defilement came to be viewed as external agents attacking from without the community of the faithful. This process of Pharisaic intensification can be fruitfully discussed bearing in mind the Durkheimian dictum—popularized in this context by Mary Douglas (1966), Edmund Leach (1964), and S.J. Tambiah (1973)—that ritual boundaries reflect social boundaries. As the number of "Christians" declined, and the size of the "pagan" class magnified, the perception of external threat intensified, leading to a progressive accumulation of pollutants. Such a "social distance" model (Leach 1964) helps to clarify parallels between defiling things and defiling people. But it fails to account for the extraordinary durability of the Old Orthodox puritanism. It is difficult to imagine that any society could sustain the exceptionally intricate and demanding pollution avoidance of the Old Believers for more than three centuries merely as a symbolic enactment of the distinction between "us" and "them". Once the persecution and hysteria of the years and decades following the *raskol* abated, when the collective suicides and hopeless insurrections gave way to a fairly secure frontier existence, why didn't the whipped-up purity precautions weaken and revert to the more manageable levels prevalent in Byzantine and early Muscovite society? Why is it that the Old Orthodox puritanism failed to consume itself—as it should have, being a "greedy ideology"—and instead has flourished, virtually unmodified, until present times?

I offer several explanations for the durability of the Old Orthodox purity system further below. One hypothesis, however, should be suggested immediately, because it provides an alternative to the Durkheimian social distance model. Instead of interpreting purity maintenance and pollution avoidance as *symbolic* statements representing ideas about social relations, we could regard them as having an inherent value, which makes them indispensable for the survival of the society in question. What I am suggesting here is to consider the possibility that the intensified puritanism developed by the Old Believers constituted and, as far as Berezovka goes, still constitutes, the prerequisite for the maintenance of Orthodoxy under the conditions imposed by the schism.

The conditions faced by the Old Believers in consequence of the *raskol* not only deepened the gulf between the "Christians" and the surrounding, "pagan" society. They also threatened to generate a gulf between the Old Believers and the very Orthodoxy defended by them. The second, far more serious danger, arose out of the determination to make do without the reformed, Nikonian, church. When Avvakum denounced the Eucharist offered by the official priests as "communion of Antichrist" (Avvakum 1974:439,447; Smirnov 1898:94-95), when he dismissed the modified baptism ritual as an invocation of the devil (Avvakum 1974:447), and finally, when he advised true Christians to gather all Nikonian liturgical objects "and together with the Host put it all in a sack and throw it into the water with a stone attached" (in Andreyev 1961:43), he and other early leaders of the *raskolniki* were generating favourable conditions for the kind of "sacramental vacuum" encountered by the Old Believers after the loss of the old priesthood. Since then, the history of Old Orthodoxy has been dominated by a search for substitutes to fill the sacramental vacuum, and I suggest that the preoccupation with purity maintenance should be seen as an important component of this search.

The link between priesthood and purity is self-evident. In so far as God is the source of perfection, and to the extent that contact with God depends on institutionalized intermediaries who administer sacraments and perform liturgical services, priesthood, at least in Eastern Orthodoxy, is a precondition for proper purity maintenance. This is made evident even by the people of Berezovka who, despite the bravado with which they claim the status of chosen people, acknowledge that the absence of priests deprives them of complete liturgy, sacraments, and other components of Christian purity maintenance. I see this recognition as the impetus for a search for alternatives. Given their greater susceptibility to pollution, it would seem mandatory that people who lack the full range of cleansing methods prescribed by the religion they follow, pay increased attention to the threat of defilement and their own responsibility for avoiding it. In this way, radical views embraced originally only by semi-fanatical clerics find their way to peasant families, purity precautions observed traditionally in church are transposed to the home environment, and what may have begun as a puritan *movement* solidifies into a durable condition that can outlast centuries.

The "sacramental deprivation" hypothesis explains important discrepancies in purity maintenance between priestly and priestless Old Believers. These emerged in the latter part of the nineteenth century when, after two centuries of a considerable shortage of priests, the *popovtsy* had managed to set up an independent church in Austria, which renewed the supply of Old Orthodox clergy. Very quickly, the leaders of this church lifted most of the purity precautions observed at home, including the ban on tea, coffee, tobacco (*Tserkov* 1911/1985, 21:20), "unclean" animals (*Tserkov* 1910/1985, 21:29,31), and modern dress (*Tserkov* 1980, 3:11). But the most revealing departure from traditional views on purity is manifested in the desegregation of "Christians" and "pagans" during meals. Arguing that the practice of preventing

contact between the two categories should be confined to the partaking of the Eucharist, the theologians of the new church dis-
turbed the overlap between natural and ritual purity maintenance
which is so characteristic of the Old Belief (Arsenii 1885:170-172;
Blomkvist & Grinkova 1930:35; *Tserkov* 1912/1980, 2:25-56).

The sacramental deprivation theory receives further support
from the work conducted by Jacob Neusner in the field of Judaic
studies. Investigating the consequences of the destruction of the
Temple for the Jewish purity system, Neusner describes a situation
that bears more than a superficial resemblance to the *raskol* and
the Old Believers' adaptation to it. Like the Old Believers, the
Jews lost access to the traditional source of purification, which
was confined to the Temple (Neusner 1983:5-13). With the disappearance of the cultic centre, the priesthood could no longer
fulfil the role of the intermediary between God and the believers,
and the responsibility for purity maintenance came to rest on the
shoulders of ordinary people (*ibid.*:61). This, according to Neusner, led to a preoccupation with defilement as a physical rather
than a metaphorical state (1973:54), and to the extension of rules
observed previously only in the Temple to the home environment
(*ibid.*:70). It was in this context that the Pharisees acquired the
reputation for puritan extremism. Insisting that the home was a
reflection of the Temple, they "arrogated to themselves—and to
all Jews equally—the status of the Temple priests and did the
things which priests must do on account of that status" (*ibid.*:65).
What Neusner describes here is exactly the same overlap between
natural and ritual purity maintenance as that so fastidiously adhered to by the Old Believers.

Ritualism

The preoccupation with purity exhibited by the Old Believers
is, for a Christian society, not only unusually elaborate but also
unexpectedly materialistic. Unlike the Calvinists of Geneva, London, or New England, or, for that matter, the American fundamentalists who play the role of puritans in contemporary
Christianity, the Old Believers seem far more interested in concrete, material details of the food they eat, the icons they pray to,

and the rituals they participate in than in abstract dogmata of faith. Indeed, western fundamentalists would have difficulty recognizing themselves in the Old Orthodox insistence on ritual exactness, or in the belief that defilement is more than a spiritual condition whose source is insufficient faith in God. In all these respects, the puritans of Berezovka have more in common with Islamic fundamentalists than with their western counterparts (Velzen & Beek 1988:5-7).

This high regard for the material aspects of religion has been associated with Russian Orthodoxy for centuries. What is particularly noteworthy about this connection is the claim advanced by many commentators that the formalism of Russian Christians goes hand in hand with, or is even the result of, ignorance of doctrinal issues. In other words, the hyper-attention to the *form* of religion is directly or indirectly attributed to an inability to discern its *content*.

This view was coined by early western travellers who, with hardly an exception, perceived the Russians as deficient Christians (Olearius 1656:275). Adam Olearius, an eminent seventeenth-century scientist, quipped that while elsewhere Christianity signified charity, in Muscovy it meant little else but the construction of churches and monasteries (*ibid.*:277). Playing on the contrast between (outer) form and (inner) content, he observed about Moscow: "From the outside, the city glistens like Jerusalem, but from within, it looks like Bethlehem" (*ibid.*:147). His contemporary, the Croatian Jesuit Juraj Krizhanich, made use of the same inner:outer dichotomy when claiming that the Muscovites cling "to the *rituals* of religion with great superstition" while being "completely ignorant of *theology*" (Letiche & Dmytryshyn 1990:54,61, my emphasis).

Modern scholarship has continued this line of interpretation. James Billington, an eminent historian of Russia, has argued that Kievan Rus' absorbed the Byzantine architecture, iconography, ceremoniousness, and other "outer" attributes of Orthodoxy, but failed to adopt its scholarship, thus encouraging the rise of a religion which emphasized "concrete beauty rather than abstract ideas" (Billington 1970:7). Similar conclusions have been reached by Russian scholars, such as Geoge Fedotov, who is the only modern historian with an eye for the Orthodox preoccupation with purity maintenance. Commenting on the "Judaistic" attention of his countrymen to ritual detail (Fedotov 1975:182), he postulated that

> From early Christian times to the present, the Russian has been finding his way to God through the bodily senses, all five of them; not only through sight by means of icons, and hearing by means of the Church chant, but also through touch by kissing, smell by means of incense...and taste by sacred bread, water, and all kinds of consecrated food. (*ibid.*:196-197)

Where should we search for the source of this interest in the "ritual side of religion"? In Fedotov's opinion, it is a *defect* associated with the "primitive mind" and the "semibarbarian" features of early Russian Christians (*ibid.*:182,196).

It will be remembered from chapter 2 that the ritualism of Kievan and Muscovite Orthodoxy became unfashionable in the course of the eighteenth century. Once the western view of spirituality as the proper expression of faith had been accepted by the reformed church, it became possible and indeed desirable to distance Russian Orthodoxy from the formalism which had been its trademark since the formative period. Those who failed to see the shortcomings of the past, such as the Old Believers, served as a warning about the consequences of what now came to be called "empty" ritualism. Accusing them of "praying with the body rather than the spirit" (Lopatinskii 1745:11), the already quoted Bishop Lopatinskii and his colleagues in the Holy Synod elevated the *raskolniki* to a symbol of theological ignorance.

The trivialization of ritualism is reflected in the changing terminology employed by the Russian government to designate the so-called schismatics. As late as 1745, state officials refused to permit the name *starovertsy* (Old *Believers*) (*Sobranie* 1858:462), and when finally the despised name *raskolniki* was dropped from official documents in 1790, the term *staroobriadtsy* (Old *Ritualists*) appeared as its substitute (*Sobranie* 1858:729). It expressed succinctly the official refusal to recognize Old Orthodoxy as a genuine rival of the reformed church. By playing up the modern bias against ritualism, late eighteenth-century Russian church and state condemned the Old *Ritualists* to the status of a relic and denied them the right to a separate set of *beliefs* and doctrines. According to a government edict issued in 1762, they were Orthodox Russians of an "old-fashioned" character (*Sobranie* 1858:587).

The view of the Old Believers as old-fashioned ritualists who differ from reformed Russian Orthodoxy merely in appearances has survived well into our times. To Paul Miliukov, they represent the "formalism of the old Russian religion" (1942:28) combined with an inability to discern "the substance of faith" (*ibid.*). In the words of Timothy Ware, Old and New Orthodoxy differ "solely in ritual, not in doctrine" (1972:123). Similar assessments are part and parcel of virtually every scholarly analysis dealing with the *raskol* and its consequences (Lane 1978:113; Lupinin 1984:123).

The reduction of the views upheld by the Old Believers to a survival from ancient times, when religion was synonymous with ritual observances, is reminiscent of nineteenth-century social evolutionism with its rigid separation of magic and religion. The pioneers of comparative religion, such as Robertson Smith (1889) and Sir James Frazer (1922), conceived of cosmologies preoccupied with concrete dangers, such as defilement, and their ritual enactments as magic, which, under favourable circumstances, could evolve into proper, that is, spiritual, religion. Mary Douglas, who has criticized the distinction between magic and religion as artificial (Douglas 1966), speaks of an "anti-ritualist prejudice" in modern society, which makes any appreciation of external forms of religion appear highly suspect (*ibid.*:60-61). This prejudice consists of the same two components which make themselves felt in official and scholarly attitudes to Old Orthodoxy, namely the assumption that interest in ritual correctness goes hand in hand with disinterest in doctrine, and that therefore ritualism is a somewhat deficient expression of religious devotion.

I would like to briefly substantiate this parallel with two examples taken from the works of prominent contemporary scholars. In both instances attention should be paid to the way in which outer and inner religiosity are presented as being mutually exclusive. It seems as though ritualism precludes interest in and knowledge of doctrinal issues. Here is an excerpt from the influential *Religion and the Decline of Magic* by the British historian Keith Thomas:

> A medieval peasant's knowledge of Biblical history or Church doctrine was, so far as one can tell, usually extremely slight. The Church was important to him not because of its formalised code of belief, but because its rites were an essential accompaniment to the important events in his own life—birth, marriage and death. It solemnised these occasions by providing appropriate rites of passage to emphasise their social significance. *Religion was a ritual method of living, not a set of dogmas.* (1971:76; my emphasis).

One is tempted to ask, "How do we know this much about a medieval peasant?", but let's postpone that question and proceed instead to my second example, taken from the best-known work of the American anthropologist Clifford Geertz, *The Interpretation of Cultures*. This is how he describes the essence of Balinese Hinduism:

> Balinese religion, even among the priests, is concrete, action-centered, thoroughly interwoven with the details of everyday life, and touched with little, if any, of the philosophical sophistication or generalized concern of classical Brahmanism or its Buddhist offshoot...The world is still enchanted and...the tangled net of magical realism is almost completely intact, broken only here and there by individual qualms and reflections...The Balinese, perpetually weaving intricate palm-leaf offerings, preparing elaborate ritual meals, decorating all sorts of temples, marching in massive processions, and falling into sudden trances, seem much too busy *practicing their religion to think (or worry) very much about it.* Beyond a minimal level, there is almost no interest in doctrine, or generalized interpretation of what is going on, at all. The stress is on orthopraxy, not orthodoxy—what is crucial is that each ritual detail should be correct and in place...You can believe virtually anything you want to actually, in-

cluding that the whole thing is rather a bore, and even say so. But if you do not perform the ritual duties for which you are responsible you will be totally ostracized, not just from the temple congregation, but from the temple community as a whole. (1973:175-177; my emphasis).

The contrast between religion as *practice* and religion as *doctrine* employed here by Thomas and Geertz encapsulates the traditional distinction between magic and religion with its emphasis on *action* versus *thought*. Whichever label we use, western scholarship differentiates between cosmologies whose practitioners attribute foremost significance to an accurate acting out of seemingly timeless rituals while showing little interest in shared beliefs, and between belief systems which, as the terminology indicates, derive meaning from shared doctrines with little attention given to ritual acts. Traditional Russian Orthodoxy in general and the Old Belief in particular are delegated to the action-oriented, ritualistic, and magic-like spectrum of the dichotomy. Here, to use Geertz's words, "orthopraxy" counts more than "orthodoxy".

There is no doubt in my mind that the Old Believers can be classified as ritualists. Mary Douglas' definition of ritualism as a "heightened appreciation of symbolic action" that is associated with a "belief in the efficacy of instituted signs" (1973:26) can be applied fruitfully to a whole range of behaviour exhibited by the people of Berezovka and their forebears. But whether this ritualism is indeed "empty" in the sense of having no or little doctrinal foundation, as implied by the contrast between "orthopraxy" and "orthodoxy", is an unanswered question, which demands serious attention not only in the interest of a better understanding of the Old Believers, but also for the sake of illuminating an important anthropological problem.

The connection between Old Orthodox ritual and dogma has never been adequately examined in western or Russian scholarship. This fundamental gap is perhaps less remarkable than it appears, for the postulated blind ritualism of the Old Believers seems to account for the willingness of millions to suffer persecution for the sake of clinging to a few ritual details. Yet any serious analysis of Old Orthodox ritualism must take into account its

Greek Orthodox roots and the substantial evidence demonstrating a tangible link between ritual and dogma, orthopraxy and orthodoxy, in Byzantine Christianity. I have already alluded to the manifold disagreements between Rome and Constantinople arising out of differences in ritual practice, and it is essential to understand that it was the connection between ritual and doctrine which made these seemingly trifling divergences solidify into lasting conflicts.

The only relatively well-known example of this proclivity is the *filioque* dispute, which was briefly mentioned in chapter 2. As I have indicated there, the Greek rejection of the addition "and the Son" to the common Christian creed was prompted not by empty ritualism, but by the fear of creating the impression that the Holy Spirit consisted of two entities (Pelikan 1974:183-198). Similar doctrinal motives led to disputes about the validity of Latin sacraments. When Greek theologians insisted on the ritual of baptism containing not just a triple gesture, but a triple *immersion*, they did so in order to underline the significance of Christ's death and resurrection (Ware 1972:284). When they condemned the Latin use of unleavened *azymes* in the Eucharist, it was explained as an attempt at setting the Christian sacrament apart from its Jewish prototype (Erickson 1970). And when Christians who were in the habit of making the sign of the cross with one rather than two fingers were assumed to be heretics, it was based on the clearly articulated connection between the two-finger sign and the rejection of the Monophysite belief in Christ as an ordinary man (Koch 1962:95). Many more examples could be enumerated from the realms of liturgy and iconography, but even the few mentioned here demonstrate the importance of ritual correctness for the doctrinal coherence of Eastern Orthodoxy.

The same insistence on treating ritual as an expression of dogma permeates much of the polemical literature produced in the seventeenth and eighteenth centuries by prominent defenders of Old Orthodoxy. This voluminous body of theological works has been conveniently overlooked by the scholars who deny any doctrinal foundation to the *raskol*, and this is a pity, because it is here that we touch the raw nerve of the radical distinction between orthopraxy and orthodoxy or magic and religion. Unfortunately, the sheer size of these unexplored early sources makes it impossible to provide here more than a cursory overview of the overlap between ritual and dogma as seen by Old Orthodox theologians.

It is a little-known fact that two of the most influential early leaders of the Old Believers, Archpriest Avvakum and Deacon Feodor, were prolific authors of considerable theological erudition. Avvakum wrote a whole series of epistles and tracts on subjects ranging from the sign of the cross, iconography, fasts, and similar "ritualistic" subjects to topics explicitly concerned with the Christian dogma, such as the creation of the world, the significance of the Eucharist, and the status of the Mother of God (Platonov 1927). What all these writings have in common is an implicit refusal to draw a line between religious form and content.

Avvakum's colleague and later rival, Deacon Feodor, made the link between ritual and doctrine explicit in the parallel he drew between the Latin *filioque* and Nikon's reforms. Repeatedly, he pointed out this connection in his attacks on the triple *alleluia*; the new designation of Christ's mother as a mere "creator of children" (*dietotvoritelnitsa*), which appeared to degrade her divine Son; and many other textual and ritual innovations (Subbotin 1881:4-15, 27, 139, 289). As he put it, these changes "nibble at God's writings like mice" (*ibid.*:32).

Doctrinal issues were also at stake in the internal conflicts that beset Old Orthodoxy very soon after the eruption of the schism. Outside commentators are fond of reducing these to seemingly meaningless squabbles over iconographic inscriptions, manufacture of crosses, the presence or absence of buttons, and similar "ritual details" (Smirnov 1898). While such disputes clearly did take place, one should not overlook truly theological questions, such as the still unresolved debate between the *popovtsy* and the *bezpopovtsy* regarding the status of post-*raskol* clergy. Another early dogmatic disagreement developed out of Avvakum's commentary on the Mother of God. In his apparent eagerness to expose Nikon's "attack" on the status of the Mother as an insult to the Son, Avvakum drew the bond between the two ever more tightly until one was left with the impression of a four-partite Holy Trinity (Platonov 1927:685-688). Deacon Feodor chastised him for that, and the ensuing debate led to a schism among their respective followers, which lasted until the early eighteenth century (Esipov 1863:230-259).

Without doubt the best testimony to the ability and willingness of Old Belief's founding fathers to interpret ritual as a reflection of dogma is enshrined in the monumental *Pomorskie otvety* by Andrei Denisov. Written in 1723 as a systematic rebuttal of all the innovations accepted by the reformed church, this encyclopedia of the divergences separating Old and New Orthodoxy leaves no doubt that its author was an excellent church historian who knew very well that his opposition to the new ritual continued a long tradition established in Byzantium. The man who speaks to us here is not some old-fashioned ritualist who hangs on blindly to prehistoric customs, but rather a scholar who skilfully guides his readers through the intricate labyrinth of a theologically grounded formalism (Chrysostomus 1957; Denisov 1912).

Unfortunately, we have no way of knowing whether the theologically grounded formalism defended by Avvakum, Feodor, Denisov, and other early leaders was the foremost reason for rejecting Nikon's reforms or whether it constituted merely a scholarly justification of "empty ritualism", with the latter being the actual cause of the dissent. It is clear from the reviewed literature that past and present scholarly opinion favours ritualism for the sake of ritualism as the only possible explanation of the rigid traditionalism of Old Orthodoxy, and while I disagree with this assessment, I do concede that the ritualism of the masses was probably less reflective than that of the movement's leaders. But I warn against adopting Keith Thomas' verdict that medieval peasants knew next to nothing about Biblical history and church doctrine and extending it to seventeenth-century Muscovy. We simply don't know enough.

What we do know is quite a deal about the ritualism of Berezovka's Old Believers, and that material clearly demonstrates a considerable awareness of Biblical history, church doctrine, and the link between ritual and dogma. The people of Berezovka rarely use the words "ritual", "dogma", or, for that matter, "religion". To them, Christianity is a state of the mind as well as of the body. To repeat one of my earlier assertions, local Old Believers insist on *demonstrating* faith through the medium of the body, and that's a long way from practicing a "ritual method of living" out of blind traditionalism.

My informants often confessed ignorance of complex doctrinal issues, such as, for example, the exact nature of the link between the humanity and divinity of Christ. Such questions were, as the humbler ones declared, beyond the grasp of semi-literate peasants. But they all displayed a good understanding of the basic Christian dogmata and a determination to repeat them over and over through various rituals. We have seen that the link between action and doctrine is the strongest and the most explicit in dominant symbols of Orthodoxy, such as the sign of the cross, the shape of the crucifix, the beard, the sacrament of baptism, and the preparation and consumption of holy water. There can be no doubt that the insistence on *dvoeperstie* has a doctrinal justification which ordinary believers are well acquainted with. The configuration of the fingers, the sequence of touching different parts of the body, the significance attached to the distinction between left and right, all these ritual details express well-articulated beliefs. The same goes for the tri-partite *krest*, which, unlike the *krizh*, conveys one's faith in the central dogma of Christianity, namely the divinity of Christ. The insistence on depicting Christ the crucified as standing rather than hanging may seem of little consequence to many, but to the Old Believers it affirms a postulate of considerable doctrinal significance. Similarly, to refrain from warming up the water used in baptism can express the required reliance on the Holy Spirit, just as beardlessness can denote apostasy.

It should not be necessary to repeat all the evidence amassed in the ethnographic chapters to conclude that the people of Berezovka do see a connection between action and belief, ritual and doctrine, orthopraxy and orthodoxy. For this very reason, traditional explanations of Old Orthodox ritualism as the result of blind formalism devoid of doctrinal undercurrents cannot be applied to the situation in Berezovka. But we must be careful not to adopt the opposite extreme of depicting the Old Believers as theologians for whom ritual is important only as a vehicle for the expression of dogma. This would be as much of a caricature as the prevalent attitude that action and belief can be divorced from one another.

Authenticity

My plea for a re-evaluation of Old Orthodox ritualism should not be seen as a departure from the repeated assertion that the Old Believers are ritualists. The fact remains that the people of Berezovka attribute religious significance to more material objects and outward acts than most other Christians, and that the expression of their doctrines depends on ritual correctness to an unusual degree. This prominence of ritualism calls for serious attention.

I suggest that ritual acts and objects are so important to the Old Believers because they serve as the main vehicle for the transmission of their culture across time. This means not merely that rituals function as a communication device—a fact well known to anthropologists and other students of religion—but that they serve as a crucial link in the "dialogue" between past and present Christians, that is, between people who cannot interact directly.

In their view of the relationship of the present to the past, the Old Believers belong to the category of societies called "repetitive" by Max Gluckman (1958) and "substantive traditionalist" by Edward Shils (1981). They appreciate "the accomplishments and wisdom of the past", and they regard "patterns inherited from the past as valid guides" (Shils 1981:21). The justifications for adhering to inherited models rather than designing new ones are manifold, but in one way or another, they all reflect one of Christianity's central commands, expressed by St. Paul in the epistle to the Corinthians: "Be imitators of me, just as I also am of Christ" (I Cor. 11:1). The utmost attention paid by the people of Berezovka to the distinction between *similar* and *dissimilar* books, icons, sacraments, and rituals results from the determination to collapse, or at least bridge, the gap that threatens to divorce the present from the past.

Although the Old Believers are unusually insistent on preserving the past to the smallest significant detail, their concern for cultural continuity and authenticity is not unique. Every society must solve the perennial problem of how to transmit traditional models of thought and behaviour—models that must be preserved in order to maintain stability and predictability and thus the continuation of society in the most basic sense. The transmission of tradition is largely a function of memory, and it is here that ritual plays an essential role.

Anthropologists agree that ritual acts are characterized by "formality (conventionality), stereotypy (rigidity), condensation (fusion), and redundancy (repetition)" (Tambiah 1979:119). These properties make ritual resemble a highly formalized language which, because of its simplicity and predictability, facilitates easy recall and repetition of the ritualized "text" (Bloch 1974; Rappaport 1974). This alone destines ritual to fulfill a very important function as a mnemonic device, which can be seen in children's rhymes and games, proverbs, folk tales, and similar stores of traditional wisdom that should not be forgotten. Since the aura of the past often automatically evokes the image of a higher authority, particularly formalized and repetitive rituals tend to acquire a religious connotation which makes the memorization of the performed ceremony even more imperative. "Sanctity, certainty and invariance", suggests Roy Rappaport, "are closely related" (1974:54).

Paul Connerton (1989) has recently analysed at length the role of ritual in the transmission of traditional models or, as he calls it comprehensively, "social memory". He distinguishes between three modes of articulation, consisting of "calendrical repetition", "verbal repetition", and "gestural repetition". The first one is expressed in rituals which commemorate past events on their exact anniversaries even centuries and millennia later. The church holidays celebrated in Berezovka belong to this category, and it will be recalled how much attention is placed on marking these events. The complex annual cycle of fasts and fast-free periods affords another example.

Connerton's inclusion of verbal repetition drives home the valuable point that rituals need not consist of acts and gestures. "The recitation of gospels and psalms, of prayers and sagas", claims Connerton, "has the same ritual value—as repeatable utterances—as have a genuflection or an offering, a gesture of benediction or a ceremonial dance" (1989:67). All of these expressions of the past must, however, be passed on in the original form in order to retain their efficacy, which rests "in their uttered repetition" (ibid.:67). This is why the Koran may not be translated from the Arabic, why the Torah must remain in Hebrew, and why the people of Berezovka insist on reciting all prayers in Church Slavonic. The power of the text vanishes when the original is copied incorrectly, whether this be in oral or in written form, not so much because its content is modified, but because the perfect harmony between the past and the present is destroyed.

The third vehicle of ritual transmission described by Connerton, gestural repetition, consists of the stuff that rituals are conventionally associated with: dance steps, genuflections, prostrations, hand-drawn signs, and similar repetitive movements. Here too, the author underlines the preservative aspect of ritual, claiming that "while physical existence is quintessentially transient, ritual gestures remain identical" (*ibid.*:70).

The link established by Connerton between ritual and the transmission of social memory corresponds rather well with the ideas and behaviour of the Old Believers. As has been pointed out on numerous occasions throughout this book, the people of Berezovka regard the sign of the cross, the double *alleluia*, the triple immersion, the public recitation of prayers, and all the other ritual details that give meaning to their social identity as a means to *authenticate* their imitation of divinely inspired models of Christian conduct which are believed to go back hundreds and thousands of years. In this sense, Old Orthodox ritualism should be seen as a variant of a universal method for the preservation of significant aspects of the past.

From research conducted by anthropologists, linguists, and psychologists, it would appear that the role of ritual in the transmission of culture is especially strong in societies where knowledge is passed on exclusively or at least primarily by oral means. In the absence of writing, particularly valuable ideas and insights must be perpetuated in an easily remembered form, such as proverbs, riddles, and other ritualized mnemonic tools, which encourage what Walter Ong has termed "formulaic thought" (Ong 1982:26, 34-35).

The kind of preoccupation exhibited by the Old Believers with the authenticity of the transmitted models is, however, rarely encountered in purely oral societies. The reliance on ritual and formulaic thought does not preclude variation and improvisation, nor does it stifle experimentation with new ideas and formulas, which may lead to the discarding of the old ones. As Jack Goody has observed, oral societies *re-create* rather than *repeat* traditional models (1987:84-85).

It will be recalled that the distinction between re-creation and repetition parallels the distinction made in Berezovka between Church Slavonic and Russian. Church Slavonic texts must be reproduced entirely in accordance with the original version, whereas texts in Russian—even when touching on religious subjects—may exhibit considerable variance from speaker to speaker, without necessarily losing their formulaic distinctiveness. The same situation prevails with respect to non-verbal rituals; those associated with religious observances must adhere to their prototypes in every detail, while secular family and community celebrations are free of such restrictions.

This contrast takes us to the use of *writing* as the second device for the transmission of "social memory" and its role in the Old Believers' quest for authentication of that transmission. We have seen that it is the written tradition of Old Orthodoxy which is regarded as the ultimate authority on all matters pertaining to authenticity, or, to use the distinction introduced above, as the primary medium in which flawless *repetition* is enshrined as the *sine qua non* of authenticity. It is possible to go further and postulate that writing is used in Berezovka in the first place as a method for perfecting and justifying the rigidity and formality characteristic of ritualism. Thus, there is a tendency for what Connerton calls "inscribing practices" to reinforce the preservative influence of the ritualized "incorporating practices". The perfectly copied word—written or spoken—continues to be a carrier of meaning, but it tends to play this role more as a mnemonic device than as an analytical tool.

This use of writing is far removed from the purpose to which it is put in truly literate societies, where it suppresses formulaic thought in favour of cognitive flexibility, skepticism, and other forms of "innovative thought" (Hallpike 1979:131; Ong 1982:76-78). The passive literacy encountered among the Old Believers—confined to the repetition of texts rather than their creation—resembles what Jack Goody has termed "restricted literacy" (1968; 1987). It is characteristic of societies which are introduced to writing and reading as a by-product of religious conversion, and where consequently the written word comes to be regarded not as an *arbitrary* symbol invented and manipulated by ordinary mortals, but rather as a divinely inspired sign which must be kept immutable in order to point to Truth. In view of the high regard in which words are held in oral societies (Ong 1982:32-33), the belief that writing is a gift of God intended to reveal and enshrine Truth is easily accepted, and the written word takes on the properties of a magical instrument with limitless powers (Goody 1968:16-17, 1987:131, 137; Ong 1982:93-95). Under such conditions, according to Goody, the written word itself becomes "oralized" and "ritualized":

> Books serve as a mnemonic and have themselves to be committed to memory before they are considered as read. Consequently, initial instruction places more emphasis on the repetition of content than the acquisition of skill...booklearning takes on an inflexibility that is the antithesis of the spirit of inquiry which literacy has elsewhere fostered. (1968:14)

Restricted literacy leads not only to "grapholatry"—reciting, reading, and writing become ends in themselves (Goody 1968:16)—but also to increased ideological rigidity. Unlike oral systems of belief, which Goody claims to be "open-ended in a meaningful way, encouraging the search, the quest, the journey after...the truth" (1986:8), literate religions take on an aura of finality, defining and guarding the truth by means of inflexible either/or boundaries and intricate distinctions between orthodoxy and heresy (*ibid.*:9-10).

Goody's reminder that literacy as it has come to be understood in contemporary western societies has little in common with the way in which it is *practised* in many parts of the world has important repercussions for our interpretation of Old Orthodoxy. The concept of "restricted literacy" is helpful in clarifying the tremendous difficulties faced by Muscovite clerics in their attempts to authenticate and correct the liturgical texts and rituals involved in the *raskol*. Treating the written word as a revelation of divine truth which had to be repeated rather than analyzed, Muscovite Christians displayed a degree of resistance to the change of sacred texts which can even today be observed in many Buddhist, Islamic, and Christian societies in which literacy remains confined to the realm of religion. In such settings, one would expect to find doctrinal issues externalized and ritualized, much as they are among the Old Believers. It is the externalization of beliefs by means of rituals which permits and indeed encourages the preoccupation with authenticity characteristic of Old Orthodoxy. As long as the configuration of fingers in the sign of the cross, the posture of crucified Christ, or the intonation of a prayer is accepted as a statement of dogma, adherence to or departure from the truth can be determined very easily by any reasonably devout person. Once the dogma is removed from visual and aural scrutiny and becomes internalized in abstract written codes, authenticity takes on an air of considerable complexity and relativity. Such is evidently the case in contemporary western Christianity, where the idea of imitation has very different connotations than in Berezovka.

Although I suggest the Old Orthodox preoccupation with authenticity be interpreted as an example of a widespread cognitive trait which emerges in consequence of a particular coexistence of orality and literacy, I wish to draw attention to a more restricted characteristic of Old Orthodoxy which must be taken into account in any discussion of this subject. What I have in mind is an "inscribing technique" of paramount significance, which has so far received minimal attention from anthropologists—Christian iconography. We have seen that pictorial images in Berezovka occupy the status of very important sacramentals, which are indispensable to daily life. This high regard for icons stems from the belief that they constitute accurate copies of divinely inspired originals which reveal in great detail the fundamentals of Christianity. By themselves, and in conjunction with the iconic principle which is closely associated with them, religious depictions provide the evidence that the insistence on an authentic representation of traditional models is far from futile. This means that iconography plays a most significant role in the externalization of dogma referred to above, and that its analysis should provide additional insights into the link between ritual and dogma under conditions of restricted literacy.

The rules governing the use of icons in Berezovka go back, as so much else of the local religious culture, to Byzantium. They evolved in the second half of the first millennium, largely in response to popular demand for material representations of divinity, which had to be reconciled with the traditional prohibition of idolatry. The result was a doctrine which postulated an explicit symmetry between the status of written and painted statements of the Christian dogma. Both the icon and the gospels were to be venerated, as they complemented one another in revealing the mysteries of the new religion (Hefele 1896:262, 370, 375; Jedin 1967:147, 152; Kitzinger 1976:105). In the wording of the Seventh Ecumenical Council held in 787, "Through these two mediums which accompany each other...we acquire the knowledge of the same realities" (quoted in Ouspensky 1978:10). Hence, as Leonide Ouspensky has put it,

> For the Church,...the icon is not an art illustrating Holy Scripture; it is a language which corresponds to Scripture, to the very contents of Scripture, to its meaning, just as do the liturgical texts. This is why the icon plays the same role as Scripture in the Church; it has the same liturgical, dogmatic, educational meaning. (1978:166).

The parallel between the icon and the book destined them to be venerated not only as sources of enlightenment but, beyond that, as objects of unusual power that could effect healing and similar miracle-like transformations (Baynes 1951:100-101; Campenhausen 1957:89; Kitzinger 1976:123-125, 153; Mango 1972:134). Such was the case especially in Muscovy, where holy books and sacred images received identical reverential treatment. The manufacture of books and icons followed very similar principles, which derived from the view that it involved a process of *copying* rather than *creating*, and that the copied "text" possessed qualities which removed it from the realm of ordinary human activity (Bolshakov 1903:18-20; Kozhanchikov 1863:128; Siniavski 1988). A large number of pollutants, ranging from sex to dogs, tobacco, and even ordinary human touch at times (Rushchinskii 1871:96; Smirnov 1914:67), were to be kept away from them for fear of adversely affecting their power. They were not allowed to be used for commercial purposes (Akademiya nauk SSSR 1941; Rushchinskii 1871:77); and once time had rendered them useless, worn-out texts and indistinct pictures had to be entrusted to the clean waters of a river (Kostomarov 1905:167; Uspensky 1976:29). In all these respects, icons and books comprised a single category of links connecting ordinary Christians with God through a long chain of copies believed to be authentic renditions of divine Truth.

The similarity between these two sources of revelation was postulated most succinctly by Avvakum in his lament and accusation: "But as the Niconians copy the European books, so do they copy their icons" (quoted in Andreyev 1961:43). We have seen that this claim still echoes in Berezovka, where the *raskol* is largely attributed to modifications of "old books" and "old icons". The Byzantine and Muscovite parallel between the interpretation and treatment of sacred texts and images survives here intact.

I regard the Old Orthodox tendency to diminish the distinctions between writing and painting as an important cause of the ritualization of dogma and the search for authentic models of tradition, which are so striking among past and present Old Believers. We have already observed that one of the consequences of "restricted literacy" makes itself felt in the tendency to appreciate written texts for their formal properties, meaning that reading and writing are guided by conventions which place a higher value upon the *repetition* than the *comprehension* of words. This is not to imply that written texts are not comprehended at all, but rather that they remain subordinate to other carriers of meaning, such as ritual. It would seem that a declaration of symmetry between writing and painting must erode even further the role played by written texts in the transmission of the Christian dogma, for if all necessary knowledge can be imparted by means of easily comprehended pictures, what incentive is there to learn how to read *analytically* rather than *ritualistically*? And to the extent that paintings, unlike written texts, must provide information about styles of clothing, the length of hair, the presence or absence of beards, the manner of signing the cross, and many more *material* details, their elevation to the status of sacred objects was bound to further encourage and legitimate the formalism of Byzantine and Muscovite Orthodoxy.

Although the theological theory behind iconography established an equivalence between sacred texts and images, the equivalence was undermined from the beginning by distinctions made between the educated devotion of the literate elite and the folk piety of the illiterate masses. Reducible to the contrast between abstract and concrete ways of approaching God, these distinctions isolated writing as the path for the educated, and painting as the medium suitable for the illiterates. In the memorable words of Pope St. Gregory the Great, uttered in the year 600,

> What the Scripture is for the man who knows how to read, the icon is for the illiterate. Through it, even uneducated men can see what they must follow. It is the book of those who do not know the alphabet. (quoted in Ouspensky 1978:134)

The value of the icon as a didactic device stemmed above all from its ability to help with the recall of Christian history and doctrine, and from doing so not as an impersonal and dry narrative, but in a manner which fostered immediacy and identification between the viewer and the contemplated scene. The Fathers assembled at the Seventh Ecumenical Council declared, "The oftener one looked on these representations, the more would the looker be stirred to the remembrance of the originals, and to the imitation of them" (quoted in Hefele 1896:375). Using the example of the famous scholar Gregory of Nyssa, who is reported to have wept after contemplating a painted depiction of the offering of Isaac, the clerics agreed on the universal appeal of iconography, but then they concluded, "If this happened to a learned man, how much more must it be useful to the unlearned, that they may be touched" (quoted in Hefele 1896:368). And lest there be any doubt about the deeper meaning of this conclusion, a bishop from Asia Minor, speaking on behalf of his educated peers, declared, "As for ourselves we have no delight in the icons" (quoted in Baynes 1951:95).

What we see in these examples is a more or less explicit denial of the equivalence of writing and painting. While it is recognized that both media serve the same purpose, the icon is described as a more concrete, immediate, evocative, blunt, and hence easily understood carrier of meaning than the written text. It is recommended for the uneducated folk as a temporary *substitute* for the more abstract, complex, and difficult book.

It is beyond the scope of this study to analyse the reasons for the immense popularity of iconography in Eastern Christendom in general and Russian Orthodoxy in particular. Such an analysis would have to take into account complex theological and philosophical questions, such as, for example, the influence of Plotinus and other neo-Platonists on Greek Orthodox views of the connection between reality and its image (Ladner 1953). But at the level of "folk religion", which is what we confront in dealing with the Old Believers, it should be justifiable to postulate a strong link between restricted literacy and the reliance on icons as a source of doctrinal knowledge. Like ritual, icons visualize and thus externalize models of tradition with an attention to concrete detail, which is rarely achieved in written statements. The latter may, as is clearly the case among the people of Berezovka, be considered the ultimate source of one's beliefs and conduct, but in the absence of a genuinely analytical study of the written tradition, the orthodoxy of daily life comes to be regulated by the iconic principle, with its emphasis on the authenticity of external markers rather than inner states.

East and West

The conclusion that I have reached now on several occasions is that the people of Berezovka transmit culture *iconically*, which means that all representations of orthodoxy must be authenticated copies of ancient and unchanging models. Having provided ample illustration of the antiquity of what I call the iconic principle, and of its apparent association with ritualism, iconography, and restricted literacy, I would like to refine it a little further by contrasting it with the dominant mode of cultural transmission prevalent in the Christian West. That contrast, I believe, is roughly equivalent to the distinction between *icons* and *symbols*.

According to Charles Peirce, one of the founders of the scientific study of signs, nowadays conventionally designated as semiotics, an iconic sign conveys meaning by virtue of a planned resemblance between the signified object and the sign that represents it (Innis 1985:8, 18; Jakobson 1971:347; Singer 1984:27). To take Old Orthodox depictions of the crucifixion as an example, what makes them icons in the semiotic sense is the belief that the *signifier*, that is, the painting, faithfully reproduces the *signified*, the crucifixion scene, as it was hundreds of years ago. Symbols, on the other hand, are arbitrary signs which convey meaning based on agreement that a given object, gesture, or sound stands for something other than what it is. Hence to many Christians, a lamb that appears to be carrying a cross represents the crucified Christ in spite of no apparent connection between the signifier and the signified. Although that connection is invented—and everybody knows it, for few Christians believe that their idol looked like a lamb—the power of symbols to evoke appropriate emotions is no less strong than that of iconic signs. But, as I am about to demonstrate, icons and symbols play a different role in the shaping of attitudes towards the past, or, as J.G.A. Pocock has put it, "past relationships" (1962:242-244). The western past-relationship has for a long time been expressed symbolically, which is a very different method from the iconic principle entrenched in Old Orthodoxy.

In anthropological circles, the contrast between iconic and symbolic representations is usually conveyed in the dichotomies of magic:religion, and ritual:belief. To the extent that Protestantism effected a shift away from the magico-ritual dimension in traditional Roman Catholicism, the Reformation is usually portrayed as triggering the first significant attack on the iconic principle in Christianity (Douglas 1973; Radcliffe-Brown 1952:155; Thomas 1971). Without doubt, the radical rejection by Protestants of ritualism in favour of faith has had a considerable effect on the Christian interpretation of religion and of the relationship between the past and the present. It is clear that people who agreed with the Lollards that the sign of the cross could "avail to nothing else but to scare away flies" (quoted in Thomas 1971:72), subscribed to a significantly different view of history than did medieval Christians. However, once we elevate ourselves above the occident-centric approach to Christianity prevalent in anthropological (and other academic) circles, we should be able to detect significant shifts in the western past-relationship long before the Reformation.

One such shift can be seen in the readiness with which Latin theologians of late antiquity and the early Middle Ages accepted and implemented changes in the ritual of the western church. Unlike in the East, ritual details such as the exact shape of the sign of the cross, the depiction of the crucifix, the distinction between pure and impure food, the presence or absence of beards, the precise sequence of baptism, the composition of the Eucharist, and many more, mattered relatively little. This is not to say that such issues were not debated or that they could not play a part in accusations of heterodoxy. Such an assertion would definitely be wrong, especially in view of the intransigence displayed by the Latin church in the *filioque* question. But the preoccupation with ritual and natural purity demonstrated, occasionally, by western churchmen was for most part characterized by a trait unknown in the East. It can be described as *ritual pluralism* in the sense that it involved an explicit recognition of the possibility of expressing orthodoxy in more than one ritual tradition. In practice this meant that while medieval Greek Christians called for the rebaptism of Latin "heretics", the latter were always willing to share their churches, tables, and beds with their eastern "brothers" and "sisters".

The willingness to tolerate ritual discrepancies may be associated with a relatively low opinion of the significance of ritual for the expression of dogma, but also with a relative lack of interest in the search for authentic models of the past, which is such a distinguishing feature of Old Orthodoxy. Thus while medieval western Christianity appears from the Protestant or modern Roman Catholic perspective as rigid ritualism infused with a considerable dose of superstition it may also be regarded as a religion which paid remarkably little attention to the manner in which tradition was transmitted and expressed, and which was unusually tolerant of alternatives. Looked at from the traditional Orthodox perspective, western Christianity encouraged the substitution of symbolic for iconic signs a long time before the Reformation.

This assertion is well substantiated by the history of Roman Catholic iconography. The first significant shift in this realm occurred when the Council of Frankfurt, held in 794 and remembered primarily as the source of the *filioque* controversy, refused to treat painted images with the degree of reverence agreed on by the Seventh Ecumenical Council a mere seven years earlier

(Hefele 1896:398-399). Foreshadowing the views of Protestant theologians seven centuries later, Charlemagne's *Libri Carolini* declared the image inferior to the word, "as, of course, man can be saved without seeing pictures, but he cannot without the knowledge of God" (quoted in Berliner 1953:265).

The repudiation of the Greek theory of symmetry and (near) equivalence between painting and writing relegated western iconography to an illustrative enterprise whose practitioners felt few of the numerous ordinances imposed on Orthodox painters. The traditional models *copied* so faithfully in the East were *re-created* in the West with much more latitude, and by the thirteenth century, the semiotic character of western religious art had become more symbolic than iconic. This state of affairs invited comments from contemporaries, such as Bishop Durand of Mende, who observed that religious motifs were painted *"pro voluntate pictorum"*, after the taste of the artists (quoted in Kollwitz 1957:124). Another thirteenth-century bishop, Luke of Tuy, concurred and justified the trend in these memorable words:

> Since the aim of religious art is to arouse the emotions of the spectator, the artist must have liberty to compose his works, so as to assure to them the greatest effectiveness. The representation should not always be forced into traditional patterns. In order to avoid the *dullness of accustomed formulas*, the artist needs freedom to devise unusual motifs and to *invent* new ideas as they seem appropriate to him with respect to the location of the work of art and to his period, *even if they contradict the literal truth.* (quoted in Berliner 1953:278; my emphasis).

This extraordinary statement indicates the extent to which the imitation of the past had fallen into disrepute in western Christendom centuries prior to the Reformation. Christ and the saints remained, of course, a source of inspiration, but their distinctiveness became more and more divorced from any exterior, visible markers. The strangeness of such a development for an Eastern Orthodox Christian is captured in this comment by the Greek cleric Gregory Melissenus: "When I enter a Latin church, I do not revere any of the saints that are there because I do not recognize any of them" (quoted in Mango 1972:254).

The Renaissance effected a complete and final abandonment of traditional iconographic models in favour of modernist motifs. The search for recognition took on another twist as the conventional view of man as an image of God was reversed by famous painters, such as Albrecht Dürer and Michelangelo, who portrayed Christ as a modern man and the past as a reflection of the present (Miles 1985:72-73; Schoene 1957:40-41; Steinberg 1983). Hence, Ruben's Christ after the crucifixion could now be taken for "a good-looking Flemish worker who has fallen from the fifth floor" (quoted in Leeuw 1963:167).

The emancipation from "the dullness of accustomed formulas" in the iconographic realm can be understood as a shift from iconic to symbolic representations, set in motion by the western belief that the *invention* of alternative models of expression and interpretation could become a better tool for the dissemination of Christian principles than the *emulation* of existing ones. The same conviction seems to underlie the treatment of the written word. To start with, the western version of the Bible emerged in the sixth century in the form of the Latin *Vulgate*, which was a work of translation unadorned but also unburdened by any direct link with God or the apostles. Unlike Hebrew, Greek, Sanskrit, Arabic, or Church Slavonic, Latin has never possessed the status of a *lingua sacra*, and this has tended to encourage a remarkably flexible view of its purpose. This is not to suggest that medieval Roman Catholics were not likely to treat the gospels as a concrete, iconic source of divine power, which could cure headaches or inflict harm (McNeill & Gamer 1938:177, 200). Such magical views were undoubtedly widespread, but the church as an institution treated them as superstitions, which lacked proper dogmatic foundation (Thomas 1971).

The flexibility with which the western church employed Latin comes to the fore in the stipulation issued in the early ninth century at the Council of Tours that in order to be fully comprehended, public readings from the Bible had to be translated into the vernacular (Illich & Sanders 1988:61-63). In view of the proximity between written Latin and spoken Romance at that time

(McKitterick 1989:22), it may be assumed that the "translation" ordered by the synod was more likely an explication.

The willingness to translate or even interpret biblical texts—a violation of the iconic principle not tolerated in seventeenth-century Muscovy—indicates that the Word, akin to the Image, was treated as a tool, which could be manipulated in order to serve the user, at a very early time and, again, definitely long before the Reformation. This suggestion is confirmed by recent research conducted by Rosamond McKitterick, which provides evidence of widespread literacy throughout all but the lowest strata of Carolingian society. "It was a society," claims McKitterick, "to which the written word was central" not just in the religious realm, but also in commerce, administration, and entertainment (1989:273).

If the Carolingian era can be regarded as the starting point for the gradual onslaught on the iconic principle in western painting and writing, the thirteenth century should be remembered as bringing about the first decisive victory. What happened in iconography with the rejection of the dull "accustomed formulas", had the same impact and source as the birth of *fiction* in western literature. The emergence of the novel was linked, as the word itself indicates, with the desire for experiencing something new, something unburdened by the weight of the past, something that could and indeed had to be *forgotten* in order to make room for a never-ending stream of new facts and ideas (Illich & Sanders 1988:86-91). The encouragement to *invent*, which triumphs in Gothic writing and painting, must be seen as effecting a revolutionary change in the western past-relationship, culminating in *modernity*. As a result of this change, medieval western writing and painting began to liberate Latin Christians from the very past which the Word and the Image had been intended to transmit.

The next and probably most decisive step towards the emancipation from tradition was taken during the Renaissance. Celebrated as an era of renewed faith in the wisdom of the past, the Renaissance began with the re-discovery of Greek and Hebrew originals of the Bible, and the call of the humanists for the correction of the Latin Vulgate (Schwarz 1955). But the scientific scrutiny of classical languages led to a scientific scrutiny of classical history and to the realization that a *text* cannot be understood without its *context*, or, put in other words, that meaning

is determined by culture (Pocock 1962:227). This insight posed a
significant problem for the translators of biblical texts. If they
opted for linguistic purity, they faced the danger of generating
texts whose meaning was obscure to readers raised in a different
culture than that of the author; on the other hand, if they chose
clarity of meaning over verbal authenticity, they exposed themselves to possible accusations of tinkering with God's words (Schwarz
1955). Either way, philology and historiography prepared the way
for the realization that the past and the present are not con-
tinuous, as had been asserted by Christian theology (Connerton
1989:100; Pocock 1962:228). The power of the iconic principle
was broken.

The remnants of the Christian past-relationship disintegrated
under the onslaught of the Reformation. The new churches
rejected the authority of tradition especially strongly in the interpretation of scripture. To Martin Luther, the Word was no longer
an iconic bond between the past and the present, but a living
symbol which could be manipulated and interpreted at will. "The
Gospel," asserted he, "should not be written but screamed"
(quoted in Miles 1985:104). Even the Latin Vulgate appeared now
as a pseudo-magical instrument on account of its association with
the literalist tradition, and it was soon replaced with translations
into the vernacular which adapted the Bible to the needs of the
modern reader (Herbert 1989).

The Protestant attack on the traditional text and interpretation of the Bible should be seen in conjunction with the
iconoclasm that swept across central and northwestern Europe in
the sixteenth century. The wholesale destruction of "papist"
religious art expressed the desire of reformers to put an end to
the conventional approach to God (Miles 1985). When Erasmus
of Rotterdam declared, "I am not such a fool that I need carved
or painted images" (quoted in Leeuw 1963:184), he was re-affirm-
ing a preference for the word that permeates the history of literate
Christianity, but he was doing so under radically different conditions. Largely as a result of the Renaissance and the Reformation,
post-medieval western Europe developed a "language-oriented
religion and culture" (Miles 1985:123), which, at least in the
Protestant countries, now affected the majority of the believers
in quite far-reaching ways. The insistence on formal education,

sobriety, introspection, abstraction, and skepticism, principles usually associated with the Reformation, could not but further undermine the already shaky faith in the view of the present as a reflection of the past. "Sacred" images, formulas, books, rituals, and other iconic props lost much of their prestige to the symbols of the emerging scientific culture, which discredited the traditional quest for authenticity. From the sixteenth century on, Truth in the minds of western Christians has come to be associated either with science or with *faith*. The latter has become a substitute for the proof of authenticity which traditions used to be thought to certify (Shils 1981). Indeed, far from serving as the bearer of Truth, tradition has taken on an air of falsehood and deception in modern social thought (Hobsbawm & Ranger 1983).

The new past-relationship carved out by the Renaissance and the Reformation was evidently involved in the Russian *raskol*. Triggered, as we have seen, by textual corrections comparable to those carried out by western philologists, the schism can be seen as an expression of clashing views of the past. Like the Reformation in the West, it caused a lasting split between "traditionalists" and "modernists", and propelled a search for new models of culture, which were supposed to replace the old iconic link between the present and the past. It is of more than passing significance that Peter the Great, the self-appointed reformer of Russia, turned not merely to the West, but to the *Protestant* West for assistance. In the ideology which he imposed on his subjects,

> a link with the memory of earlier cultural development
> was called ignorance, while a break with that memory
> was perceived as "enlightenment". "To remember"
> meant being an ignoramus, and "to forget" was to be
> enlightened. (Lotman & Uspenskii 1985:50)

It is entirely possible that the organized forgetting demanded by the tsar in order to rid the country of its "barbaric" past may have been inspired by Peter's fieldwork in Holland, the bulwark of the Reformation.

Those who refused to engage in collective forgetting most sensibly attributed the radically changed climate to the antichrist himself. In a society which had not experienced the Carolingian

Renaissance, the innovations of the Gothic, the triumphs of humanism, a society which possessed at the end of the eighteenth century an estimated twelve thousand "active readers" (Sevastianov 1985:91), the radical departure from the traditional models of culture and history must have appeared as machinations of the devil, intended to bring about a complete breakdown of the Christian order. We have seen this opinion at work among the people of Berezovka who, surviving in the antichrist's shadow, so to speak, go to great lengths to nurture the ancient iconic relationship with God and the past, determined to withstand the onslaught of modernity.

NOTES

1. The name Josephville is a pseudonym. The Old Believers do not wish their location to be widely known, and I have removed all indicators that might disclose it.

2. The *filioque* dispute erupted in 794 at the Council of Frankfurt, at which Latin theologians adopted a modification of the common Christian creed. In its traditional wording, the creed expressed the belief in "God, the Father Almighty...,and in Jesus Christ...in the Holy Spirit, the Lord, the Giver of Life, *who proceeds from the Father*, who with the Father and the Son together is worshipped and together glorified." The new version inserted the addition "and the son" (*filioque* in Latin) after the phrase "from the Father", creating the impression that there were two Holy Spirits and thus four entities within the Holy Trinity (Geanakoplos 1984:205-212; Ware 1972:58-59).

3. The manner in which religious differences helped create the political and social tensions between Russia and western Europe remains to be documented in all its details. Some of the empirical evidence can be found in Fedotov (1975), Koncevicius (1927), Popov (1875).

4. The religious motif in Muscovy's wars with its western neighbours is nicely reflected in the *Story of Stephen Bathory's Campaign Against Pskov*, summarized by Serge Zenkovsky (1974).

5. The historical justification for the "Third Rome" doctrine is provided in the late fifteenth century *Tale of the White Cowl* (in Zenkovsky 1974:323-332). The first formulation of the doctrine itself is attributed to one Monk Pilotheus, who wrote in the first half of the sixteenth century: "All Christian realms will come to an end and will unite into the one single realm of our sovereign, that is, into the Russian realm, according to the prophetic books. Both Romes fell, the third endures, and a fourth there will never be" (in Zenkovsky 1974:323).

6. The tendency to lump all foreigners into the "pagan" class notwithstanding, Muscovite state officials did distinguish between categories of foreigners when it proved expedient. Dignitaries of the Greek church, for example, were permitted to enter the royal palace via a route that took them along the tsar's private chapel — an honour denied other emissaries, who were compelled to use a side entrance (Aleppo 1873:97; Olearius 1656:32). Some tsars expressed their regard for eastern patriarchs by kissing their mouth and even hand (Aleppo 1873:97-98); at the ambassadorial level, only European envoys received permission to kiss the tsar's hand (Herberstein 1926:216; Olearius 1656:34). The contempt felt for Moslems precluded not only direct physical contact but even the use of the Turkish language in the presence of the ruler (Aleppo 1873:98). The bottom of the ethno-religious hierarchy was occupied by the Jews; they are reported to have been barred from residing in or even travelling through Muscovy (Staden 1964:103).

7. The seriousness of this problem is illustrated by the "Maxim the Greek" affair, an episode that encapsulates the uneasy relationship between Russian and Greek churchmen in the sixteenth century. Maxim the Greek, or, as he came to be known in Russian, *Maksim Grek*, was a theologian lent to Tsar Ivan III by the Patriarch of Constantinople in 1518. His mandate was to assist with the translation and authentication of the written tradition, which was then in its initial phase. After several years of great productivity, Maksim was removed from the project, tried, condemned as a heretic, and banished to a monastery in 1525. Officially, he was accused of translation errors, criticism of the tsar and the church, and, most revealingly, of "Greek and Jewish philosophizing" (Koch 1962:88). It has been suggested that his real crime was to express doubts about his Russian colleagues' ability to carry out the assigned task, and to insist on correcting previously completed translations. Hence, precisely when politicians and churchmen were beginning to construct the ideology of the Third Rome, Maksim was undermining that ideology by pointing out the fragility of its foundation (Herberstein 1926:91; Hoesch 1975:131-133; Koch 1962:87-88).

8. The belief in the authenticity of God's word had an interesting parallel in the insistence that the tsar's word was also divine and had to be protected from adulteration (Olearius 1656:222). The tsar was represented by his title, and state officials expected a faithful repetition of the long and intricate title whenever the ruler was

addressed by a foreign potentate or representative (Herberstein 1926:212; Olearius 1656:189).

9. It would be wrong to imply that all of Russian Orthodoxy was entirely formalistic. Several important figures attacked Muscovite formalism and attempted to carve out a different channel of religious devotion. The outstanding representative of this dissenting faction was Nil Sorskii (1433-1508), the founder of Russian ascetic monasticism. He advocated a flexible, individualistic form of worship which emphasized spiritual over physical duties, with the soul rather than the book regarded as the real source of faith. Nil Sorskii's theology did play a role in sixteenth- and seventeenth-century Russia, but it was overshadowed by the ritualistic approach, advocated by Sorskii's main opponent, Iosif Volotskii.

10. More about the distinction between *dvoe-* and *troeperstie* is said in chapters 5 and 6.

11. The defence of Old Orthodoxy played a part in virtually every major popular uprising between the late seventeenth and the late eighteenth centuries. Stenka Razin, who revolted in 1669-1671, was held to be an Old Believer blessed by Avvakum himself (Eliasov 1963:302). The famous 1682 rebellion of the *strel'tsy* — the royal life-guard — generated hopes that the old faith was about to be restored (Palmer 1873:436). Bulavin's army, which fought against Peter the Great, contained numerous Old Believers (Call 1979:144), and the program of Pugachev's insurrection of 1772-1775 called for the restoration of Old Orthodoxy as Russia's official religion (Siegelbaum 1979:230). The topic is ably dealt with by Michael Cherniavsky (1966).

12. The extent to which the defenders of the old faith meant to rebel against the *tsar* — rather than a presumed imposter or anonymous official — is debatable. The available evidence suggests that they saw him as a victim of Nikon's machinations rather than a genuine ally. That's why the monks appealed to him in the humblest language, "Great gossudar and tsar, be gracious, be merciful!" (in Palmer 1873:459). The belief in the justice of the ruler generated a legend which claimed that the tsar wanted to pardon the monks, and that he died after learning that the courier he had dispatched with the pardon arrived too late to prevent a bloodbath (Palmer 1873:447). For a discussion of the relationship between the Old Believers and the state, see Scheffel (1989c).

13. The most detailed exposition of the differences between pre- and post-Nikonian liturgical books remains the monumental defence of Old Orthodoxy, *Pomorskie otvety*, written by Andrei Denisov (1912 [1723]). This rare book is summarized in several more recent works (e.g. Chrysostomus 1957).

14. The demographic data are based on material obtained from the Department of Manpower and Immigration of the Government of Canada.

Bibliography

Akademiya Nauk SSSR. *Pamiatniki istorii staroobriadchestva xvii v.*
1927   Russkaia istoricheskaia biblioteka, vol. 39, Leningrad.
1941   Istoriia russkoi literatury. Vol. 1. and Vol. 3, pt. 1.
1947   *Istoriia russkoi literatury.* Vol. 4, pt. 2.
1948   *Istoriia russkoi literatury.* Vol. 2, pt. 2.

Aleppo, Paul of.
1873   Travels of the Patriarch Macarius of Antioch. In Palmer , ed., *The Patriarch and the Tsar.* London: Trübner.

Ammann, A.
1937   Bei den Altgläubigen am Peipus-See. *Stimmen der Zeit.*
1950   *Abriss der Ostslawischen Kirchengeschichte.* Vienna: Herder.

Andreev, V.V.
1870   *Raskol i ego znachenie v narodnoi russkoi istorii.* St. Petersburg.

Andreyev, N.
1961. Nikon and Avvakum on icon-painting. *Revue des etudes slaves,* 38:37-44.

Anonymous
1694   Prigovor ili ulozhenie novgorodskogo sobora 1694 goda. *See* Vasilev 1694.
1865   Neskolko slov o raskolnikakh irkutskoi epartkhii. *Pravoslavnyi sobesednik,* 3:309-318.

Arkheograficheskaya Kommissiya.
1897   Letopisnyi sbornik, imenuemyi patriarsheiu ili nikonovskoiu letopisiu. *Polnoe sobranie russkikh letopisei,* 11:22-108, St. Petersburg.

Arsenii.
1885 *Istinnost staroobriadstvuiushchei ierarkhii.* Manuilovsko-Nikolskii Monastery.

Avvakum.
1974 Life of Archpriest Avvakum by himself. In S. Zenkovsky, ed., *Medieval Russia's epics, chronicles, and tales.* New York: E.P. Dutton & Co.

Badone, E. ed.
1990 *Religious orthodoxy & popular faith in European society.* Princeton: Princeton University Press.

Baron, S. ed.
1967 *The travels of Olearius in seventeenth-century Russia.* Stanford: Stanford University Press.

Barskov, Y. ed.
1912 *Pamiatniki pervykh let russkago staroobriadchestva.* St. Petersburg.

Basargin, O.
1984 *A story of Nikolaevsk.* Nikolaevsk: Kenai Peninsula Borough School.

Baynes, N.
1951 The icons before iconoclasm. *Harvard Theological Review,* 44:93-106.

Begunov, Y.
1969 Auf der Suche nach altrussischen Handschriften bei den Altgläubigen am Estnischen Ufer des Peipussees. *Zeitschrift für Slawistik,* 14:506-518.

Berliner, R.
1953 The freedom of medieval art. *Gazette des beaux-arts,* ser. 6, no. 28:263-288.

Biggins, M.
1985 Linguistic aspects of the *Turchane* of Oregon. Manuscript.

Billington, J.
1970 *The icon and the axe: An interpretive history of Russian culture.* New York: Alfred Knopf.

Bloch, M.
1974 Symbols, song, dance and features of articulation. *Archives Européennes de Sociologie,* 15:55-81.

Blomkvist, E. & Grinkova, N.
1930 Kto takie bukhtarminskie staroobriadtsy. In S.I. Rudenko, ed., *Bukhtarminskie staroobriadtsy*. Leningrad.

Boeckenhoff, K.
1903 *Das apostolische Speisegesetz in den ersten fünf Jahrhunderten*. Paderborn: Schöningh.

Bolshakov {Bolshakoff], S.
1903 *Podlinik ikonopisnyi*. St. Petersburg.
1950 *Russian Nonconformity*. Philadelphia: Westminster.

Bullough, S.
1963 *Roman Catholicism*. Harmondsworth: Penguin.

Buslaev, F.
1861 *Istoricheskie ocherki russkoi narodnoi slovesnosti i iskusstva*. vol 1, *Russkaia narodnaia poeziia*. St. Petersburg. vol 2, *Drevne-russkaia narodnaia literatura i iskusstvo*.

Cabrol, F. & Leclercq, H.
1914 "Croix et Crucifix", "Croix (signe de la)". *Dictionnaire d'archéologie chrétienne et de liturgie*. Paris.

Call, P.
1979 *Vasily L. Kelsiev: An encounter between the Russian revolutionaries and the Old Believers*. Belmont: Nordland.

Campenhausen, H. von
1957 Die Bilderfrage als theologishes Problem der alten Kirche. In Schöne, J. Kollwitz, H. von Campenhausen, eds. *Das Gottesbild im Abendland*, Witten: Eckart.

Cherniavsky, M.
1966 The Old Believers and the new religion. *Slavic Review*. 25: 1-39.

Chrysostomus, J.
1957 Die "Pomorskie Otvety" als Denkmal der Anschauungen der russischen Altgläubigen gegen Ende des 1. Viertels des XVIII. Jahrhunderts. *Orientalia Christiana Analecta*, no. 148.

Cochrane, A.
1974 *Eating and drinking with Jesus: An ethical and bibilical inquiry*. Philadelphia: Westminster.

Connerton, P.
1989 *How societies remember*. Cambridge: Cambridge University Press.

Conybeare, F.
1962   *Russian dissenters*. New York: Russell & Russell.

Cooper, W.
1971   *Hair*. New York: Stein & Day.

Cross, F.L., ed.
1958   *The Oxford dictionary of the Christian church*. London: Oxford University Press.

Crummey, R.
1970   *The Old Believers and the world of antichrist*. Madison: University of Wisconsin Press.

Cudell, R.
1927   *Das Buch vom Tabak*. Köln: Haus Neuerburg.

Curtiss, J.S.
1940   Church and State in Russia—The Last Years of the Empire: 1900-1917. New York: Columbia University Press.

Dal, V.I.
1862   Poslovitsy russkago naroda. In *Chteniia v imperatorskom obshchestve istorii i drevnostei rossiiskikh pri moskovskom universitete*, 1:687-1095.

Denisov, A.
1912 [1723]   *Pomorskie otvety*. Moscow: Rabushinskii.

Dix, G.
1953   *Jew and Greek: A study in the primitive church*. London: Dacre.

Douglas, M.
1966   *Purity and danger*. London: Routledge & Kegan Paul. Reprinted ARK Paperbacks 1984.
1973   *Natural symbols: Explorations in cosmology*. 2nd ed. London: Barrie & Jenkins.

Durkheim, E. & Mauss, M.
1903   *De quelques formes primitives de classification*. Paris.

Dvornik, F.
1961   *The ecumenical councils*. New York: Hawthorn.

Eliasov, L.E.
1963   *Folklor semeiskikh*. Ulan-Ude.

Erickson, J.
1970   Leavened and unleavened: Some theological implications of the schism of 1054. *St. Vladimir's Theological Quarterly*, 14:155-176.

Esipov, G.V.
1863 Ruskaia boroda i niemetskoe platie. *Raskolnichi diela XVIII stoletia*. Vol. 2. St. Petersburg.

Fedotov, G.
1975 *The Russian religious mind*, Vol. 1, *Kievan Christianity*. Belmont: Nordland.

Fisher, R.
1939 *The odyssey of tobacco*. Litchfield: The Prospect Press.

Fortes, M.
1949 Time and social structure—An Ashanti case study. *Social structure*. Oxford: Clarendon Press.

Foster, G.
1965 Peasant society and the image of limited good. *American Anthropologist*, 67:293-315.

Frazer, J.
1922 *The Golden Bough*. London.

Friedrich, P.
1963 An evolutionary sketch of Russian kinship. In V. Garfield & W. Chafe, eds., *Proceedings of the AES Meeting*, Seattle: American Ethnological Society.
1964 Semantic structure and social structure: An instance from Russian. In W.H. Goodenough, ed., *Explorations in cultural anthropology*. New York.

Fuhrmann, J.
1982 *Tsar Alexis: His reign and his Russia*. Gulf Breeze: Academic International.

Geanakoplos, D.
1976 *Interaction of the "sibling" Byzantine and Western cultures in the Middle Ages and Italian Renaissance*. New Haven: Yale University Press.
1984 *Byzantium: Church, society and civilization seen through contemporary eyes*. Chicago: University of Chicago Press.

Geertz, C.
1973 *The interpretation of cultures*. New York: Basic.

Gerss, M.
1909 Die Philipponen. *Zeitschrift der Altertumsgesellschaft Insterburg*, F. Tetzner, ed. no. 11: 44-84.
1910 Die Glaubenslehren der Philipponen zur Zeit ihrer Einwanderung in Ostpreussen. *Mitteilungen der Literarischen Gesellschaft Masovia*, 15:1-27.

Gluckman, M.
1958   *Analysis of a social situation in modern Zululand.* Rhodes-Livingston Papers, no. 28. Manchester: Manchester University Press.

Goehlert, J.V.
1863   Die Lipowaner in der Bukowina. *Kaiserliche Akademie der Wissenschaften*, 41:478-488.

Goetz, L.
1905   *Pamiatniki Drevne-Russkago Kanonichaskago Prava.* Stuttgart:Enke.

Goody, J.
1968   Restricted literacy in northern Ghana. In J. Goody, ed., *Literacy in traditional societies.* Cambridge: Cambridge University Press.
1986   *The logic of writing and the organization of society.* Cambridge: Cambridge University Press.
1987   *The interface between the written and the oral.* Cambridge: Cambridge University Press.

Haberland, K.
1887/88   Ueber Gebräuche und Aberglauben beim Essen. *Zeitschrift für Völkerpsychologie und Sprachwissenschaft.* vol. 17/18.

Hall, R.
1970   Population biology of the Russian Old Believers of Marion County, Oregon. Ph.D. diss, anthropology, University of Oregon.

Hallpike, C.
1979   *The foundations of primitive thought.* Oxford: Clarendon.

Halpern, J.
1967   *A Serbian village.* Rev. ed. New York: Harper & Row.

Hattox, R.
1985   *Coffee and Coffeehouses: The origins of a social beverage in the medieval Near East.* Seattle: University of Washington Press.

Hauptmann, P.
1963   *Altrussischer Glaube.* Göttingen: Vandenhoeck & Ruprecht.
1984   Das Gemeindeleiteramt bei den priesterlosen Altgläubigen. In P. Hauptmann, ed., *Unser ganzes Leben Christus unserm Gott überantworten: Studien zur ostkirchlichen Spiritualität*, Göttingen: Vandenhoeck & Ruprecht.

Haussig, H.W.
1971 *A history of Byzantine civilization*, New York: Praeger.

Hefele, C.
1896 *A history of the councils of the church*. Vol. 5. Edinburgh: T & T Clark.

Hein, K.
1973 *Eucharist and excommunication*. Frankfurt: Peter Lang.

Hennisch, R.
1976 *Fast and feast: Food in medieval society*. University Park: Pennsylvania State University.

Herberstein, S.
1926 *Rerum Moscoviticarum Commentarii oder Moscovia*. Edited by H. Kauders. Erlangen: Verlag der Philosophischen Akademie.

Herbert, R.
1989 The way of angels. *Parabola*, 14:77-86.

Hobsbawm, E. & Ranger, T, eds.
1983 *The invention of tradition*. Cambridge: Cambridge University Press.

Hoesch, E.
1975 *Orthodoxie und heresie im alten Russland*. Wiesbaden: Otto Harrassowitz.

Illich, I., & Sanders, B.
1988 *The alphabetization of the popular mind*, San Francisco: North Point.

Innis, R. ed.
1985 *Semiotics: An introductory anthology*. Bloomington: Indiana University Press.

Iosif [Basargin]
1985 Vozvanie ko vsem zhiteliam Aliaski. Mimeo.

Iwaniec, E.
1977 *Z dziejow staroobrzedowcow na zemiach polskich XVII-XX w.* Warsaw: Wydawnictwo Naukowe.

Jakobson, R.
1971 *Selected writings: Word and language II.* The Hague: Mouton.

Jedin, H.
1967 *Crisis and closure of the Council of Trent.* London: Sheed & Ward.

Kaindl, R.
1897 Das Entstehen und die Entwicklung der Lippowaner-Colonien in der Bukowina. *Archiv für österreichische Geschichte*, 83:235-383.

Katunskii, A.E.
1972 *Staroobriadchestvo*, Moscow: Izdatelstvo politicheskoi literatury.

Kelsiev, V. ed.
1860 *Sbornik pravitelstvennykh sviedenii o raskolnikakh*. London: Trübner & Co.
1866 Russkoe selo v maloi Azii. *Russkii vestnik*, 63:413-451.

Kitzinger, E.
1976 *The art of Byzantium and the Medieval West*, Bloomington: Indiana University Press.

Kniga o vere
1648 *(edinnoi istinnoi prevoslavnoi)*. Moscow.

Koch, H.
1962 Die Slavisierung der griechischen Kirche im Moskauer Staate als bodenständige Voraussetzung des russischen Raskol. In *Kleine Schriften zur Kirchen- und Geistesgeschichte Osteuropas*. Wiesbaden: Otto Harrassowitz.

Kolarz, W.
1961 *Religion in the Soviet Union*. London: Macmillan.

Kollwitz, J.
1957 Bild und Bildertheologie im Mittelalter. In W. Schöne, J. Kollwitz, & H. von Campenhausen, ed., *Das Gottesbild im Abendland*, Witten: Eckart Verlag.

Koncevicius, J.
1927 *Russia's attitude towards union with Rome*. Washington.

Kormchaia kniga (Nomokanon).
1650 Moscow: Preobrazhensk. Reprinted 1914.

Kostomarov, N., ed.
1860 *Pamiatniki starinnoi russkoi literatury*. vols. 1 & 2, St. Petersburg.
1871 Istoriia raskola u raskolnikov. *Vestnik Evropy*. April 1871:469-536.
1905 *Sobranie sochinenii*, vol. 8, St. Petersburg.

Kozhanchikov, D.E., ed.
1863 *Stoglav*. St. Petersburg.

Ladner, G.
1953 The concept of the image in the Greek Fathers and the Byzantine iconoclastic controversy. *Dumbarton Oaks Papers*, 7:3-34.

Lane, C.
1978 *Christian religion in the Soviet Union*. Albany: State University of New York Press.

Laufer, B.
1924 *Introduction of tobacco into Europe*. Anthropology Leaflet no. 19. Chicago: Field Museum of Natural History.

Leach, E.
1964 Anthropological aspects of language: Animal categories and verbal abuse. In E.H. Lenneberg, ed., *New Directions in the study of language*, Cambridge: MIT Press.

Leeuw, G. van der
1963 *Sacred and Profane*, New York: Holt, Rinehart & Winston.

Letiche, J. & Dmytryshyn, B.
1990 Krizanic's memorandum on the mission to Moscow. *Slavonic and East European Review*, 68, 1: 51-68.

Lopatinskii, F.
1745 *Oblichenie nepravdy raskolnicheskiia*, St. Petersburg.

Lopukhin, I.V.
1862 Tserkovno-Istoricheskoe izsledovanie o drevnei oblasti Viatitsei.... In *Chteniia v imperatorskom obshchestve istorii i drevnostei rossiiskikh pri moskovskom universitete*, 2:1-156.

Lotman, I. & Uspenskii, B.
1985 Binary models in the dynamics of Russian culture. In Alexander Nakhimovsky & A. Stone Nakhimovsky, eds., *The semiotics of Russian cultural history*. Ithaca: Cornell University Press.

Lupinin, N.
1984 *Religious revolt in the XVIIth century: The schism of the Russian church*. Princeton: The Kingston Press.

Mackenzie, C.
1957 *Sublime tobacco*. London: Chatto & Windus.

Malaya rodoslovna.
1920 Manuscript.

Mango, C. ed.
1972 *The art of the Byzantine Empire 312-1453: Sources and documents.* Englewood Cliffs: Prentice-Hall.
1980 *Byzantium: The empire of New Rome.* London: Weidenfeld & Nicolson.

Marchadier, B.
1977 Les vieux-croyants de Wojnowo. *Cahiers du Monde russe et sovietique*, 18, 4:435-448.

Markell.
1862 O zhitii eretika Feofana Prokopovitcha. *Chteniia v imperatorskom obshchestve istorii i drevnostei rossiiskikh pri moskovskom universitete*, vol. 1:1-11.

Masaryk, T.
1919 *The Spirit of Russia.* London: Allen & Unwin.

Matejka, L.
1984 Church Slavonic as a national language. In Halle et al., eds., *Semiosis: Semiotics and the history of culture.* Michigan Slavic Contributions. University of Michigan.

McKitterick, R.
1989 *The Carolingians and the written word.* Cambridge: Cambridge University Press.

McNeill, J. & Gamer, H., ed.
1938 *Medieval handbooks of penance.* New York: Columbia University Press.

Miles, M.
1985 *Image as insight.* Boston: Beacon.

Miliukov, P.
1942 *Outlines of Russian culture,* Part 1, *Religion and the Church.* Philadelphia: University of Pennsylvania Press.

Mitrovits, T.
1898 *Nomokanon der slavischen morgenländischen Kirche oder die Kormtschaja Kniga.* Vienna: Braunmüller.

Morris, R.
1981 Three Russian groups in Oregon: A comparison of boundaries in a pluralistic environment. Ph.D. diss. University of Oregon.

Murdock, G.
1949 *Social Structure.* New York: Free Press.

Neusner, J.
1973 *The idea of purity in ancient Judaism.* Leiden: E.J. Brill.
1983 *Ancient Israel after catastrophe: The religious world view of the Mishnah.* Charlottesville: University Press of Virginia.

Olearius, A.
1656 *Vermehrte Newe Beschreibung Der Muscowitischen und Persischen Reyse.* Schleswig. Reprinted Max Niemayer, Tübingen, 1971.

Ong, W.
1982 *Orality and literacy.* New York: Methuen.

Ouspensky, L.
1978 *Theology of the icon.* Crestwood: St. Vladimir's Seminary Press.

Palmer, W.
1873 *The patriarch and the tsar.* Vol. 2. London: Trübner.

Pascal, P.
1938 *Avvakum et les debuts du raskol.* Paris.

Pavlov, A.S., ed.
1908 *Pamiatniki drevne-russkago kanonicheskago prava.* 2nd ed., 1st pt. St. Petersburg.

Pelikan, J.
1974 *The spirit of Eastern Christendom (600-1700).* Chicago: University of Chicago Press.
1985 *Jesus through the centuries.* New Haven: Yale University Press.

Pesheva. R.
1971 Late patrimonial traditions in the social organization of the Slavs. *Ethnologia Slavica*, 3:159-165.

Peskov, V.
1982 Taezhnyi tupik. *Komsomolskaya Pravda*, October 9-22.

Piepkorn, A.
1977 The Russian Old Believers. In *Profiles in belief: The religious bodies of the United States and Canada*, 1:108-116. New York: Harper & Row.

Platonov, S.F., ed.
1927 *Pamiatniki istorii staroobriadchestva xvii v.* Russkaia istoricheskaia biblioteka vol. xxxix. Leningrad: Akademiya nauk SSSR.

Pleyer, V.
1961 *Das russische Altgläubigentum: Geschichte; Darstellung in der Literatur.* Munich: Otto Sanger.

Pocock, J.G.A.
1962 The origins of study of the past: A comparative approach. *Comparative Studies in Society and History,* 4:209-246.

Polek, J.
1885 Die Lippowaner-Colonien in der Bukowina. *Mitteilungen der kaiserlich-königlichen Geographischen Gesellschaft,* 28:301-312.

Popov, A.
1875 *Istoriko-literaturnyi obzor drevne-russkikh polemicheskikh sochinenii protiv latinian.* Moscow.

Popova, A.M.
1928 *Semeiskie (Zabaikalskie staroobriadtsy).* Verkhneudinsk.

Radcliffe-Brown, A.R.
1952 *Structure and function in primitive society.* London: Cohen & West.

Raeff, M.
1984 *Understanding Imperial Russia.* New York: Columbia University Press.

Rappaport, R.
1974 Obvious aspects of ritual. *Cambridge Anthropology,* 2, 1:3-69.

Reardon, J.
1972 A bit of Russia takes root in Alaska. *National Geographic,* September 1972.

Reynolds, R.
1950 *Beards.* London: Allen & Unwin.

Robertson Smith, W
1889 *The religion of the Semites.* London.

Rochow auf Reckan
1799 Einige Nachrichten über die in Neu-ostpreussen befindlichen Philipponen. *Neue Berlinische Monatsschrift,* 2:403-422.

Rushchinskii, L.P.
1871 *Religioznyi byt russkikh po sviedeniam inostrannykh pisatelei XVI i XVII vekov.* Moscow.

Russell, J.
1981 *Satan: The early Christian tradition.* Ithaca: Cornell Univer-

sity Press.
1984 *Lucifer: The devil in the Middle Ages.* Ithaca: Cornell University Press.

Sabey, R.
1969 Starovery and school: A case study of the education of Russian immigrant children in a rural Oregon community. Ph.D. diss., University of Oregon.

Scheffel, D.
1989a Russian Old Believers and Canada: A historical sketch. *Canadian Ethnic Studies,* 21, 1:1-18.
1989b Russische Altgläubige in der Mandschurei. *Kirche im Osten,* Band 32:109-119.
1989c There is always somewhere to go — Russian Old Believers and the state. In *Outwitting the State,* Peter Skalnik, ed., Political Anthropology 8, New Brunswick: Transaction.
1991a "Bezpopovtsy". *Modern Encyclopedia of Religions in Russia and the Soviet Union.* Gulf Breeze: Academic International Press.
1991b "Chasovennye". *Modern Enclyclopedia of Religions in Russia and the Soviet Union.* Gulf Breeze: Academic International Press.

Schoene, W.
1957 Die Bildergeschichte der christlichen Gottesgestalten in abendländischer Kunst. In W. Schöne, J. Kollwitz, & H. von Campenhausen, eds., *Das Gottesbild im Abendland.* Witten: Eckart.

Schwarz, W.
1955 *Principles and problems of biblical translation.* Cambridge: Cambridge University Press.

Schurtz, H.
1893 Die Speiseverbote: Ein Problem der Völkerkunde. In R. Virchow & W. Wattenbach, eds., *Sammlung gemeinverständlicher wissenschaftlicher Vorträge,* no. 184:1-46.

Sevastianov, A.N.
1985 Kniga, chitatel' i literatura vo vtoroi polovine xviii veka v Rossii. In K.V. Liutova, ed., *Kniga v Rossii do serediny XIX veka.* Leningrad: Akademiya nauk SSSR.

Shamaro, A.
1964 Kazaki vernulis v Rossiyu. *Nauka i religiia,* 8:26-32.

Shchapov, A.P.
1906 Russkii raskol staroobriadchestva. *Sochineniia.* Vol 1. St. Petersburg.

Shils, E.

1981 *Tradition*. Chicago: University of Chicago Press.

Siegelbaum, L.

1979 Peasant disorders and the myth of the tsar: Russian variations on a millenarian theme. *The Journal of Religious History*, 10:223-235.

Singer, M.

1984 *Man's glassy essence: Explorations in semiotic anthropology*. Bloomington: Indiana University Press.

Siniavski, A.

1988 Apofeoz knigi. *Cahiers du Monde russe et soviétique*, 19, 3-4:293-301.

Smirnov, P.S.

1898 *Vnutrennie voprosy v raskole v XVII veke*. St. Petersburg.

1914 *Drevne-russkii dukhovnik: izsledovanie po istorii tserkovnago byta*. St. Petersburg.

Smith, R.E.F.

1977 *Peasant farming in Muscovy*. Cambridge: Cambridge University Press.

Smith, R.E.F. & Christian, D.

1984 *Bread and salt: A social and economic history of food and drink in Russia*. Cambridge: Cambridge University Press.

Smithson, M.

1976 Of icons and motorcycles: A sociological study of acculturation among Russian Old Believers in central Oregon and Alaska. Ph.D. diss. Univeristy of Oregon.

Sobranie postanovlenii po chasti raskola.

1858 Vols. 1 & 2. St. Petersburg.

Staden, H. von

1964 *Aufzeichnungen über den Moskauer Staat*. 2nd ed. Ed. F. Epstein. Hamburg: Cram, de Gruyter & Co.

Stavrou, T. & Weisensel, P.

1986 *Russian travellers to the Christian East from the twelfth to the twentieth century*. Columbus: Slavica.

Steinberg, L.

1983 *The sexuality of Christ in Renaissance art and in modern oblivion*. New York: Pantheon.

Subbotin, N.I.
1881 *Materialy dlia istorii raskola za pervoe vremia ego sush-chestvovania*. Vol. 6. Moscow.

Sviedenia
1862 Sviedenia o Raskolnikakh, izvlechennyia iz Ukazov v Nov-gorodskuiu Gubernskuiu Kantselariu i Olonetskuiu Voevodskuiu. *Chteniia v imperatorskom obshchestve istorii i drevnostei rossiiskikh pri moskovskom universitete*, 4:11-32.

Tambiah, S.J.
1973 Classification of animals in Thailand. In Mary Douglas, ed., *Rules and meanings*. Harmondsworth: Penguin.
1979 A performative approach to ritual. *Proceedings of the British Academy*, 65:113-169.

Tetzner, F.
1899 Die Philipponen in Ostpreussen. *Globus*. 76, 12:181-192.
1908 Philipponische Legenden. *Globus*. 94, 8:117-119 & 241-243.

Thomas, K.
1971 *Religion and the decline of magic*. New York: Charles Scribner's Sons.

Tserkov.
1980 O vkushenii pishchi s inakoveruiushchimi. Vol. 1, no. 2. Kakaia odezhda prilichna khristianinu. Vol 5, no. 21.
1985 Vosmikonechnyi krest Khristov i borba protiv nego. Vol. 5, no. 20. Raziasnenia o chae i tabake. Vol. 5, no. 21.

Unkrieg, W.A.
1933 Volkskundliche Beobachtungen aus dem Gouvernement Kostroma. *Zeitschrift für Ethnologie,* 65:80-92.

Uspenskii, M.I.
1905 Staroobriadcheskoe sochinenie xviii stoletiia ob odezhde. *Izvestiya otdeleniya russkogo iazyka i slovesnosti akademii nauk.* St. Petersburg.

Uspensky, B.
1976 The semiotics of the Russian icon. Lisse: de Ridder.

Vasilev.
1694 Prigovor ili ulozhenie novgorodskogo sobora 1694 goda. Reprinted in Smirnov 1898.

Velzen, H.U.E. van & Beek, W. van
1988 Purity, a greedy ideology. In *The quest for purity*. W. van Beek, ed., Amsterdam: Mouton de Gruyter.

Vernadsky, G. ed.
1972   *A source book for Russian history from early times to 1917.*
Vols. 1 & 2. New Haven: Yale University Press.

Ware, T.
1972   *The Orthodox Church.* Harmondsworth: Penguin.

Wigowsky, P.
1982   *Freedom for an Old Believer.* Woodburn.

Zelenin, D.
1927   *Russische (Ostslavische) Volkskunde.* Berlin: de Gruyter.

Zenkovsky, S.
1957   The Russian church schism: Its background and repercussions. *The Russian Review,* 16, 4:37-58.
1970   *Russkoe staroobriadchestvo.* Munich: Wilhelm Fink.
1974   ed., *Medieval Russia's epics, chronicals, and tales.* Revised ed. New York: E.P. Dutton & Co.

Zhuravlev, A.I.
1831   *Polnoe istoricheskoe izvestie o drevnikh strigolnikakh, i novykh raskolnikakh, tak nazyvaemykh staroobriadtsakh, o ikh uchenii, delakh i razglasiakh.* St. Petersburg.